Body as Psychoanalytic Object

This book explores the role of bodily phenomena in mental life and in the psychoanalytic encounter, encouraging further dialog within psychoanalysis, philosophy, and the humanities, and contributing new clinical and theoretical perspectives to the recent resurgence of psychoanalytic interest in the body.

Presented in six parts in which diverse meanings are explored, *Body as Psychoanalytic Object* focuses on the clinical psychoanalytic encounter and the body as object of psychoanalytic inquiry, spanning from the prenatal experience to death. The contributors explore key themes including mind–body relations in Winnicott, Bion, and beyond; oneiric body; nascent body in early object relations; body and psychosensory experience; body in breakdown; and body in virtual space. With clinical vignettes throughout, each chapter provides unique insight into how different analysts work with bodily phenomena in the clinical situation and how it is conceived theoretically.

Building on the thinking of Winnicott and Bion, as well as contributions from French psychoanalysis, *Body as Psychoanalytic Object* offers a way forward in a body-based understanding of object relations theory for psychoanalysts and psychotherapists.

Caron Harrang, LICSW, FIPA is a board-certified training and supervising psychoanalyst of the Northwestern Psychoanalytic Society and Institute in Seattle, Washington, USA.

Drew Tillotson, PsyD, FIPA is a board-certified psychoanalyst and a graduate and Past President of the Psychoanalytic Institute of Northern California in San Francisco, California, USA.

Nancy C. Winters, MD, FIPA is a training and supervising psychoanalyst of the Oregon Psychoanalytic Institute and Clinical Professor of Psychiatry and Child/Adolescent Psychiatry at the Oregon Health and Science University in Portland, Oregon, USA.

Body as Psychoanalytic Object

Clinical Applications from Winnicott to Bion and Beyond

Edited by
Caron Harrang, Drew Tillotson, and
Nancy C. Winters

R Routledge
Taylor & Francis Group

LONDON AND NEW YORK

First published 2022
by Routledge
2 Park Square, Milton Park, Abingdon, Oxon, OX14 4RN

and by Routledge
605 Third Avenue, New York, NY 10158

Routledge is an imprint of the Taylor & Francis Group, an informa business

© 2022 selection and editorial matter, Nancy Winters, Caron Harrang and Drew Tillotson; individual chapters, the contributors

Library of Congress Cataloging-in-Publication Data
A catalog record for this title has been requested

ISBN: 978-1-032-04915-1 (hbk)
ISBN: 978-0-367-41844-1 (pbk)
ISBN: 978-1-003-19555-9 (ebk)

DOI: 10.4324/9781003195559

Typeset in Baskerville
by codeMantra

"It is paradoxical and intriguing that after a century of existence psychoanalysis is still so uncomfortable saying what it knows about the body. Paradoxical because psychoanalysis was born giving voice to the body of hysterics. Yet over time, the picture became that of a disincarnate analyst for a disincarnate patient, prompting Paula Heimann to remind us that the purpose of psychoanalysis is not to transform the analyst into a mechanical brain, which produces interpretations purely on the basis of intellectual procedures. In her classic 1949 essay on countertransference, Heimann denounces a split not yet resolved in psychoanalytic theorizing on the link between mind and body. Otherwise one would not understand why a book like *Body as Psychoanalytic Object* can be so intriguing. The fact is, this remains an exciting frontier of research in psychoanalysis. How body and mind communicate remains quite mysterious. We know that the body that interests us does not speak in words; still it 'speaks' and cannot be placed entirely outside the field of the symbolic even when it is deprived of the ability to communicate lexically, as is the case with small children. It is not at all obvious that even the body of the infant, that is, the child who does not yet have access to words, is already touched by culture; which means that it starts immediately (even before birth) to exist as a body that has its own intentionality, a body that dreams, a body that communicates. Nor is it clear what relation there is between intersubjectivity based on instinct, what Bion calls the proto-mental system—the ability of individuals to connect with each other on the basis of certain 'valences'—and intersubjectivity based on language. This outstanding book co-authored and edited by Caron Harrang, Drew Tillotson, and Nancy Winters promises readers an extraordinary journey in which, little by little, they will be able to reflect on these issues and see them in the light of a series of rigorous, provocative, and sophisticated essays that make up the volume. I recommend this splendid book to psychotherapists, to psychoanalysts, and to all those in philosophy and the humanities who reflect on the mystery of what constitutes the essence of our humanity."

— **Giuseppe Civitarese, MD, FIPA, author of Sublime Subjects: Aesthetic Experience and Intersubjectivity in Psychoanalysis**

"In this theoretically intricate, clinically rich and challenging collection of essays, edited by Caron Harrang, Drew Tillotson, and Nancy Winters, we are exposed to new and evolving ideas on the creative forms of body–mind engagement. With Bion and Winnicott as guiding lodestars, authors here take us on fascinating journeys. Body–mind emergence in prenatal and perinatal life, at the end of life, in the process of growth and development, at points of breakdown, and even, quite presciently, in the transformed clinical scenes of teletherapy and screens. I was struck by the complexity and challenge of the many clinical moments in this book, used to push the reader towards new imaginings of the body and mind in their complex and profound encountering. We are presented here with troubling and inspiring stories, through a complex theoretical perspective in which psychoanalysis is about opening the capacity to dream, to need, to want, as well as to know."

— **Adrienne Harris, PhD, Director, Sandor Ferenczi Center of the New School**

To our patients, whose embodied lives inspired us to explore *body* in its limitless capacity to speak, dream, desire, and grieve.

Contents

Notes on contributors

Editors

Caron Harrang, LICSW, FIPA is a board-certified psychoanalyst and an IPA training and supervising psychoanalyst on faculty at Northwestern Psychoanalytic Society and Institute in Seattle, Washington. She maintains a full-time practice offering clinical consultation and psychoanalysis to mothers and infants, adolescents, and adults. Trained in bioenergetic analysis prior to becoming a psychoanalyst, she has a longstanding interest in the body as it relates to clinical process and technique. Publications related to bodymind phenomena include "Painting Poppies: On the relationship between concrete and metaphorical thinking" (2012); "Psychic skin and narcissistic rage: Reflections on Almodóvar's *The Skin I Live In*" (2012); and *From Reverie to Interpretation: Transforming Thought into the Action of Psychoanalysis* (2016).

Drew Tillotson, PsyD, FIPA is a board-certified psychoanalyst, Past President of the Psychoanalytic Institute of Northern California, and past Vice President of the North American Psychoanalytic Confederation (NAPsaC). He serves on the boards of the Confederation of Independent Psychoanalytic Societies (CIPS) and NAPsaC. He teaches widely in the Bay Area and maintains a full-time private practice in San Francisco, California, offering psychoanalysis and clinical consultation. He has published on masculinity, aging, intercultural phenomena, book reviews for the *International Journal of Psychoanalysis* and *Fort Da*, and is a chapter author in Routledge's forthcoming publication, *Braving the Erotic Field in the Treatment of Adolescents and Children*, edited by Mary T. Brady, PhD.

Nancy C. Winters, MD, FIPA is an APsaA training and supervising psychoanalyst of the Oregon Psychoanalytic Institute and a Clinical Professor of Psychiatry at the Oregon Health and Science University, where she previously directed the Child and Adolescent Psychiatry residency program. She maintains a full-time practice of adult psychoanalysis, consultation, and supervision in Portland, Oregon (USA). She is on the Editorial Boards of the *International Journal of Psychoanalysis* and the *Psychoanalytic Quarterly* and is recipient of APsaA's Edith Sabshin Teaching Award (2014). Publications include *The Handbook of Child and Adolescent Systems of Care: The New Community Psychiatry*

(2002), review of *Sexual Difference in Debate: Bodies, Desires, and Fictions* (Glocer Fiorini, 2017), and articles on early childhood feeding problems, adolescent depression, and the 'wraparound' model.

Authors

Patricia K. Antin, LCSW, PhD, FIPA is an IPA training and supervising psychoanalyst at the Psychoanalytic Center of California where she has served as Society President and Secretary-Treasurer. She has also served as Co-Chair of the Infant Observation Committee. She is a member of the Executive Committee of the North American Tavistock Observational Link which represents infant observation facilitators trained in the Tavistock method of infant observation. She maintains a private practice in Los Angeles, California offering psychoanalysis to adults as well as supervision to students and analysts-in-training at the Psychoanalytic Center of California. She presents on the clinical relevance of infant observation throughout North America.

Dana M. Blue, LICSW, FIPA is a board-certified psychoanalyst and an IPA training and supervising psychoanalyst on faculty at Northwestern Psychoanalytic Society and Institute in Seattle, Washington. In private practice in Seattle, she offers clinical consultation and psychoanalysis to adults and mother/infant couples. Before becoming a psychoanalyst, she worked as a doula, a most somatic ground from which to observe psychic growth. Prior publications include *From Reverie to Interpretation: Transforming Thought into the Action of Psychoanalysis* (2016).

David M. Brooks, PhD, PsyD, FIPA is a Fellow of the International Psychoanalytical Association, former Dean of the Psychoanalytic Center of California, Member of the Psychoanalytic Institute of Northern California Society, and Clinical Associate of the Neuropsychoanalysis Association. He serves on the boards of directors for the AK Rice Institute for the Study of Social Systems and its West Coast Affiliate, GREX. He maintains a private practice in Los Angeles and Chicago (USA) offering psychoanalysis to adults and clinical consultation specializing in chronic depression, bipolar, borderline, and schizoid personality disorders. Recent publications include "The Barbed-Wire Hole of Despair: Retreat from Aesthetic Conflict" (2018).

Lesley Caldwell, PhD, FIPA is a fellow of the International Psychoanalytical Association, member of the British Psychoanalytic Association, and an Academic Associate of the British Psychoanalytic Society. She is a corresponding member of the Los Angeles Institute and Society for Psychoanalytic Studies, serves on the IPA Women and Psychoanalysis Committee (COWAP), and is a Visiting Professor in the Psychoanalysis Unit at University College, London. With Helen Taylor Robinson she is Joint General Editor of the *Collected Works of Donald Winnicott* (2016) and is responsible for more than 100 further additions uploaded to the freely available Volume 12 of the online edition (2020).

Other recent publications include "From Psychoanalysis to Being and Doing" (2020) and "From Symbolism to Symbol Formation and Illusion" (2020).

Jeffrey L. Eaton, MA, FIPA is a graduate and faculty member of the Northwestern Psychoanalytic Society and Institute. He is author of *A Fruitful Harvest: Essays after Bion* published by The Alliance Press as well as several other book chapters. He lectures and teaches widely and provides consultation to psychotherapists and psychoanalysts internationally.

Judy K. Eekhoff, PhD, FIPA is an IPA-certified training and supervising psychoanalyst and a licensed child psychologist who has a private practice in Seattle, Washington, USA. She is a full faculty member of Northwestern Psychoanalytic Society & Institute, of Seattle Psychoanalytic Society and Institute, and of COR Northwest Family Development Center. She is the author of numerous articles and book chapters and of the book: *Trauma & Primitive Mental States, an Object Relations Perspective*. Her second book, *Between the Real and the Imaginary* is nearing completion. Dr. Eekhoff believes unrepresented and poorly represented states are amenable to psychoanalysis.

Peter Goldberg, PhD, FIPA is a personal and supervising psychoanalyst at the Psychoanalytic Institute of Northern California, is Chair of Faculty at the San Francisco Center for Psychoanalysis, and on the faculty of the Wright Institute in Berkeley. He maintains a full-time practice of psychoanalysis in Berkeley, California. Prior publications related to psyche-soma phenomena include "Successful dissociation, pseudo-vitality and inauthentic use of the senses" (1995), "Fabricated bodies: A model for the somatic false self" (2004), and "Active perception and the search for sensory symbiosis" (2012).

Adrian Jarreau[†], LMHC, FIPA is a graduate of Northwestern Psychoanalytic Society and Institute and served as Treasurer on the Board of Directors as well as teaching in the Institute. Previous publications include "Intuiting the Unknown" (2016). He maintained a private practice in Seattle, Washington until his death in April 22, 2018.

Andrea Marzi, MD, PhD, FIPA is a member of the Italian Psychoanalytical Society and the American Psychoanalytic Association. He is a member of the IPA Task Force on Remote Analysis in Training and the IPS Ethical Code Committee. He maintains a fulltime private practice in Siena, Italy. Previous positions include Visiting Fellow at the University of Cambridge (England), consultant to the Department of Forensic Psychopathology, and Professor of Developmental Psychology at the University of Siena (Italy). He has published numerous scientific papers in national and international journals. Recent edited and co-authored books include *Ciak si gira, Psicoanalisi al cinema* (2013), and *Psychoanalysis, Identity and the Internet* (2016); and a chapter titled "Light and shadow in online analysis" with Giuseppe Fiorentini (2017).

Robert Oelsner, MD, FIPA is a training and supervising psychoanalyst of the Psychoanalytic Institute of Northern California and Northwestern

† The author is deceased.

Psychoanalytic Society and Institute. He maintains a private practice offering psychoanalysis to children and adults and clinical consultation in Seattle, Washington. Recent papers include "Melanie Klein and Bion's Cat, an Essay on Kleinian Ethics" presented to the Buenos Aires Psychoanalytic Society (2019). He is editor and co-author of *Transference and Countertransference Today* (2013) and numerous book chapters on the works of Wilfred Bion and Donald Meltzer.

Rikki Ricard, LMHC, FIPA is a graduate of Northwestern Psychoanalytic Society and Institute. She maintains a private practice in Seattle, Washington working with adults, adolescents, mothers and infants, and couples. Rikki is a Washington State-approved supervisor and teaches frequently at Northwestern Psychoanalytic Society and Institute (NPSI) and other psychoanalytic organizations in Seattle. Rikki's first career was as a professional actress and she is on honorary withdrawal from the Screen Actors Guild: American Federation of Television and Radio Artists (SAG-AFTRA). Although dying and grief have taken a significant place in her life over the last few years, they are topics that have been meaningful in her work for a long time, particularly in relation to body and the unconscious. She is currently working on a memoir.

Oscar H. Romero, MD, FIPA is a training and supervising analyst of the Northwestern Psychoanalytic Society and Institute and the Seattle Psychoanalytic Society and Institute, and a clinical associate professor of psychiatry at the University of Washington. Bilingual in Spanish and English, he is an active member of the Colombian Psychoanalytic Society and the Federation of Psychoanalytic Societies of Latin America (FEPAL). He has written on topics related to early mental phenomena including reparation through the work of forgiveness, "Bi-logic and the Metapsychology of Forgiveness" (2004); "Reverie in psychoanalysis and in the poem 'Zone' by Apollinaire" (2014); and a psychoanalytic understanding of non-religious experience, "De la metafísica a la metapsicología: Lo spiritual no religioso en el psicoanálisis" (2016). He maintains a private practice offering psychoanalysis to adults and clinical consultation in Seattle, Washington.

Acknowledgments

This book arose from selected papers presented at the Twelfth International Evolving British Object Relations Conference sponsored by Northwestern Psychoanalytic Society and Institute (NPSI) in Seattle, Washington. The theme of the 2018 conference was "The Body as Psychoanalytic Object: Clinical Applications from Winnicott to Bion and Beyond" and featured Lesley Caldwell and Robert Oelsner as plenary presenters along with psychoanalyst and psychotherapist colleagues from North America, Europe, and the Middle East. The conference organizing committee consisted of Caron Harrang (Chair), Drew Tillotson, Nancy C. Winters, and then NPSI Administrator Hollee Sweet. The committee was assisted by numerous volunteer members of the NPSI Society who generously gave of their time and talent to create a remarkably intimate and generative conference experience.

Reflecting on the aliveness and passionate discourse generated by large and small group discussion of the conference theme as explicated by individual authors, it became clear to the organizers that the body's role in the psychoanalytic encounter necessitated further exploration theoretically and clinically. The organizers formed a workgroup becoming co-editors and chapter authors of this book with 12 additional contributors who presented papers at EBOR. The editors' conviction of the importance of the body's role in psychoanalysis was further confirmed by observing that numerous international psychoanalytic conferences worldwide have chosen to focus on the body since 2018.

In developing the current volume, we wish to acknowledge the extraordinary camaraderie that developed in the editing group with one another and with our chapter authors. In addition, we wish to thank the following individuals who have lent their professional or personal support to us at various moments in the sojourn of bringing this project to fruition: Maxine Anderson, Sigrid Asmus, Rachel Blass, Erin Carruth, Anna Christopoulos, John Edmiston, Malena Harrang, Adrienne Harris, Frank Lachmann, Patrick Miller, Scott Murray, Bruce Reis, and Willie Anne Wright. Lastly, we are grateful to Routledge for their support and professionalism throughout the development and publication process, including Russell George and Alec Selwyn.

General introduction

Caron Harrang, Drew Tillotson, and Nancy C. Winters

Beginnings

Harrang, Tillotson, and Winters' title for this collection, *Body as Psychoanalytic Object: Clinical Applications from Winnicott to Bion and Beyond* may raise questions in the reader's mind as to what is meant by *body as psychoanalytic object* and the use of *body* instead of *the body*, which is more typical in psychoanalytic writing. In the following pages we explain these choices emanating from a series of après-coups for the editors. At the time of this writing in August, 2020 we are in the midst of the COVID-19 pandemic, unlike any known during our lifetimes. The lived experience of the pandemic has unearthed, après-coup, previously inaccessible understandings about the body and a further appreciation of the uniqueness of this collection. We hope these chapters will afford readers a similar après-coup lifting a kind of denial, an inability to be in direct contact with bodily phenomena.

This book contributes new clinical and theoretical perspectives to the recent resurgence of psychoanalytic interest in the body. Understanding the body's role in psychic development over the lifespan has yet to be integrated into theory and clinical technique. As Caldwell observes (Chapter 2), despite Freud's declaration that the body ego is first and foremost, the body receded in importance relative to the mind in contemporary psychoanalysis. Caldwell suggests this trend parallels the marginalization of sexuality and the female body. Intensification of interest in the body (examples include Lemma, 2014; Miller, 2014; Press, 2019; Tsolas and Anzieu-Premmereur, 2018) has been seen as a restoration of the relationship between body, the drives, and psychic life (Tsolas and Anzieu-Premmereur, 2018). We posit this welcome trend as an effort to revive a potentially dissociated aspect of human aliveness and early somatopsychic experience residing in the body or *bodymind*. *Bodymind*, a term used in this book for the indivisibility of body and mind, recalls Winnicott's *psyche-soma* (1965), the "indwelling of the psyche in the soma" (p. 45).

The Twelfth International Evolving British Object Relations Conference (Seattle, 2018) from which this book derives was one of the first body-themed international psychoanalytic conferences. Its title "The body as psychoanalytic object: clinical applications from Winnicott to Bion and beyond" ignited interest from authors throughout the United States and abroad and yielded an unusually varied, original, and clinically rich collection of papers. Eight of these were

DOI: 10.4324/9781003195559

selected to develop further for this book, with the addition of new chapters by Goldberg, Harrang, Tillotson, and Winters. With Winnicott and Bion as a starting point for the authors' diverse clinical and theoretical excursions, the body or *bodymind* emerges here in its kaleidoscopic complexity, from its intrauterine beginnings, its nascence in psychic life, its oneiric functions and psychosensory states, its dematerialization in remote analysis, to the body in somatic illness and ultimately death.

Returning to the initial questions—why *body* and not *the body* and what is meant by *body as psychoanalytic* object—each après-coup widened our understanding of the presentation and representation of *body* in the chapters. Here we use two meanings of après-coup as described by Sodré (2005): the "long-time-span" version as in Freud's *Nachträglichkeit*, "seems to transform the past, so that 'old' relationships and events are seen in a new light, and this transformation, involving substantial and therefore more permanent psychic change, will have lasting consequences for the future ..." (p. 8), whereas the "short-time-span" après-coup also described by Faimberg (2005) "refers to the moment-to-moment changes which take place continuously in an object relationship, involving different identifications, different projections both of internal objects and parts of the self, changes of mood and affect ..." (ibid.) The latter makes the sudden discoveries of après-coup possible.

The most dramatic après-coup of the first type as described above was the inrush of the pandemic and ensuing physical lockdowns (shelter in place) as we were preparing the book, and chapters were in the editing process. All at once the body and its now undeniable primacy took center stage, albeit traumatically. Our collective fantasies of invulnerability and 'mind over matter' were precipitously punctured. We had to face that our well-toned, clothed, and photographed bodies unconsciously experienced as providing a barrier between our insides and the outer world could be penetrated by a microscopic particle invisible to the human eye that could sneak into our cells like a thief in the night, colonize us, and make us acutely ill even unto death. Death anxiety cannot be forestalled when we realize we can contract a potentially fatal virus by simply inhaling droplets or aerosolized particles from another person coughing, singing, or speaking to us. Fortuitously invoked by Caldwell (Chapter 2), Carla de Toffoli (2011) writes

> [breath] spreads throughout the body, goes beyond it and is not in itself containable, it moves freely from I to you, like the psychic, eluding the customs barriers of the single individual ... necessitating a constant oscillation between being one and being two in the analytic pair.
>
> (p. 601)

How disheartening for practitioners of the talking cure to have the nuances and intimacy of in-person analysis becomes suddenly dangerous to our patients' and our own health.

The pandemic brought to the foreground the body's role in human touch, connectedness, and separation. The most poignant of bodily separations are between those who are sick or dying, from their loved ones. Ironically, the virus connects us as a worldwide human 'herd' striving for immunity and 'touching' each other through transmission of the virus. We are also connected by our shared anxieties, defenses, and hopefully positive ways of coping such as slowing down and becoming more present and embodied in our daily lives. Après-coup, the pandemic brought new meaning to chapters already written on body in remote analysis (Marzi, Chapter 19), psychic dysregulation of the immune system (Winters, Chapter 17), and conscious experience of impending death (Eaton, Chapter 6; Ricard and Jarreau, Chapter 7).

As we read and re-read the chapters in an iterative process described in the second type of après-coup, the editors realized this book is not about *the body*, which implies distance, abstraction, and dualism of body and mind, but about *body*. *Body* as a presence intimately constitutive of subjectivity and of life itself. Analogously, we say 'me' and not 'the me' when referring to ourselves. This view of *body* is one of immanence, the quality of being within us as opposed to transcendence, whereas *the body* is apprehended as separate from the mind. Body is also multitudinous, fitting its etymology which refers to the human form, but also to the main part of a group, any number of individuals spoken of collectively.

As several chapters in this book elaborate (Harrang, Chapter 13; Oelsner, Chapter 3), *body* in its communicative capacity speaks for itself. When recognized and given voice by the analyst it expands the analytic dialog, often in startling ways.

Body has the paradoxical quality of being at once knowable and unknowable. We know body through what we can see, feel, hear, smell, and taste. Our bodily 'envelope' and the sensory information we receive from internal states, for example, hunger or pain, are entry points into the unknown. *Body's* internal structure and complex inner workings that keep us alive as a dynamic organism interacting with the environment remain largely unknown to us.

This paradox of the knowable and unknowable is relevant to *body as psychoanalytic object* and its application to the book. Bion (1962) writes of psychoanalytic objects: "it is with the detection and observation of these objects that the psycho-analyst must concern himself in the conduct of an analysis" (p. 68). Such objects, like the selected fact, evolve in the shared emotional experience of the session. Reminiscent of the unknowable quality of *body,* Bion notes the psychoanalytic object, the "thing in itself … following Kant, cannot be known to us" (ibid.).

For Bion, interpretations of psychoanalytic objects contain the domains of sense, myth, and passion (Bion, 1963, p. 11). He explains these domains as follows: what the analyst says to the analysand must be "audible, visible, palpable or odoriferous" (ibid., p. 12), must involve a narrative meaningful to the analysand, and must represent "an emotion experienced with intensity and warmth though without any suggestion of violence" (ibid., p. 13).

In preparing this book, we came to see each chapter as a 'psychoanalytic session' in which *body* made its appearance as a psychoanalytic object, with sense, myth, and passion. Bion's emphasis on the role of sensing in the analytic encounter is echoed especially by Harrang (Chapter 13) and Goldberg (Chapter 12) in their descriptions of shared psychosensory states and technical implications thereof. *Body's* capacity to speak its myth through dreams as emissary to the mind is present in chapters by Eekhoff (Chapter 5), and Ricard and Jarreau (Chapter 7). The embodied emotional intensity of the analytic encounter comes through in detailed clinical vignettes throughout the book.

The excitement of après-coup occurred for us in the editorial process as we experienced *body* emerge with infinite meanings in the 'session,' so to speak, of our collective reading and rereading of the chapters. We hope readers will have an equally rich experience of the myriad meanings of body as a psychoanalytic concept.

Contents

In noting all of the different ways body is explored within these chapters, significant commonalities emerged. In fact, each book part emerged organically by observing authors' investigation of similar themes from different vertices. Consequently, we organized the book into six parts depicting *body as psychoanalytic object* as having diverse meanings explored in a variety of ways.

Each book part begins with its own introduction in the form of chapter synopses. Thus, the following descriptions are meant to present a more general sense of the book's organization. Part I, "Mind–body relations in Winnicott, Bion, and beyond" consists of two chapters (Caldwell, and Oelsner), both with clinical examples examining the contributions of Winnicott and Bion from the perspective of bodily phenomena while moving us forward (the 'beyond') in evolving psychoanalytic theory and clinical technique. Part II, "Oneiric body," contains two chapters (Eekhoff, and Ricard and Jarreau) in which dreaming's communicative potential is considered as a function of body, and not only of mind. Part III is "Nascent body in early object relations" with two chapters (Brooks and Antin, and Blue) that consider body as carrier of meaning in primitive or pre-verbal mental states. Part IV is "Body and psychosensory experience" with two chapters (Goldberg, and Harrang) illustrating theory and technique in the exploration of body as communicator of both sub-symbolic and symbolic communication. Part V, "Body in breakdown," contains three chapters (Romero, Tillotson, and Winters) involving psychosomatics. Bodily illness in all three provides analytic opportunities to examine body as an object of psychoanalytic inquiry, and in two of these chapters, transient somatization emerges during treatment. Finally, Part VI, "Body in virtual space" contains one chapter (Marzi) which examines remote analysis and offers new ways of thinking about body in virtual space as a dream space, and cyberspace as a dimension of the analytic field.

Convergences

In organizing the chapters into sections, we noticed significant convergences both within and *across* sections that were revealed and elucidated by the authors. Several themes emerged in these convergences worth noting.

An overarching theme we see in many of the chapters concerns the psychoanalyst's embodied experience and its application to clinical technique. Several chapters address the register conceptualized as existing before or 'beyond' somatic countertransference used to inform verbal interventions. Goldberg (Chapter 12) and Harrang (Chapter 13), for example, describe ways in which body participates in the analytic encounter prior to, or independent of, symbolically or lexically represented communication. Both suggest there are limitations to the clinical efficacy of typical analytic interventions based on mentalization and verbalization with some analysands. In their clinical examples the medium of shared psychosensory experience allows for spontaneous participation of the analyst's body, such as entering the session in an "improvisational state of physical readiness" (Goldberg) or spontaneously leaning in *towards* rather than *away from* an enraged analysand (Harrang). In these body-to-body moments, new possibilities emerge in the analytic encounter. Antin and Brooks (Chapter 9) describe situations when "visceral receptive observation" is needed in lieu of verbal interpretation which may be experienced by the analysand at certain moments as a chokehold.

Blue (Chapter 10) and Romero (Chapter 15) describe analytic hours when the analyst develops unexplained physical symptoms in what might be described as somatic reverie. Immersed in embodied experience inaccessible through verbal channels, they come to understand these symptoms as projective communications of their analysands' unconscious inchoate state or internal object representations. In one of Blue's vignettes it was only après-coup that she was able to interpret the meaning of the intense bodily dread she experienced during labor and delivery of a birth she attended. Similarly, Tillotson (Chapter 16) writes that his physical experience of dread in response to the obsessive verbal 'looping' of his analysand's ruminations served as a portal to understanding the psychosomatic illness he suffered from.

Another theme we noticed is bodily pain and illness as container of unmourned losses, internal trauma, or the analytic transference/countertransference matrix. Clinical vignettes by Romero (Chapter 15), Tillotson (Chapter 16), and Winters (Chapter 17) present analysands all of whom experienced early life traumatic losses. For each, it appeared that mourning and recovery were compromised as long as body held frozen un-mourned loss. Bodily pain and illness in this case serve as a negative container, obscuring linkages and preventing psychic growth and development. In Oelsner's clinical vignette (Chapter 3) the analysand's neck pain may be seen as container for his phantasy of a lost or damaged body part.

Controversies

This book represents two sorts of controversies; one conscious and intended, and others coincidental that came to light in observing the diversity of ways chapter authors define body psychoanalytically and perceive these phenomena and work with it in the clinical encounter. As previously noted, it was through noticing this multiplicity that we realized *body* is experienced as personal and infinitely various, rather than *the body* which implies a discrete, predetermined, singular entity.

The intended controversy has to do with the stance reflected in the book's title that rejects the premise that a focus on the object or object relations (necessarily) excludes body or leaves behind the Freudian drives as claimed by Tsolas and Anzieu-Premmereur (2018) among others. They argue that body has been "extinguished from contemporary psychoanalysis as a consequence of leaving behind the Freudian drives in favor of privileging the object" (ibid., p. 4). By inviting authors to employ Winnicott's and Bion's contributions as a springboard for presenting their own views on body as it evolves in the clinical situation, we are taking the position in this debate that infantile sexuality and drive theory is compatible with a contemporary object relations approach.

López-Corvo (2003) notes that Klein (who was Bion's analyst and Winnicott's supervisor) understood *drives as object representations* expressed through an infinite variety of body-based unconscious phantasies. Moreover, Klein (1930) believed the infant's aggressive phantasies *involving the mother's body* result in excessive anxiety that interferes with symbol formation. Although body is clearly implicated in Kleinian theory, the focus historically has been on interpreting the patient's deepest anxieties as a means of supporting psychic development evidenced by one's capacity for symbolization and communicating lexically.

A different view presented by Caldwell (Chapter 2) suggests bodily phenomena has been ignored for some time by all psychoanalytic schools as a consequence of our "insistence on the [analysand's] capacity to think, to reflect, to mentalise as the foundations of psychic awareness" without including the consanguinity of body and mind. At the same time, a reexamination of both Winnicott's and Bion's theoretical contributions reveals a direct concern with body not previously appreciated; they both—in similar and different ways—explore states of *being* and its implications for how the analyst engages the analysand and views the goals of treatment. Harrang (Chapter 13) comes to a similar conclusion in challenging the commonly held assumption that Bion considered 'at-one-ment' an intersubjective experience unrelated to bodily phenomena. As a counter point, she notes that Bion places beta elements or raw sense impressions before they acquire (full) psychical significance in Row A of his grid (1963) and designates this positioning as closest to O or ultimate reality. Brooks and Antin (Chapter 9) and Goldberg (Chapter 12) observe Winnicott's close attention to bodily phenomena in his clinical work even as certain concepts (e.g. direct communication) remained undeveloped theoretically. Winters (Chapter 17) considers a possible relation between Winnicott's (1949) notion of the "live body" as the "core of the imaginative self" (p. 244) and the libidinal body of erotic experience.

It is our hope that a careful review of the contributions of these two psychoanalytic luminaries through the lens of our chapter authors' attention to body and states of being may contribute to an evolving conversation in psychoanalysis; one that allows for fuller integration of object relations and drive theory as well as opening the door to debate of other controversies related to bodymind, briefly mentioned below.

Of the controversies we discovered in the chapters to follow, the most signif-icant pertains to what authors view as the fundamental aim of psychoanalysis vis-à-vis bodily phenomena. Is the aim of treatment to facilitate transformation of protomental states into symbolic thought and verbal speech? In Bionian terms, do we think that beta elements or sense impressions need always to be trans-formed into alpha elements or dream thoughts to achieve meaning? Or, is there now sufficient clinical data to suggest the body's capacity for unconscious intra-psychic and intersubjective communication extends to registers that do not need to be mediated by symbolic thought to be significant? If so, what is the signifi-cance of bodily experience that is lived in the realm of the senses; experience that is *presented* rather than *represented*?

In some chapters the abovementioned controversy is taken up directly and in others the author's position is evident only if the reader is on the lookout. For example, when Goldberg (Chapter 12) says, "the soma has psychical qualities of its own, its own way of ordering things" it is clear he believes not all experience needs to become mentalized to be meaningful. Or, when Oelsner (Chapter 2) titles his chapter "Does the body have a mind?" without a doubt he is suggesting body has a 'mind of its own' separate from and in dynamic tension with psyche. Harrang (Chapter 13) similarly aligns with those who perceive body as capable of 'speaking' for itself and being spoken to independent of or contemporaneous with experience that can be mentalized and communicated lexically.

By contrast, Romero (Chapter 15) and Eekhoff (Chapter 5) suggest that sym-bolization, although not always possible, is nevertheless what analytic treatment aims for. For example, when Eekhoff says, "The body is a dream space where sensory and emotional experience is transformed into representations that can be used to make personal meaning," it is evident she honors body as the ground of being and works to facilitate a transformational process that fosters thinking as the apex of meaning. Romero too allies with representation as the desired aim of analytic treatment when he says,

> In my view, it is possible for the analyst and patient to emerge from a primi-tive world without symbols into the symbolic order where poetry can emerge after a prolonged period in which the analyst is immersed in the psychoso-matic world of bodily illness concretely expressed. As this progression occurs, the analyst becomes for the psychosomatic patient the internal projective identification welcoming object that provides the alpha function necessary to transform unrepresented experience into lived experience symbolized and shared through language.

An additional controversy revealed in this collection has to do not only with the historical controversy over the existence of a death instinct, but whether it is an inborn destructive drive as Freud and Klein believed, or related to fear of dying as Bion held. Several chapters further explore the bodily basis of the death instinct. Blue (Chapter 10) writes about the death instinct from the perspective of the fetus' fear of annihilation in the process of birth, which she suggests may be projectively communicated to the mother through somatic channels. Alternatively, Winters (Chapter 17) finds support in the biology of autoimmunity for an inherent tendency toward destructiveness that is kept in check by regulatory mechanisms. Psychic developments leading to an unbinding of drives, she suggests, unleash this destructive potential. Although Ricard and Jarreau (Chapter 7) do not posit the death instinct as the source for Jarreau's dreams of his own death, one could postulate an inherent body-based death drive that communicates body's anxiety about its fate oneirically. It is noteworthy that four chapters of the book take up death as a theme; this stands in contrast to its lesser prominence generally in psychoanalytic theory and praxis. The death instinct and its possible biological roots are particularly relevant now in the face of the worldwide death toll of COVID-19 and emerging evidence that the most severe illnesses from the virus relate to the body's excessive immune response, that is, attack against itself.

A final controversy revealed in these chapters has to do with the analytic setting and impact of working remotely. Ironically, the final part of the book titled "Body in virtual space" has only a single chapter. This configuration speaks to a longstanding controversy in psychoanalysis about the efficacy of psychoanalysis conducted via remote technology and the relative inattention given to studying its impact on analytic treatment. Enter the COVID-19 pandemic on December 31, 2019 in Wuhan, China and suddenly, in a matter of months, psychoanalysts worldwide were confronted with the need to conduct analysis remotely to mitigate contracting and spreading the virus. Although many aspects of this situation are important to consider, the one taken up by Marzi (Chapter 19) has to do with bodily experience and the identity of the analyst in remote analysis. Does the body as psychoanalytic object vanish when analyst and analysand are separated spatially? Does the lack of physical contiguity render bodily phenomena (apart from sound and speech) inaccessible? Or, does introduction of the digital realm in the analytic field provide opportunities to learn more about body and its relation to mental life? In other words, does cyberspace provide access to new ways of thinking about the mind's 'virtual spaces' and about psychoanalysis itself? For Marzi, remote analysis is not synonymous with disembodied analysis. In fact, for some analysands working remotely seems to allow greater access and freedom of expression of intimate bodily experience. Regardless of where readers land on this controversy, all will agree it is an issue that deserves a great deal of careful thought and continued debate.

Beyond

The 'beyond' in our book's title acknowledges the continually evolving nature of psychoanalytic theory and clinical technique standing on the shoulders of our ancestors beginning with Freud and extending to Winnicott and Bion, among many others. Beyond also draws attention to the future and where we go from here in what we hope is an ongoing dialog among psychoanalysts worldwide as to the significance of bodily phenomena in human emotional development from conception to inevitable mortality.

We hope the diverse ways our chapter authors have delineated body as psycho-analytic object and sought to apply it in their work with analysands enhance the utility of this concept as an important analytic tool. Additionally, we hope the clinical vignettes contained in all of the chapters of this volume give specificity to how uniquely different analysts work with bodily phenomena in the clinical situation and conceive of it theoretically. In so doing, we hope that bodily phenomena first presented in the nonverbal 'song and dance' of the analytic encounter may receive greater attention and become further integrated into evolving clinical theory.

As previously mentioned (Controversies) and demonstrated in many of the chapters of this book, we see a path forward that no longer insists on incompatibility between Freudian drive theory and a body-based understanding of object relations theory. In this regard, we hope the individual and collective voices expressed in the volume fosters further dialog of this and other controversies related to the role of bodily phenomena in mental life and well-being within psychoanalysis, and in related fields such as philosophy, sociology, and political science. Additionally, given the necessity of modifications to the analytic setting during the pandemic and likely beyond (including remote analysis) as well as our increasing reliance on various forms of artificial intelligence (e.g. computers, smartphones), it behooves us to continue analyzing the somatopsychic impact associated with these increasingly complex forms of communication.

Finally, as demonstrated by the collection of voices that defines our approach for exploring body as psychoanalytic object in this volume, we suggest the strength of our collective understanding as psychoanalysts, now and going forward, is only possible through respectful dialog and debate with one another; body as group phenomenon, rather than individual entity.

References

Bion, W.R. (1962). *Learning from experience.* William Heinemann Medical Books Ltd.

Bion, W.R. (1963). *Elements of psycho-analysis.* Basic Books Publishing Co., Inc.

de Toffoli, C. (2011). The living body in the psychoanalytic experience. *Psychoanalytic Quarterly, 80*(3):595–618.

Faimberg, H. (2005). Après-coup. *The International Journal of Psychoanalysis, 86*(1):1–6.

Klein, M. (1930 [1975]). The importance of symbol-formation in the development of the ego. In *The writings of Melanie Klein* (Vol.1). Hogarth Press.

Lemma, A. (2014). *Minding the body: The body in psychoanalysis and beyond.* Routledge.

López-Corvo, R. (2003). *The dictionary of the work of W. R. Bion.* Karnac Books.

Miller, P. (2014). *Driving soma: A transformational process in the analytic encounter.* Karnac Books.

Press, J. (2019). *Experiencing the body: A psychoanalytic dialogue on psychosomatics.* Routledge.

Sodré, I. (2005). 'As I was walking down the stair, I saw a concept which wasn't there …' Or, après-coup: A missing concept? *The International Journal of Psychoanalysis, 86*(1):7–10.

Tsolas, V. and Anzieu-Premmereur, C. (2018). *A psychoanalytic exploration of the body in today's world.* Routledge.

Winnicott, D.W. (1949 [1975]) Mind and its relation to the psyche-soma. In *Through paediatrics to psycho-analysis* (pp. 243–254). Hogarth Press.

Winnicott, D.W. (1965) *The maturational processes and the facilitating environment: Studies in the theory of emotional development.* Hogarth Press.

Part I

Mind–body relations in Winnicott, Bion, and beyond

1 Introduction

Caron Harrang, Drew Tillotson, and Nancy C. Winters

In this first part of the book, we offer two views of body as psychoanalytic object from Lesley Caldwell and Robert Oelsner, scholars in the published work of Donald Winnicott and Wilfred Bion, respectively. Their critical engagement with these psychoanalytic luminaries gives us a fresh look back at Winnicott's and Bion's contributions through the lens of bodily phenomena as well as pointing the way forward to the constantly evolving 'beyond' in psychoanalytic theory and clinical technique.

Lesley Caldwell begins her chapter "Being after Winnicott: minding the body, embodying the mind" with an evocative quote from Didier Anzieu (2016) to introduce her exploration of how, until more recent times, psychoanalytic interest in the body has been largely disregarded: "In Freud's time it was sex, but in the [1980s] it was the body that was ignored" (p. 23). Caldwell primarily utilizes the work of Donald Winnicott and Wilfred Bion to elucidate how the body was not incorporated or developed by prominent theoreticians of post-Freudian, British psychoanalysis. By also integrating insights from authors not belonging to the British School, Caldwell constructs an investigation into how the body in psychoanalysis has been mainly overlooked until recent times due primarily to the theoretical privileging of conscious and unconscious processes, an analytic "insistence on the capacity to think, to reflect, to mentalise as the foundations of psychic awareness" without including the consanguinity of body and mind. Caldwell acknowledges Winnicott's and Bion's direct concern with the body in their theoretical contributions was not immediately obvious; they both—in similar and different ways—explored the term 'being' and its implications for what analysts do.

Caldwell's most important contribution is her focus on the integration of the body into "what analysts do." Her main interest is what actually occurs in the consulting room between patient and analyst *beyond* language and more in the realm of the body and "states of being" (Mawson, 2019, p. 79). She posits *being with* our patients can be very demanding, perhaps more demanding than *thinking about* them and with them through offering interpretations. Germane to her focus on inhabiting states of being with patients, her use of Winnicott's concepts of "going on being" (1954, p. 274; 1960, p. 149) and "continuity of being" (1960, p. 54) are especially helpful in thinking about the discovery of one's own body starting at

DOI: 10.4324/9781003195559-1

infancy, which may later be evoked in the transference and countertransference during analysis. Caldwell pays particularly close attention in her chapter to theories regarding women's bodies and the mother's body, drawing upon the work of Rosine Perelberg and Marion Milner. In an especially fortuitous passage in light of the COVID-19 pandemic, Caldwell invokes Carla De Toffoli's (2011) conceptions of breathing in approaching some aspects of analytic work:

> [breath] spreads throughout the body, goes beyond it and is not in itself containable, it moves freely from I to you, like the psychic, eluding the customs barriers of the single individual... necessitating a constant oscillation between being one and being two in the analytic pair.
>
> (p. 601)

Caldwell describes an analytic encounter that evokes powerful feelings of hate, boredom, and helplessness on her part with wishes "to get rid of him" during two short periods of a patient's analysis. She describes her countertransference as "intensely physical" and thinks it is related to her patient's early mother–infant experiences. However, this insight is not enough to alter this somatic countertransference dynamic. Reflecting upon her discussion of the body in this chapter, Caldwell wonders what might have occurred with this patient had she been able to pay closer attention to the patient's bodily impact on her at the time, hence to *being with* rather than *knowing about*.

Robert Oelsner's title "Does the body have a mind?" is like a Zen koan, opening a kaleidoscope of possibilities with no easy answers. Oelsner's exploration of what he calls "body mentality" and "somato-logic" evinces a central concern of this book, the role of body in generating meaning. He begins with a quote from Bion's *Memoir of the Future* (1991): "MIND (speaking to BODY) What is that amusing little affair sticking out? I like it. It has a mind of its own—just like me" (p. 434). We are thus reminded, the amusing little affair that has shaped psychoanalytic theory since its inception *truly* has a mind of its own.

In Oelsner's consulting room we meet Mark who has a sore neck. This material, Oelsner says, "brings in a condensed manner the whole history of the body in relation to the mind." Mark insists his sore neck has no relation to his unconscious. He imagines his aging analyst would not complain of such pain. Mark's associations are to other problems with his body, especially dislike of his penis, which he believes causes pain to others; there is confusion between his penis and his tongue which hurts others with words. Oelsner observes diverse meanings of Mark's symptoms. To begin with his symptom is somatic (*not* psychosomatic) and evolves into a hysterical conversive phenomenon of being possessed by a sadistic sexual predator, and lastly hypochondriacal identification with an analyst in pain.

Oelsner further explores the distinction between somatic, hysteric, and hypochondriacal phenomena in a lucid review of psychoanalytic ideas about mind–body relations from Freud to Klein to Bion, noting Freud's understanding of hysteria as "a disease of the nerves without fever" led him from neuroscience to a science of the mind. Also considered are the French somaticists Marty and de M'Uzan; Piera Aulagnier; and Donald Meltzer. Oelsner employs clinical illustrations from Freud and Klein. For example, the hypochondria of Freud's Wolf Man (1918) is seen as an identification with his ailing mother. Oelsner adds, Klein later posits hypochondriacal anxiety "comes from an unconscious identification with objects that have been damaged as well as the damaged objects retaliating and damaging the inside of the body." In Klein's (1961) analysis of young Richard recovering from a sore throat, she shows there is "actual physical illness, hypochondria and hysteria," making an often-neglected connection between hysterical symptoms and hypochondriacal anxieties.

In the second part of the chapter Oelsner reviews selected concepts relevant to 'body mentality' from Bion's early, mid-term, and late work. Early Bion (1961), Oelsner tells us, posits a proto-mental system functioning at the body level "in which physical and psychological or mental are undifferentiated" (p. 101). Mid-term Bion describes how the evacuation of beta elements projected into the body causes psychosomatic symptoms. As an example, Oelsner's patient Mr. K has indigestion. Oelsner wonders, "can the analyst speak to the indigestion so that his gastrointestinal system would understand?" Harrang's chapter later in the book also takes up this question.

Oelsner quotes generously from Bion's enigmatic late work *Memoir of the Future* (1991) in which Body and Mind are in dialog. However, they speak different languages, revealing an unbridgeable caesura between them. Oelsner concludes his incisive synthesis of Bion's early, mid-term, and late views of body and mind with questions. "Can psychoanalysis tame these characters with their wild thoughts?" "Can the impenetrable diaphragm become a friendly contact barrier?" As Bion came to believe, Oelsner suggests the vertex of psychoanalysis is to "integrate parts of the self in discord" and the quest for language that "speaks to all, from Body to Mind."

References

Anzieu, D. (2016). *The skin ego* (Trans. N. Segal). Karnac Books.
Bion, W.R. (1961). *Experiences in groups*. Tavistock Publications.
Bion, W.R. (1991). *A memoir of the future*. Karnac Books.
De Toffoli, C. (2011). The living body in the psychoanalytic experience. *Psychoanalytic Quarterly*, 80(3):595–618.
Freud, S. (1918). From the history of an infantile neurosis. In J. Strachey (Ed. & Trans.). *The standard edition of the complete psychological works of Sigmund Freud* (Vol. 17, pp. 1–124). Hogarth Press.
Klein, M. (1961 [1984]). *Narrative of a child analysis: The conduct of the psycho-analysis of children as seen in the treatment of a ten-year-old boy*. The Free Press.
Mawson, C. (2019). *Psychoanalysis and anxiety: From knowing to being*. Routledge.
Winnicott, D.W. (2016 [1954]). Character types: The foolhardy and the cautious: On funfairs, thrills and regressions, by Michael Balint. In L. Caldwell & H. Taylor Robinson (Eds.). *The collected works of D. W. Winnicott* (Vol. 4, pp. 273–278). Oxford University Press.
Winnicott, D.W. (2016 [1960]). The theory of the parent infant relationship. In L. Caldwell & H. Taylor Robinson (Eds.). *The collected works of D. W. Winnicott* (Vol. 6, pp. 141–158). Oxford University Press.

2 Being after Winnicott

Minding the body, embodying the mind

Lesley Caldwell

"In Freud's time it was sex," claimed Didier Anzieu (2016), "but in the eighties it was the body that was ignored. The body as a vital element of human reality, as a general, irreducible, pre-sexual given, as the thing that all psychical functions lean on analytically" (p. 23).

It is logical to oppose psyche and soma and therefore to oppose the emotional development and the bodily development of an individual. It is not logical however to oppose the mental and the physical as these are not of the same stuff. Mental phenomena are complications of variable importance in psyche soma continuity of being, in that which adds up to the individual's 'self' (Winnicott, 1949, p. 254).

Contemporary psychoanalytic concern with the body followed the explosion of interest in the body in the human sciences in the seventies and eighties, and it is a development related to the body's "eclipse," to use Armando Ferrari's (2004) word, in much post-war psychoanalytic theorizing, especially that of British object relations. As Ferrari himself pointed out, an eclipse is not a disappearance or an actual absence, since what is eclipsed is always there. Even in a total eclipse the object is there in shadow (il corpo viene posto in ombra, si eclisse: non sparisce (p. 278)).

In this chapter, I approach this eclipse from the British tradition, particularly the work of Donald Winnicott, but also that of Wilfred Bion, two theorists whose increasingly convergent interests have until recently been overlooked in London, if not in Europe and Latin America. I do not trace a complete trajectory of their work, but rather use it to introduce some related themes that are worthy of consideration, together with some insights from authors who do not belong to the British school. On the basis of the work of the Italian analyst Carla de Toffoli, I revisit a case of my own in which I speculate / free associate to material in which, despite my awareness of the patient's bodily impact, I did not develop the possible meanings of what may have elicited my response at the time.

The foundations of psychoanalysis in the interrelation of body and mind, and the affective life of the patient being spoken through the body as in Dora's use of her reticule as negating her denial of her masturbation, had Freud (1905) stating, "He that has eyes to see and ears to hear may convince himself that no mortal can keep a secret. If his lips are silent he chatters with his fingertips; betrayal

DOI: 10.4324/9781003195559-2

oozes out of him at every pore" (pp. 77–78). And yet a major orientation of the discursive formations of post-war psychoanalysis did seem to overlook the impact of the body's very bodilyness, as material presence, and as carrier of other dimensions of what being human means.

The noted anthropologist Mary Douglas (2002) claimed the body provides the primary symbolic system for signifying other aspects of personal and social life. She proposed two intimately related bodies, the social body and the physical body, with the experience of the physical body always linked with and dependent on changing perceptions of both. Boundaries and margins are central to her understanding of both social and physical bodies, but psychoanalysis also considers the psychological body and the impact of the unconscious meanings it carries. While the psyche's participation in the symbolic systems clustering around the constitution of bodily boundaries and margins and the sense of interiority they carry has always been recognized, it has also been consistently overlooked.

Bodies change in form as do the meanings ascribed to those forms and the social contexts in which they are understood. For instance, current preoccupations with the gym and fitness foreground a particular body as did the bodies of the middle ages that lactated, produced the stigmata, and so on, but what is so significant for the contemporary body is the extreme concentration on the body itself and its links with ideas of identity and the self, in ways that the suffering and/ or ecstatic bodies of the Europe of the late middle ages were not: arguably, they may have been a way of further losing that self in the godhead. Modern conditions of psychological disturbance and difficulty however, gather increasingly around the body, bodily symptoms, bodily change and its limits, claims for bodily modification and rejection of what the sexed, biological body has traditionally signified.

While both Winnicott and Bion contributed significantly to the general field of psychoanalytic enquiry approached through the specificity of the analytic relation, the analytic setting, and the shifting temporalities present in every session, their direct concern with the body is less immediately obvious. For them, conceptions of the body, the self, the mind, and being come in and out of focus, singly and together, and the totality of these terms maps a network of multiply inflected investigations that each pursues in similar and different ways around the term *being*, and its implications for what each of them understands as the project of psychoanalysis and of what analysts do.

For instance, Winnicott's (1949) description of psychosomatic conditions as "counteracting a seduction of the psyche into the mind" (p. 254) in his paper "Mind and its relation to the psyche soma" is both suggestive of some patients' need to keep their body in the foreground for themselves and for their analysts, but it also highlights some recent strands in psychoanalysis which, on occasion, seem to have been seduced into a preferred reading of psychoanalytic understanding and treatment as focused especially on the mind and its primacy. In acknowledging this stage however, Damasio (2012) referred to it as now passed: "The classical association of psychoanalysis with the investigation of language processes is no longer the limit of investigative approaches" (p. 591). Didier Anzieu, working within a different tradition, argued that the influence of Jacques

Lacan's concern with language in the Francophone world had shifted the focus to a more exclusive emphasis on discourse, words, and their conditions of existence, conditions in which the body was "eclipsed."

The contemporary resort to descriptions like keeping patients in mind, having a place in someone's mind, finding a place in our minds, holding someone in mind, and so on, together with an insistence on the capacity to think, to reflect, to mentalize as the foundations of psychic awareness also need to be questioned, and the approaches they endorse explicitly and implicitly subjected to historical contextualization to understand both the parameters and the origins of this very widespread tendency and its relation to a concern with the body. For instance, when an experienced clinician interpreted the patient had missed "the analyst's analytic mind" over a weekend, a common type of formulation, I was struck anew by just how much the narrowness of what it prioritises blots out the texture of the experience of the analytic relation. When we miss something or, more particularly someone, what are we missing? Can a person's self, her personality, her being, whether analyst or analysand, be summed up in this way? In such an intervention it is as if the analyst had abandoned the challenge continuingly posed to be in contact with her patient.

The consistent recourse to thinking and to states of mind now found in most psychoanalytic discourse, written or spoken, may also register a shift in the psychoanalytic enterprise, a shift that may parallel the body's eclipse, but certainly needs to be thought in conjunction with it.

Mind over body

Widespread interest in theories of thinking developed in the wake of Bion's paper at the International Psychoanalytical Association congress in 1960. It was later reinforced by a particular developmental perspective emphasizing the extended interest in attachment, and the cognitive and affective concerns with which it has become linked (demonstrated in my own department, The Psychoanalysis Unit at University College London's, focus on mentalization and reflective functioning). Together with the interest in neuroscience and the development of neuropsychoanalysis, these strands have contributed to the shaping of psychoanalytic accounts that tended to omit the body, though Damasio (1999) himself, as mentioned earlier, often insisted on its primacy. For instance,

> I have proposed (without thinking of Freud but coincident with him), that the body, real, and as represented in the brain, is the theater for the emotions, and that feelings are largely read-outs of body changes 'really' enacted in the body *and* 'really' constructed in an 'as-if' mode in body-mapping brain structures.
>
> (p. 38)

We now know that *by its very functioning* the body starts a reflective process that ends with the birth of human subjectivity, that cognitive, emotional, and socializing capacities are intertwined in the architecture of the brain (Luyten, spoken presentation UCL, 2013), but what follows clinically in the sessions of an intensive treatment seems less clear.

This was first raised for me in 2010 in an event on Winnicott and Bion on holding and containing, when the organizer wrote to the speakers, "Eventually these features could be summed up or expressed as the comparison of the respective theories of thinking of these outstanding theoreticians of British psychoanalysis." But I doubted then and continue to doubt whether Winnicott was ever particularly concerned with a theory of thinking, least of all in his attention to holding, though holding may provide the kind of start that will enable thinking of a creative rather than a defensive kind.

In his new book, Chris Mawson (2019) approaches the area I am concerned with here in his discussion of an example reported by Michael Parsons (2014, p. 117), where Parsons misremembered what a prospective patient, an artist, had said. The artist wanted help in understanding what lay behind his blocked creativity and his loss of capacity to respond emotionally in his work. After the consultation, Parsons remembered the artist's words, "He had become a maker of things rather than an investigator of states of mind" as having made an impression on him around the possible parallels in being an artist and being a psychoanalyst. When he looked at his notes however, he found that the patient had actually said, "He had become a maker of things rather than an investigator of states of being." Parsons thought he had assimilated the patient's words to the "apparently more manageable idea of an analyst as one who deals with states of mind" (quoted in Mawson, 2019, p. 79).

Mawson was struck by Parsons' willingness to scrutinize himself about this mistake, which led him to wonder,

> If this experienced analyst had identified closely with the patient's description of the creative task shared by both of them, which he evidently had done, it seems possible that he had also partaken of the mood of angst at the possibility of its loss.
>
> (p. 80)

In line with his own account of the foundational position of anxiety in human subjectivity, Mawson asks if the misremembered phrase,

> was a realisation of the ontological despair of losing the vital functions of creativity and potency, which lie at the heart of purpose and meaning for the artist and the psychoanalyst, and the recognition of the loss of these not as 'ontical losses' but as losses of being, of being what one is.
>
> (p. 80)

Parsons' (2014) own thought was, "What this man actually said gave me a momentary sense, not just of understanding, but of recognition. Then I let go of it, opting instead to deal with states of mind" (p. 117, quoted in Mawson, 2019, p. 80).

Parsons here sees himself approaching the disquieting array of emotions involved for both protagonists in the realization of "recognition" in the consulting room and the profound emotions it carries. Mawson too realizes what is at stake; "A 'state of mind' is something that we can opt to deal with; and it constitutes something that can, in fact, be 'dealt with'" (p. 80).

Parsons and Mawson seem to imply, and I agree with them, that "states of being" call up something very different, and that involves a much more demanding role for the analyst. Mawson's own reflection reinforces the need for a questioning of our current ways of speaking raised above:

> 'State of mind' is extremely common and verging on the automatic in the English-speaking world. It is a serviceable enough term but it does predispose us more strongly in our thinking towards knowing-about and the ontic, than it does towards becoming attuned in contact with the ontological anxiety which is disclosive of the being of the patient.
>
> (p. 81)

Being and the body

In his account of the origins of being in his composite text, *Human Nature*, much of which is directly or indirectly concerned with the terms, psyche, soma, being, and self, Winnicott (1988) asks, "What is the state of the human individual as the being emerges out of non-being?" (p. 131). He then adds an apparently different question: "What is the fundamental state to which every individual however old and with whatever experiences can return in order to start again?" (p. 132). He answers that it is "essential aloneness under specific conditions of dependency which provide a continuity of being with awareness, a condition that is never again precisely repeated" (p. 132). For Winnicott, becoming aware of this state of aloneness precisely involves coming into being in the first place and he further elaborates, "The life of an individual is an interval between two states of unaliveness. The first of these, out of which aliveness arises, colours ideas people have about the second, death" (p. 132).

It is how the baby emerges from unaliveness into aliveness that shapes and organizes the living and experiencing human being. Such an emphasis certainly does not discount the mind, rather, the mind is its guarantor, but for Winnicott, if all goes well, it develops as part of the psyche: "The psyche begins as an imaginative elaboration of physical functioning having its most important duty the binding together of past experiences, potentialities, and the present moment awareness and expectancy for the future. Thus the self comes into existence" (p. 19).

Such a condensed statement begins to raise the complexity of the analyst's task in terms of a consistently attuned awareness for the individual forms of communication brought by each patient in any session and which demands much of the clinician. Winnicott endorses a psychoanalytic account of human subjectivity that assigns a continuing task to the psyche of containing and further elaborating the simultaneously coexistent temporalities of the individual in the session, the difficulties which can arise in the analytic encounter, and what analysis can offer in the consolidation of the self.

Winnicott's colleague and friend, the Canadian analyst Clifford Scott's (1949) account of the "body scheme" identifies it as

> the whole in which parts develop and boundaries arise as time goes on. It contains and enables a disorganised array of parts such as ego, non-ego, psyche soma, psyche, soul, that, over time come to be organized and for which the body boundary is perhaps the most important aspect. The self becomes connected with what is within the body boundary, and the 'not self' with what is outside it. Sooner or later imagination comes to be felt as a part of the self.
>
> (p. 148)

Scott was in sustained dialogue with Winnicott in those years and their themes show evidence of a continuing collaboration.

Whereas the index to *The Collected Works of Donald Winnicott* (2016) gives an array of references to the body, the index to *The Complete Works of W.R. Bion* (2014) gives only two[1] though Chris Mawson kindly provided me with 20 further references, all dating from the sixties and seventies, and mostly clustering around the different possibilities allowed by medical description and what might be enabled if psychoanalysis were able to demonstrate its findings scientifically. Bion (1973) offered the fantasy of a psychoanalysis that could work in two directions

> Suppose such a questionnaire, based on the extremely important nature of the central nervous system, revealed a kind of mental X-ray which showed that the patient concerned was liable to develop, say, cancer or a duodenal ulcer; the parasympathetic nervous system could reveal things not about the mind, but about the future of that particular corporeal body. That is, psychoanalysis would not be concerned only with the human mind, but also with revealing the physical condition of the patient... there might be analysts who were concerned to reveal the physical health of the patient in a way which no medical science or procedure could, as well as those who were concerned with the operation of the mind with regard to the mental world. Thus, there could be a physical psychoanalysis just as there could be a psychological psychoanalysis.
>
> (p. 65)

An extremely challenging proposal!

In "Penetrating silence" (Bion, 2014 [1976]), of great interest for its approach to silence and its similarities with Winnicott's statements in "Communicating and not communicating," Bion contrasts physical doctors with psychoanalysts,

> ... concerned with what we suppose is the human mind. If he believes there is such a thing as the mind which he is supposed to investigate, he has very

little indeed to fall back on ... we don't in fact deal with bodies or minds: we deal with the totality of a person or of a group. And there the amount of information we get is infinite: it has no boundaries whatsoever.

(*The Complete Works of W.R. Bion*, Volume XV, p. 34)

Bion presents us with the task that the analyst undertakes every day in grappling with the totality of the human being through choices, selections, and priorities, made on the basis of his or her own experience and understanding of what analysis is.

The first half of my title, 'Minding the body' carries the meanings of 'paying attention to,' 'looking out for' the body, and the comparatively recent explosion of interest in gender identities and gender disorders and their apparently close but now often disputed association with actual bodies, together with the primacy of sexuality for Freud and psychoanalysis had initially led me to think that the woman's body might be my central focus. Rosine Perelberg's (2018) "Love and Melancholia in the analysis of women by women" draws attention not only to how the lost primary object may be found and reconstituted in the course of the transference counter transference dynamic, but the extent to which psychical separation from the mother so often involves bodily symptoms for women, a finding evident in the articles in the earlier collection, *Female Experience* (Leff, J. & Perelberg, R., (Eds.), 1997). Perelberg proposes that women analysands' bodily experiences seem to represent an attempt to have a body and a self that are separate from the mother while their symptoms simultaneously condense early conflicts of fusion and separation and their links with the original primary erotic relationship (p. 107).

This perspective was consistently there in the work of that older generation of British women analysts, Dinora Pines, Enid Balint, Nina Colthart, and its grounding in the body distinguishes it from Winnicott and Bion, for both of whom a close attention to the adult body, particularly that of the woman, and even more the woman as mother, is definitely missing. For, while Winnicott's primary maternal preoccupation proposes both a bodily and an affective state in the woman as mother involving an intense concentration on her baby for a short period of time, it omits or overrides the woman as *never only mother*: even in the earliest stages the new mother is other than mother, to herself and others. For the woman, and especially for our women patients, being both "mother" and "other than mother," whether they (or we) are actually mothers or not, needs to be considered in the psychological effects of that ever present duality and its conflicted consequences far more thoroughly than was ever done by Winnicott, or most later analysts.

But British women analysts did maintain an awareness of the body and what it signifies. For instance, Marion Milner's (1969) extraordinary case history of her patient Susan, *The Hands of the Living God*, attends acutely to the body, drawing powerfully on her readings of the image, "a particularly condensed way of communicating with oneself and with another, analytically and otherwise," as Milner calls it. The 154 images reproduced in a book of almost 500 pages are only a small selection of the almost 4,000 the patient brought to her in the course of about eight years, beginning in 1950, eight years into a twenty-year analysis begun in 1942. In itself, the timing of this shift in the focus of the analysis is of interest since the image-producing years were framed by years of analysis, both before and after, marking Milner's treating, thinking about, and living with her patient and her patient's drawings, which are intensely concentrated on the body, as a specific aspect of this long analysis.

If Winnicott paid scant attention to the adult woman's body, he certainly insisted on the centrality of the body when it came to children and babies, discussing physical complaints and conditions with such close attention to their emotional and psychological aspects, and their psychological origins, that his confidence must surely still occasion a challenge to paediatricians. And his insistence that, "It cannot be urged too often that the child must be seen naked; in no other way is it possible to avoid missing important and yet quite obvious disease signals" (*The Collected Works of D. W. Winnicott*, Volume 1, 3:2, p. 190), would almost certainly find a questioning voice in the anxious world of today.

Winnicott's claims for the primacy of motor activity in the infant as the first instance of the centrality of aggression, and his claims that the development of a sense of self and the growth of psychic life is arrived at through bodily action and sensation and what it delivers in the infant, insist on the body and its responses as the origins of the psyche. For him, clinicians must be attentive both to the place of instinctual life, moods, and the shifts in affective and psychical states delivered by bodily changes. From that first motricity onwards to the enormous changes effected by reaching out, standing upright, and walking, and then through the continuing demands of the life cycle, the body both records and embodies not only the self but the whole of unconscious life.

An early paper to dermatologists (Winnicott, 1938) addressed not only the skin, a vital aspect for any discussion of bodies, but breathing and breath, a much less studied dimension. His statement, "Every skin or other bodily phenomenon that has a relation to feelings must have a relation to the whole personality" (*The Collected Works of D. W. Winnicott*, Volume 1, 4:18, p. 452) is discussed from two perspectives: the way the skin becomes involved in the child's or adult's fantasies as a boundary for what is inside the body, what has to be got in or out of the body, and how this should be done (p. 454), and the part played by the skin in feelings and changes of feeling in us all, a topic he approaches through excitement, while agreeing that "rage, fear, apprehensiveness and desire" also deserve study (p. 455).

The skin is the borderline between physiology and psychology that keeps together the body and what in this paper Winnicott calls "the soul." Esther Bick's (1968) work develops this with a more Kleinian emphasis, though her argument is similar:

> In its most primitive form the parts of the personality are felt to have no binding force amongst themselves and must therefore be held together in a way that is experienced by them passively, by the skin functioning as a boundary.
> (p. 484)

Didier Anzieu regarded his work as similar to Bick's, but he particularly built on Winnicott's (1962) statement, "It is only when all goes well that the person of the baby starts to be linked with the body and the body functions, with the skin as the limiting membrane" (quoted in Anzieu, 2016, p. 59). Anzieu gathers his evidence for the skin ego from four different sets of data, the first from projective testing, where two variables among responses to Rorschach ink blot tests, "barrier and penetration scores" are especially interesting for any discussion of the body. Where the barrier score "implies a protective surface such as a membrane shell or skin which can be linked symbolically to the perception of the borders of the body image," "the penetration variable refers to responses that may express symbolically a sense that the body is weak protective covering." Fischer and Cleveland (1958, quoted in Anzieu, 2016) found that in people suffering from psychosomatic conditions, those whose symptoms were located on the outside imagined a body surrounded by a strong defensive wall, while those with internal symptoms had an idea of the body as easily penetrated, lacking a protective barrier. What seems compelling about their work is that these imaginary representations precede the symptoms.

Anzieu suggests that if we see the body image as a representation developed by the nascent ego through the mother's handling and holding, what is involved is what Rene Angelergues (1975) terms

> the symbolic process of representing a boundary that functions as both 'stabilising image' and protective wrapping. This action posits the body as an object of cathexis and its image as the product of that cathexis. This cathexis captures an object that is not interchangeable, except in states of delusion, and must at all costs be kept intact. The function of borders is connected to the imperative of maintaining integrity. The body image belongs to the order of phantasy and secondary elaboration; it is a representation that acts upon the body.
>
> (quoted in Anzieu 2016, p. 35)

Within that boundary, imaginative elaboration and its coming into being through the coming together of psyche, soma, and mind may lead to specific symptoms which have already been imagined.

Being, and Winnicott's phrases "going on being" (1954, p. 274; 1960, p. 149) and "continuity of being" (1960, p. 54) emphasize his interest in the totality of the patient before us in the consulting room, and Marion Milner (1972), in thinking about the relation of body and self, wonders at the interrelation of both with being:

> Linked to this question of the discovery of the self is the discovery of one's own body. So, the question arises what is the relation of the sense of being which he (Winnicott) says must precede the finding of the self to the awareness of one's own body? … here I am thinking of enjoying one's own breathing as an example of creativity.
>
> (Milner archive, BPAS)

I will return to breathing below, but Winnicott (1970) goes some way towards advancing Milner's question about whether being precedes the realization of the self through awareness of the body in a late paper, "On the basis for self in body," in a discussion of two cases, Iiro, aged nine, and Jill, who is 17. For both Iiro and Jill a sense of their being appears to have preceded their awareness that the body that carries that being, the physical location of the self, is in some way, physically imperfect. For both this awareness arises from their respective encounters with the external environment, and the impact of actual events on the body and what it carries in such a way as to challenge each in their sense of self, of who they are, and how they experience being in the world. Where Iiro's physical condition, syndactyly, had resulted in continuous interventions since infancy, the tiny difference in the length of one of Jill's limbs is unobservable, but has become the unconscious representative of something missing in the self. This symbolic sense of something not there in Jill, embodied in the small difference in length of one leg, had gathered in an absence in her that carried the death of her father at three years, and its accompanying unconscious fantasies. This was then manifested in the adolescent girl in an inability to complete things. Winnicott separated the reality of losing her father at three and what the growing child had come to make of this, and this leads him to distinguishing between the internally constructed foundations of a self-organized around the body and its functions, and external events and Jill's understanding of them as shifting the balance between psyche and soma, which results in the girl's body as the symbolic representation of emotional conflicts that happened elsewhere.

Milner's idea of "enjoying one's breath" rather than merely engaging in it without thought associates breath and breathing with human creativity, and returns her to Winnicott, whose account of the infant had linked it to the centrality of "illusion," and with a child's interest in "bubbles, clouds, rainbows and all mysterious phenomena …/along with the interest in breath which never decides whether it comes primarily from within or without and which provides a basis for the conception of spirit, soul, anima" (1945, p. 154).

Breathing may be a condition of being alive, but it has not formed a major emphasis in psychoanalytic thinking about bodies, except for certain specific conditions like asthma. The American analyst Michael Eigen (1977) addresses this lack of attention to the experience of breathing in Western approaches to the body and personality, identifying their concentration "almost exclusively with the experience of appetite … a raw material to be transformed by the higher functions of will, reason, or faith" (p. 43). This neglect of breathing and the focus on appetite is also present in psychoanalysis, but Eigen himself sees the experience of breathing as a central bridging experience of the ego,

> as the ego gradually allows itself to participate deeply, at least periodically, in the flow of breathing qua experienced breathing, it more securely grasps its own basic ambiguity of being both within and without the body: I am but am not my body … The sense of self is extended to encompass not only

the ambiguity of being both out of and in the body but also the awareness of being rooted in two fundamentally different kinds of body experiences.

(p. 46)

The analytic concern with being, of the person as always occupying internal and external worlds, both in and out of the body, was a primary interest of Milner, who entered into an extended dialogue with Eigen around these very issues. More recently the Italian analyst, Carla De Toffoli (2011) developed a discussion of breath and breathing to approach some dimensions of analytic work. She compared the common recourse to a feeding model for the analyst patient relationship with the absence of respiratory metaphors, "it (breath) spreads throughout the body, goes beyond it and is not in itself containable, it moves freely from I to you, like the psychic, eluding the customs barriers of the single individual" (p. 601). Respiratory exchanges she says,

> imply the being and the becoming of the self and the other, the communication and the thing communicated are not sensorially perceptible and they transit freely in both directions ... The soma is given physical life and the psyche is represented in the body, necessitating a constant oscillation between being one and being two in the analytic pair.

(p. 601)

She offers two clinical examples, on the basis of the first of which, she thought she could manage the second.

In his initial consultation, on seeing the large plant in her office, a man of 25 said, "My problem is that I don't know what to give back to plants in return for what they give to me" (p. 602). After a lot of thinking the analyst understood this as his asking to exchange "only or mainly air, which, through breath, coincides with life, pervading the body, penetrating the cells, and at the same time consciousness which brings matter alive" (p. 602). She found herself thinking of childbirth, but when she finally spoke she said, "Good, this is a perfect equilibrium: the plants giving you oxygen and you give them carbon dioxide which they need." He replied, "My name is Lan-Freud." She thought that for him "the oxygen of life was my being Freud while he breathed in, to the point of incorporating it, becoming it" (p. 603). That is, she thought he was "asking me to recognise breath as a metaphor for the relationship more than language, the air round us as a vector of transformation" (p. 603). His insane waste produce, the CO_2, was central for him and she would have to breathe it without judging him. Like the plant, she was to breathe in his insanity (p. 603). A few months into treatment he told her his name, "Lamberto." She said, "I am Dr De Toffoli," which she explained as having accepted the function that her patient was asking her to perform, to first be at one with him in order to help him to travel to a dual dimension where there could be two bodies and two minds, which the exchange of names represents (p. 605).

After this experience she describes herself as being able to be with another young student who came for around nine months, four times a week, and slept. During his sessions she distinguished 12 types of breathing, noticed variations in rhythm, tempo, and intensity in his respiratory activity—she lived with him through groaning, wheezing, and exclamations. She imagined obstacles to oxygenation, stoppages in blood flow, crushings of the umbilical cord until, "they came to 'the tranquil flow of air from one to the other'" and she saw, "the texture of the self emerge contextually from the relationship and from the body ... his bodily presence and my mind prefigured themselves and modelled themselves in turn" (p. 606). One day he looked round and stroked the wall near the couch. He had woken up and emerged from inside her.

De Toffoli proposes body and psyche as two ways of experiencing the complex reality of the human being and of what can happen in the consulting room and while her case reports take us into the area of the unknown and the highly speculative, she opens up a profound discussion of the presence of the bodies of analyst and analysand that deserves far wider consideration.

Rethinking a clinical encounter

With De Toffoli's thought-provoking work in mind, I turn to an experience I wrote up some years ago (Caldwell, 2017) about my intense responses to a patient on two periods, each lasting about six weeks. They were totally at odds with the general tenor of the analysis, which was slow, often boring, and had left me with the sense that very little was done, that in eight years we had scarcely begun.

In both periods I felt a growing sense of negativity become an active dislike, marked by the effort required to be there in the session and not retaliate. This would be followed by coldness, detachment and increased silence on my part. I would have moments of withdrawal, hopelessness, and above all, the wish to give up the analysis, and, especially and notably, physically get away from him. These negative sessions and their violently fluctuating emotions were extremely demanding, and they brought me forcefully up against myself and my way of being in the world and in the session. But, since they provided such a sustained contrast to the rest of the work, they also elicited a theoretical interest, which proved a kind of lifeline.

The opportunity to enact my hate through the end of the session had me looking forward to it when I felt myself withdrawing, curling up inside, unable or unwilling to respond. It seemed the only thing I could do for myself (and him?) was to get to the end of the session and shut the door on him. On perhaps half a dozen occasions I felt the encounters were making me physically ill and it is this physical effect that struck me in returning to this material, because at the time, I had not focussed on the bodily sensations of illness and nausea. Although my strong physical responses and the insecurity they occasioned in me had led me to consultations with a senior analyst, we did not really explore the physicality in itself, except in relation to his and my states of mind. I would now say that the body itself, my body, and his effect on it, was eclipsed by the discussion of states of mind!

I had been struck at the time, and again now, by the timing: two periods, two years apart, at the same time, late September, early October, each lasting about six weeks, and each containing perhaps three or four occasions of this intensely physical response of mine. I was sure that they were related to early experience, but I could do little with this vivid impression. I did realize that these highly un-usual responses signified a lot more than ordinary hatred, that this dense affect, seeking, and perhaps succeeding in driving a wedge into what Winnicott (1959) calls "the professional attitude" was something in a very different register. But there it was left.

In relating those physical experiences to this discussion of the body, I realize it had been my anticipation of my bodily frailty that had so worried me, alerting me to the power of what was happening between me and my patient. Now I won-der, if I had thought more centrally then of his powerful bodily impact on me, might something more foundational have been arrived at in this analysis? For my associations now are to morning sickness and the stark contrast, also noticed then, between these overwhelming feelings in my body, and the dull plodding on of the rest of the analysis. Could my wish to get rid of him perhaps have regis-tered something about his mother's possible reception of this pregnancy, coming, as it did, very soon after the birth of her first child?

Roger Money-Kyrle (1956) proposes that if the analyst is disturbed, it is likely that the patient has contributed to it and is, in turn, disturbed by it. In identifying the analyst's emotional disturbance, the patient's part in bringing it about, and finally the effect of both on the patient, he suggests the analyst may be more likely to respond to a patient's mood precisely because he has lost his empathy with it, the patient then picks up the negativity "that may be linked to a temporary fail-ure to understand the patient so that the patient becomes a persecution because he is felt to be incurable." Might this also be an approximate description of a young Catholic mother, faced soon after the birth of a first child, with a second pregnancy?

My relief at the end of the session, sometimes accompanied by a wish for a cleansing walk in the fresh air to shake off an experience of sheer nastiness and hatred, a kind of contamination, almost certainly overlooked its influence on, and registration in, the patient's unconscious. I was aware of my own intensely negative feelings and tried to work on them, but I overlooked their impact on the patient. Money-Kyrle elaborated, "I came to feel that the occasions on which my patient repudiated me with more than ordinary violence followed, rather than preceded, moments when I really would have been glad to see the last of him" (pp. 338–339). This man always spoke very slowly as if weighing every word, but the words amounted to very little, and they tended to give the often-irritating impression of checking if I were listening. Even the most banal of statements was weighted with a challenge about who was in charge, whether I had been lis-tening, but, given this patient's history, what seemed more important to me was what may have been an anxiety about whether he could ever get anyone to be interested enough in him to want more information. That is, his irritating challenges may equally have registered a concealed wish to make the other curious about him as if no one ever had been; a possible symptom developed over many years may have resulted in a consolidation of early deprivation that had hardened into a dense grievance.

Conclusion

Both Winnicott and Bion extended their investigations about the work of psychoanalysis over a lifetime. Although their approaches to the body did not directly place it at the centre of their thinking in regard to adult patients, their interest in what happens in the consulting room and its realities for both analyst and analysand offer a consistently questioning arena about the work and being of the analyst. In the current psychoanalytic world, their work continues to provide signposts for how to take forward a psychoanalysis that acknowledges the body as a central marker of identity and seeks to understand the variety of ways that analytic communication proceeds through bodily phenomena and bodily presence and their relation to what, in the quote mentioned at the beginning of this paper, Winnicott (1949) describes as "mental phenomena" that is, "complications of variable importance in psyche soma continuity of being" (p. 254).

Notes

1 These are the two references to the body in Bion's Complete Works: body, language of (Mawson, C. (Ed.), 2014, Vol. 15, p. 34) and body and mind, relationship between (11:302) appear respectively in a formerly unpublished paper, "Penetrating silence" (1976) and in *Cogitations* (Mawson, C. (Ed.), 2014, Vol. 11, p. 302).

References

Angelergues, R. (1975). *Réflexions critiques sur la notion de schéma corporel in psychologie de la connaissance de soi.* [From talk given at Acts of Paris Symposium of September, 1973]. Presses Universitaires de France.

Anzieu, D. (2016). *The skin ego* (translated by Naomi Segal). Routledge.

Bick, E. (1968). The experience of the skin in early object relations. *The International Journal of Psychoanalysis,* 49: 484–486.

Bion, W.R. (2014 [1973]). Brazilian lectures.8. Sao Paolo. In C. Mawson (Ed.), *The complete works of W.R. Bion,* (Vol. 7, pp. 62–70). Karnac Books.

Bion, W.R. (2014 [1976]). Penetrating silence. In C. Mawson (Ed.), *The complete works of W.R. Bion,* (Vol, 15, pp. 31–34). Karnac Books.

Caldwell, L. (2017). Dalla psicoanalisi all'essere e al fare. In C. Barbaglio, A. Macchia & A.M. Nicolò (Eds.), *Winnicott e la psicoanalisi del futuro Roma: Andhalas, trazzere, Strosi* (pp. 143–154). Alpes Italia.

Caldwell, L. (2018). A 221–239.

Carignani, P.

Carignani, P. & Romano, F. (Eds.) (2011). *Prendere corpo. Il dialogo tra corpo e mente in psicoanalisi: teoria e clinica.* Franco Angeli.

Damasio, A. (1999). Commentary by Antonio R. Damasio (Iowa City). *Neuropsychoanalysis*, *1*(1): 38–39.

Damasio, A. (2012). Neuroscience and psychoanalysis: A natural alliance. *The Psychoanalytic Review*, *99*(4): 591–594.

De Toffoli, C. (2011). The living body in the psychoanalytic experience. *Psychoanalytic Quarterly*, *80*(3): 595–618.

Douglas, M. (2002). *Purity and danger: An analysis of concepts of pollution and taboo*. Routledge Classics (Original work published 1966).

Eigen, M. (1977 [1993]). Breathing and identity. In *The electrified tightrope*, (pp. 43–48). Aronson.

Ferrari, A.B. (2004). *From the eclipse of the body to the dawn of thought*. Free Association Books.

Fischer, S. & Cleveland, S.E. (1958). *Body images and personality*. Van Nostrand Co. Inc.

Freud, S. (1905). Fragment of an analysis of a case of hysteria (1905 [1901]). In J. Strachey (Ed. and Trans.), *The standard edition of the complete psychological works of Sigmund Freud* (Vol. 7, pp. 77–78). Hogarth Press.

Leff, J. & Perelberg, R. (Eds.) (1997). *Female experience: Three generations of British women psychoanalysts on work with women*. Taylor & Francis.

Mawson, C. (Ed.) (2014). *The Complete Works of W. R. Bion*. Karnac Books.

Mawson, C. (2019) *Psychoanalysis and anxiety: From knowing to being*. Routledge.

Milner, M. (1969). *The hands of the living God*. Hogarth Press.

Milner, M. (1972). *Tribute to Donald Winnciott*. [Talk given at the Donald Winnicott Memorial Meeting contained in the archives of the British Psychoanalytic Society]. January 19, 1972, The British Psychoanalytic Society. London, England.

Money-Kyrle, R. (1956). Normal counter-transference and some of its deviations. *International Journal of Psycho-Analysis*, *37*:360–366.

Parsons, M. (2014). *Living psychoanalysis: From theory to experience*. Routledge.

Perelberg, R. (2018). Love and melancholia in the analysis of women by women. In R. Perelberg (Ed.), *Psychic bisexuality: A British-French dialogue* (pp. 103–121). Routledge.

Pines, *Generations of British Women Psychoanalysts on Work with Women* (pp. 130–143). Routledge.

Scott, C. (1949). The 'body scheme in psychotherapy.' *British Journal of Medical Psychology*, *22*(part 3–4): 139–150.

Winnicott, D.W. (2016 [1931]). Treating the whole person. Child psychiatry. In L. Caldwell & H. Taylor Robinson (Eds.) *The collected works of D. W. Winnicott*, (Vol. 1, pp. 159–160). Oxford University Press.

Winnicott, D.W. (2016 [1938]). Skin changes in relation to emotional disorder. In L. Caldwell & H. Taylor Robinson (Eds.) *The collected works of D. W. Winnicott*, (Vol. 1, pp. 449–462). Oxford University Press.

Winnicott, D.W. (2016 [1945]). Primitive emotional development. In L. Caldwell & H. Taylor Robinson (Eds.), *The collected works of D. W. Winnicott*, (Vol. 2, pp. 357–368). Oxford University Press.

Winnicott, D.W. (2016 [1949]). The mind and its relation to the Psyche Soma. In L. Caldwell & H. Taylor Robinson (Eds.). *The collected works of D. W. Winnicott* (Vol. 3, pp. 245–258). Oxford University Press.

Winnicott, D.W. (2016 [1954]). Character types: The foolhardy and the cautious: On funfairs, thrills and regressions, edited by Michael Balint. In L. Caldwell & H. Taylor Robinson (Eds.), *The collected works of D. W. Winnicott* (Vol. 4, pp. 273–278).

Winnicott, D.W. (2016 [1959]). Countertransference. In L. Caldwell & H. Taylor Robinson (Eds.), *The collected works of D. W. Winnicott* (Vol. 5, pp. 508–515). Oxford University Press.

Winnicott, D.W. (2016 [1960]). The theory of the parent infant relationship. In L. Caldwell & H. Taylor Robinson (Eds.), *The collected works of D. W. Winnicott* (Vol. 6, pp. 141–158). Oxford University Press.

Winnicott, D.W. (2016 [1962]). Ego integration in child development. In L. Caldwell & H. Taylor Robinson (Eds.), *The collected works of D.W. Winnicott* (Vol. 6, pp. 389–398). Oxford University Press.

Winnicott D.W. (2016 [1970]). Basis for self in body. In L. Caldwell & H. Taylor Robinson (Eds.), *The collected works of D. W. Winnicott* (Vol. 9, pp. 225–234). Oxford University Press.

Winnicott, D.W. (2016 [1988]). Human nature. In L. Caldwell & H. Taylor Robinson (Eds.), *The collected works of D. W. Winnicott* (Vol. 11, pp. 53–58). Oxford University Press.

3   Does the body have a mind?

Robert Oelsner

> MIND (speaking to BODY) What is that amusing little affair sticking out? I like
> it. It has a mind of its own – just like me.
>
> (Bion, 1991, p. 434)

Getting started

I found myself thinking what contribution to write for this volume on the body
and lamenting not having a current case of a psychosomatic illness. In comes my
patient Mark – 20 plus years old – lies down and starts:

> I woke up this morning with a sore neck. It is hurting now. And I don't know
> what to do about it. It is nothing related to the unconscious; it is just physical
> pain and you have to deal with it. When I was younger I had sometimes my
> body hurting but that was not a reason to stop doing the things you needed
> to do … I also know that when you get older – like yourself – you sometimes
> do wake up with physical pains here or there and it's normal. I imagine your
> having body pain. But you never cancelled a session because of that.

I am struck time and again when a patient seems to read my mind or I, his.
Whatever it was, Mark, who is pretty smart and likes the talking cure, certainly
gave me a gift here.

He went on to say that he knows what his dad would say if he complained about
neck pain. He would say take an aspirin. Or put a warm bottle around your neck.
"What else can one do with just a sore neck? I don't know" he finished saying.

I responded that he was trying me out – *'you have to deal with it'* – to see how
I dealt with his pain. But that he was also prompt to put himself in my shoes,
becoming me, the older person having to deal with physical pains due to aging.

Now with hindsight I notice how compressed this brief communication was.
For once there was some direct mysterious transmission of thoughts – which is
what Freud early on termed *Gedankenübertragung*, thought transference, an ESP-
like phenomenon. Then there was the patient's claim that a physical pain may
be *nothing related to the unconscious*, which I was ready to consider coming from
him. It followed with his recalling a time where he kept going, no matter what.

DOI: 10.4324/9781003195559-3

Then, there was his empathizing with me having body pains and yet not letting him down. At this point he could identify with me and have us be together in a deep way while at the same time embodying the man he may become in the future, an older analyst like his analyst.

The hour continued with his saying that he noticed he had a broader problem with his body. He subordinates himself to other people's imagined wishes and tries to please them. He does that for the sake of being possessed rather than to possess. He also dislikes his penis and his erections. He believes that it causes pain to others though men may be more resilient to pain than women, he said, which is why he refrains from having sex with girls. At this point he does what I have seen him do many times before: he covers his mouth for an instant with the collar of his shirt and wipes his lips. This has led us to entertain the possibility of a confusion between his anus and his mouth and between defecating and speaking, but as this was already known to both there was no need for me to repeat it. But now he also showed an equation between using his tongue to talk and his penis to cause pain. I could see that the moment he made a firm statement he behaved as if he had hurt me. I will get back to these confusions later in this chapter.

He then said that he'd always conceived of the vagina as a wound, and once when he was a child he asked his mother if intercourse did not cause her pain. She replied it did not, but she added some other comment he could not recall. (Of course, he had read Freud and was trying to please me with his assumed castration anxiety. That was now him using his mouth and speech to make me happy. A form of oral sex, as I had shown him in the past. But this was already known to us as well, so I let it go.)

I only mentioned that mother's reply seemed not to have changed his idea that he would inflict pain in an already tender wound with his penis – or with his tongue and words for that matter. This made it difficult for him to use his genital in intercourse or his tongue to speak to me, other than to give me pleasure.

Multiple dimensions of the body as a clinical fact

The interest of this material is that it brings in a condensed manner the whole history of the body in relation to the mind. It begins with just a somatic experience – the sore neck – without or prior to it being absorbed by the mind. It is short-lived in its pure state as it is brought to me to deal with. That is to bring the stray somatic pain in relation to an idea. While I took him at his word with regard to it not having an unconscious meaning, Mark spoke about an intentionality that was hoping I could deal with his physical symptom. A sign of trust. His reference to the time when he dealt with his pains all alone belonged to the time when he had his first manic psychotic episode. He had estranged himself from his family, being pulled away by his own narcissistic omnipotent and cruel organization. Now instead – in his third year of a five times weekly analysis – he has found his way back home to quite a remarkable warm and caring father, alluded to by the warm bottle. His imagining my waking up with body pains but still being there, was also an acknowledgement of what he had recently recognized as my and the parents' selfless availability. At that point he was ready to swiftly move on to the more burning matter, which was the sadistic conflict that had taken over his sexuality since childhood. Now we were ready to pursue the psychoanalytic work of the hour. The beginning of the hour brought a somatic symptom –inaccurately called "psychosomatic" – the sore neck. He then moved into a hysteric conversive phenomenon, namely being sexually possessed and hurt by a sadistic predator giving him the sore neck. He had indeed complained of pains after being passively possessed. And then he moved swiftly to his hypochondriacal identification with a hurting analyst. By myself I could not have laid out the distinction between somatic, hysteric, and hypochondriacal phenomena any better than with Mark's help. I will get back to these distinctions in a moment.

The body in the history of psychoanalysis: from neuroscience to the science of the mind

Before turning to the work of Bion, the history of psychoanalytic ideas will help to frame the clinical and theoretical problems I wish to discuss. I am persuaded that Klein cannot be understood without reference to Freud, or Bion without reference to Klein. Take this as a note of apology for affording the reader's patience.

The term neurosis comes from the old Greek word *Neuron* meaning nerve, and the suffix *sis* meaning disease. Hence, historically *neurosis* applied to a disease of the nerves, an idea that neuroscientists nowadays are trying to resuscitate.

Freud came from a neurological background and his Project for a Scientific Psychology[1] (1895) was all about neuroscience: the language is about different types of neurons, neuronal paths, connections and synapses making *'contact barriers'* – yes, 60 years before Bion – that facilitated or resisted the path of nervous impulses measured by their quantity. By 1896 however he put the whole manuscript away into a drawer to devote himself to the matters of the soul (*Seele*). Just to note, there is no word for mind in the German language, hence Freud using the terms soul or psychic apparatus in its stead. In German, psychiatrists used to be called *Nervenärtze*, that is doctors of the nerves. You can see that early on medicine could not conceive of the mind distinct from the physical body. Freud's amazing leap from the concreteness of the nervous system to the matters of the mind has still not been sufficiently acknowledged.

Hysteria was Freud's and Breuer's beginning to realize that some patients suffered from odd physical dysfunctions for which no organic cause could be found. Hysterical paralysis, aphonia, coughing, some types of hallucinations, and even transitory blindness responded well to hypnosis while not to medical treatments. They soon learned that these phenomena had a meaning that was hidden from consciousness and could be retrieved with some work to defeat the resistance of forgetfulness. We have heard of Anna O., Elizabeth von R., Irma, Dora to name just a few. What seemed odd in these cases was the low if not absent degree of anxiety, which Charcot in his time labeled as *'belle indifference.'* The conclusion was that hysteric conversions are phantasies that would normally cause anxiety and have been converted through somatic innervations into physical symptoms keeping the mind beautifully free and even.

In his paper "On narcissism" (1914) Freud wrote about a different illness affecting the body, namely hypochondria. From his dynamic point of view this was a regression of the libido from objects back to the body. In that paper he also considered that the libidinization of a body organ could bring about an actual physical alteration to it, similar to the excitation of the genitals in sexual arousal. But that was the consequence rather than the cause of hypochondria.

Subsequently in the Wolf Man (1918) he described the patient's hypochondria as an identification with the ailing mother thus:

> ... after hearing that when you have dysentery you find blood in your stool he became very nervous and declared that there was blood in his own stool; he was afraid he would die of dysentery, but allowed himself to be convinced by an examination that he had made a mistake and had no need to be frightened. We can see that in this dread he was trying to put into effect an identification with his mother, whose haemorrhages he had heard about in the conversation with her doctor.
>
> [p. 76]

Freud's new conception of hypochondria is akin to melancholia, only that here the shadow of the object has fallen on the body instead of the ego. This led Klein later to posit that hypochondriacal anxiety comes from an unconscious identification with objects that have been damaged as well as the damaged objects retaliating and damaging the inside of the body. This explains why hypochondria, unlike hysteric symptoms, causes great anxiety, the content of which is ultimately fear of dying.

In her "Narrative of a Child Analysis," Klein (1961) made important observations on the relation between somatic illness and its relation to the mind as well as the relation between actual physical illness, hypochondria, and hysteria. Consider this note (Klein, 1961, Note I, p. 216) at the end of a reported hour where young Richard was recovering from his sore throat.

> The improvement which Richard was reporting consisted not only in a lessening of his hypochondriacal anxiety, but in a disappearance of an actual physical symptom. Considering that this child had been suffering since early infancy from colds, it is interesting to see how psychological factors contributed to these colds. It seems likely that without analysis he might at this point actually have developed a sore throat. Another more general consideration enters here. In my experience, hypochondria, which was very strong in Richard, is not necessarily a preoccupation with non-existent symptoms but can develop around actual physical symptoms by exaggerating and distorting their significance. The question arises whether such symptoms in hypochondriacal people are largely the result of their hypochondriacal anxieties.

This would imply a connection between hysterical symptoms and hypochondria, a connection which I have repeatedly suggested.

(cf. Klein, The Psycho-Analysis of Children and Developments in Psycho-Analysis, pp. 225–226)

Somatic illness like Richard's early colds, as Klein states, might be the expression of anxiety, and thereafter lead to hypochondriacal concerns. Was she thinking of precursors of anxiety whose only area of expression is the physical body? Wait until we get to Bion.

As we know, in practice hypochondria, somatic illness, and conversive disorders may present themselves in mixed forms, yet the distinction is technically important to help us understand the state of mind a patient is in at a given time and address his anxiety at the right level.

Getting back to Klein and the body, recall that her renowned concept of projective identification and introjection strongly leaned on the experience of expulsion of the feces and feeding from the breast, respectively. This should remind us of Winnicott's (1965) "imaginative elaboration of physical experience" (p. 60).

On a different note, I mention the French somaticists, who found a kind of thinking where unconscious symbolic representation and meaning are inexistent and named it "*pensée operatoire,*" operatory thinking (Marty and de M'Uzan, 1978). Language, they claim, in such patients, is not alluding to or representing anything, just mirroring facts that are being stated without emotional resonance. This condition opens the door to somatic vulnerability. They posit that in psychosomatic propensities there is a missing link between the mind and the body where a sort of blindness of emotions occurs. Alexithymia – emotion illiteracy – is a term also used to describe the dysfunction (Nemiah and Sifneos, 1970). In such cases, the soma is left alone burdened with "pre-motions," as Bion (1963) calls the precursors of emotion.

Piera Aulagnier (2001, 2015), another French author, has called *originary or primal process* a process related to the body rather than the mind, that precedes our primary process and mental functioning. She coined the term *pictogram* for some pure somatic form of perception that lays the ground for the function of phantasy and later thinking. The relevance of this formulation is that it gives Freud's primary narcissism a content and function. Aulagnier's pictogram is congruent with Bion's ideographs, beta elements, or sense data from which phantasy, thinking, and communication will spring. We will get there soon.

Thus far I have argued for the existence of a form of "body mentality," which we may call for now 'somato-logic.'

We can certainly not leave this section of the chapter without considering Donald Meltzer's (1967) concept of zonal confusions. He elaborates on the state of affairs when the infant has his early erogenous somatic experiences and confusions of mouth, tongue, anus, feces, and genitals, and how equivocal the somato-logic by itself is – the shortcomings of thinking with your body alone. The mind is afforded to make sense of bodily experiences out of a primary confusional state that has to be laboriously worked-through. In the beginning of any psychoanalytic process, Meltzer argues, this confusion becomes apparent, accompanied by geographical confusions where distinctions between inside and outside, self and objects are yet to happen. The vignette of my patient Mark sheds light on this question.

What we commonly refer to as symbiosis, autistic-contiguous position, merger, or fusion, are all attempts at conceptualizing the earliest stages of development.

Thus far I have discussed the role the body has played in the development of psychoanalytic concepts since its inception. One may conclude that a mind could not ensue without a body and that the perception of the body functions sets the psychic apparatus in motion. I referred to Freud's trajectory from neuroscience to a science of the mind, which was his response to the understanding of hysteria, "a disease of the nerves without fever" as it has been called.

I touched on the matter of hypochondria and what it teaches us about identification processes, from Freud to Klein. Meltzer added the problem of an initial confusion of erogenous zones at an early stage of development observable in the first steps of an analytic process. In this he also followed Klein, shifting from Abraham's and Freud's linear model of development of the libido.

On passing I made a detour toward the French authors Marty and de M'Uzan apropos of the concepts of operatory thinking and alexithymia, as I believe they are relevant contributions to the metapsychology of psychosomatics. I also mentioned Piera Aulagnier who posited that the foundation for Freud's primary and secondary processes is what she has described as the "originary," based on the earliest stimuli stimulating a sense organ. In a sense, this is my modest homage to France.

For the psychopathologist these considerations are intended to make distinctions between a primary lack of engagement of the body to the mind, pure somatic phenomena, and the body *in* the mind, used hypochondriacally or hysterically, which is the familiar territory where psychoanalysts feel most at ease.

The way to Bion and Bion's ways

For our purposes I divide the discussion of Bion's work into early, mid-term, and late Bion.

Early Bion

While Bion is best known for his writings on container and contained, reverie or alpha function, beta and alpha elements, the psychotic part of the personality, and his theory of thinking, there is less known about the pretty fascinating Bion that belongs to his pre-psychoanalytic times, and that congealed into his book *Experiences in Groups* (Bion, 1961), the last chapter of which is a 're-view' he added after completing his psychoanalytic training and becoming a Kleinian analyst. In his last decade of life, his California years, he would come back to the same issues with his experience over the course of a lifetime. From all his rich work I will only select those concepts relevant to our topic.

In *Experiences in Groups* (1961, p. 101) Bion posited the existence of a proto-mental system

> [...] one in which physical and psychological or mental are undifferentiated. It is a matrix from which spring the phenomena which at first appear – on a psychological level and in the light of psychological investigation – to be discrete feelings only loosely associated with one another.

At the proto-mental level of functioning, behaviors are driven by what Bion has called "*basic assumptions.*" They are basic because they are the foundation for more evolved or sophisticated actions that result from the process of thinking. They are basic because they are primitive. Viewed from the perspective of the evolution of thoughts, they are also rudimentary, like the tools in the Stone Age compared to artificial intelligence. They are assumptions because they are not the result of reality checking. Basic assumptions manifest themselves in groups and lay the ground for group dynamics. In a psychoanalysis they become manifest in the group of two, analyst and analysand, and the dynamics of transference and countertransference. They belong to the individual from primeval times when our ancestors were part of what Freud (1913) referred to as the "*primal horde.*" It follows that the proto-mental system is a relic of the times when man had not yet developed a mind and his functioning was driven by impulses, tropisms, and autonomic responses like those of the adrenal glands and the hypothalamus. The principle of our autonomic nervous system is all about proto-mentality. For instance, the discharge of adrenalin into the blood stream is an autonomic response to life threats and makes us fit for either fight or flight.

Bion also states that the proto-mental system is the matrix of physical as well as of mental diseases before the development of a differentiated state in which a psychiatrist or a physical doctor could make a diagnosis. For instance, a cancer and a persecutory delusion both spring from the same matrix, namely, the proto-mental basic assumption of fight-flight. Space does not allow further elaboration on Bion's theory of groups; however, it bears mentioning that the proto-mental system that governs does its conducting at a mindless body level. Bion's model is that of the mind organized like a group – originally unconscious (not repressed) – that does not make mental representations of emotional experiences; it only catalogs them as physical phenomena and reacts to them with unthought automatic actions. Not only does that apply to the fight-flight principle but also to the 'pairing' basic assumption – the ground for sexual reproduction and the primal scene – and the 'dependence' basic assumption which governs the relation to mother and father in infancy.

It bears repeating that as far as these are innate tendencies in the individual they are not mental, but in Bion's terms proto-mental – unconscious, but not repressed.[2]

Bion's proto-mental system is consistent with Freud's (1923) statement that in the first instance the ego is a body-ego.[3] Freud was not clear about how the leap from body-ego to a psychological ego occurs but posited that initially the nervous system deals with just *quantities* of stimuli while *qualities* are a condition of consciousness, that is, the psychic apparatus. Klein tackled the matter by stating that we have an ego since birth, which she called early-ego. I have argued that she caused misunderstandings by calling it 'early-ego' rather than ego-precursor or rudimentary ego. She did not state that the ego is present early on but that there is a germinal psyche which will progressively evolve into the ego. Her early-ego is grounded in the experience of the infant's own body and its mother's. Bion's proto-mental system is different in that it comes from our animal ancestry. To know more about how the transformation from biology to psychology occurs we need to look into the mid-term Bion.

Mid-term Bion

During the period between 1962 and 1970, that is from *Learning from Experience* to *Attention and Interpretation*, Bion developed the theory of *alpha function*, a function of the mind occurring under the pressure of pure somatic stimuli which he called *sense data* and *beta elements*. But earlier on, in his paper "Differentiation of the psychotic from the non-psychotic personalities" (1957, pp. 268–269) he brings the expression *ideograph* in relation to his patient of the dark glasses, quite intriguing since he never used this wonderful term again. In that context *ideograph* looks much like his beta element or sense data – think of any stimuli impacting a sense organ. Two years later in a private note entitled *dream-work-alpha* he mentions an *ideogram* (Bion, 1992, pp. 64–65). He says that the ideogram needs to be "ideogrammaticized," that is, subjected to the grammar of the mind to become an idea. One would guess that ideogram is the word for alpha elements. Dream-work-alpha is then the ongoing function of the mind stringing ideograms into a chain or narrative to produce dreams and thoughts. I think ideogram and dream-work-alpha are much more appealing terms than alpha function. Regretfully, only in some notes that his widow collected posthumously in the book *Cogitations* will you find these two expressions.

Our rudimentary minds – the early egos of Klein – get started with the assistance of the mother that has hopefully the skill of dream-work-alpha. Bion called this *reverie*, from the French, meaning daydreaming or also lost in dreams. Winnicott's *good-enough-mother* in a state of *primary maternal preoccupation* is in the best position to provide that reverie. By way of internalizing this function of reverie, does the baby little by little learn from the mother to develop a thinking mind.

However, our minds are limited and not all sense data emanating from our insides or the outside world can successfully be submitted to dream-work-alpha. The residue is either evacuated in the form of beta elements into the external world of objects or into the body. When beta elements are projected into the body psychosomatic symptoms ensue. Whether psychosomatic phenomena carry also some relic of a symbol lies probably in the eye of the beholder but when this sounds to be the case the expression *archaic hysteria* (McDougall, 1993, p. 216) seems appropriate. The body becomes a buffer to the mind such that a painful idea converts into a physical symptom, freeing the mind from it. This sounds a bit like hysteria.

One day Mr. K has indigestion after an hour where some painful aspects of his personality were addressed. He complains about a restaurant down the street: "The indigestion happened for real. I can even indicate to you the Teriyaki place down the street where I ate," he assures. "Not a phantasy." Can indigestion speak? Can the analyst speak to the indigestion so that his gastrointestinal system would understand? In addition to this problem, the analyst smells an odor in the room, while Mr. K has arrived as usual brandishing his coffee-mug with which he tends to lecture the analyst in the hour, self-reliant and calm. But you can see his wet armpits revealing through his shirt and you could feel his hand was wet and cold. (I always shake hands with my patients both when they arrive and when they leave, not just out of courtesy.) We not only see or hear our patients but should also be able to feel their smell, their temperature, the humidity and texture of their skin, their posture and walk, and any other physical signs. These clues speak a language of their own. They are a valuable source of information from the unconscious and are missed when patient and analyst are not in the same room.

The analyst may feel lethargy during a particular hour that dissipates after the patient is gone. He may feel anxious, confused, commit repeated breaches of technique he has long learned not to make; run over the time or systematically find himself in the toilet when the patient arrives. I trust that the reader has experienced some of this too.

All of the above should give us a taste of what unprocessed sense data or beta elements can do when projected into the depth of the body and mind of the analyst.

As happens with psychosomatic phenomena, Mr. K's lay clearly outside the realm of alpha function or meaning, which needed to be conveyed by the analyst in response to his observation of the phenomena and the context.

Under the pressure of anxiety, meaning-making or alpha function may reverse its course and then psychosomatic and also psychotic phenomena become manifest. To indicate the reversibility Bion plays with the pun "psycho-somatic and somato-psychotic" in his next period in *A Memoir of the Future*. But in his mid-term works he called this "alpha function in reverse," which results in a kind of beta elements which he also called "bizarre objects."

Late Bion

This period of Bion's writings corresponds to his ten-year stay in Los Angeles. There stands out his astounding trilogy, *A Memoir of the Future*, quite incomprehensible, annoying, but also funny. To forewarn us of what we are to find in the book, Bion starts with an imaginary dialog between the reader and himself, the author:

Q CAN YOU GIVE ME AN IDEA WHAT THIS IS ABOUT?

A PSYCHOANALYSIS, I BELIEVE.

Q ARE YOU SURE? IT LOOKS LIKE A QUEER AFFAIR?

A IT IS A QUEER AFFAIR – LIKE PSYCHOANALYSIS. YOU'D HAVE TO READ IT.

(Bion, 1991, p. 2)

In the form of three plays with plenty of characters one has to just immerse one-self to realize how exciting, unsettling, mysterious, and intelligent this opus is. It goes back to Bion's lifetime topics, this time on a theatrical stage. One can guess that the stage is Klein's internal world and the characters are parts of the self and internal objects while the plot resembles what Susan Isaacs (1948) and Klein have called *unconscious phantasy*. It is indeed also like psychoanalysis. You have to make your own experience reading the book, just like you have to make your own experience if you want to know what psychoanalysis is. There is no substitute for the experience itself.

The Dawn of Oblivion, the title of the last volume, presents to us pre-natal parts of the personality, starting with *Somites* and *Embryos* through all stages of intra-uterine development to baby at *Term*. Each one is personified as a character in-teracting with each other and with post-natal characters that are also part of the cast. The Prenatals argue and get upset with the Postnatals when the caesura of birth fails to keep them apart. This collision, the reader is invited to understand, stands for Bion's concept of *catastrophic change*. These Prenatals are now what, in *Experiences in Groups*, were the Protomentals, with their basic assumptions, and their automatic and autonomic behaviors. Listen to these fragments of the drama:

Em-mature (the mature Embryo as a character) introduces himself thus:

> ... my ancestors had a long and disreputable history extending to the day when an ancestral sperm, swimming characteristically against the current, lodged in a fallopian tube to lie in wait for an unknown ovum. ... My sperm impetuously penetrated a Graafian follicle before my ovum had time itself to escape penetration...
>
> My earliest experiences were of something touching what I later heard was 'me'. The changes in pressure in the fluid surrounding me varied from what Me called pressure to what Me called pain. My optic and auditory pits at the age of three or four somites received sound and light, dark and silent, not usually increasingly beyond nice and nasty, but sometimes making Me feel more inanimate than animate.

PRE-MATURE Get on with it – when were you born?
EM-MATURE Don't hurry; I was coming to that.
EIGHT YEARS You always are, but do not arrive.
EM When I was only three somites old –
TWENTY-FOUR YEARS That's not an age.
EM Don't talk about matters you don't understand. If you have some respect for your fore-bears –
EIGHT YEARS YOU'VE SPELLED IT WRONG.
EM When I spell it, it is right; when you spell it is wrong.
EIGHT YEARS That is not how it seems to me, looking at it from my side of the barrier.

(Bion, 1991, pp. 429–430)

One can see that quite a bit of misunderstandings ensue when Prenatals and Postnatals try to talk to each other since they live in different worlds, different sides of the caesura. Will a civilized conversation among them be ever possible?

Would a psychoanalyst – also a character in the play – have the ability to help?

When Body and Mind come on stage more conflicts occur. Hear this scene from their first meeting:

MIND Hullo! Where have you sprung from?

BODY What – you again? I am Body; you can call me Soma if you like. Who are you?

MIND Call me Psyche – Psyche-Soma.

BODY Soma-Psyche.

MIND We must be related.

BODY Never – not if I can help it.

MIND Oh, come. Not as bad as that, is it?

BODY Worse. You got us into this air. Luckily I brought some liquid with me. What are you doing?

MIND Nothing; it must be my phrenes, that diaphragm going up and down. I'm breathing in air – fluid, not liquid.

(Bion, 1991, p. 433)

Bion's implication – unlike Freud and Winnicott – seems to be that deep down in our unconscious Body and Mind cannot truly cooperate as they speak different languages and are governed by different rules of grammar. It's in their nature, seems to be the conclusion. Consider this next dialog:

BODY Typical of Mind – all words and no content. Where did you find them?

MIND Borrowed from the future – you are borrowing them from me; do you get them through your diaphragm?

BODY *They* penetrate *it*. But the meaning does not get through. Where did you get your pains from?

MIND Borrowed – from the past. The meaning does not get through the barrier though. Funny – the meaning does not get through whether it is from you to me, or from me to you.

BODY It is the meaning of pain that I am sending to you; the words get through – which I have not sent – but the meaning is lost.

(Bion, 1991, pp. 433–434)

Can psychoanalysis help to tame these characters with their wild thoughts? Can the impenetrable diaphragm become a friendly contact barrier?

In this last period of his life Bion's vertex of psychoanalysis has shifted from curing the sick to attempting to integrate parts of the self in discord, trying to find a language that speaks to all, from Body to Mind, from Prenatals to Old Age, from Protomentals to Shakespeare and Albert Einstein, from the Past to the Future.

The play ends with Psychoanalyst making this closing remark:

> P.A. Because unless the human animal learns to become expert in discrimination, he will be in imminent danger of the wrong choice. .... There is no substitute for the growth of wisdom, Wisdom or oblivion – take your choice. From that warfare there is no release.
>
> (Bion, 1991, p. 576)

I think that the title *The Dawn of Oblivion* for his last volume conveyed Bion's skepticism about man's ability to learn from experience. He had been through WWI, experienced dying in the battle of Wipers, then WWII, the British Psychoanalytic Society with its controversies, and hoped he would escape psychoanalytic politics in North and South America. Here then is the epilog – not without sarcasm – of this volume finished shortly before his death, again with the same question and answer as in the foreword:

> Q .... how was America – North and South?
> A Marvellous; a nice change from the Third Battle of Wipers.
> Q Lots more since then. And more to come – which reminds me; I must rush; I have a date with Fate.
> A Bye-bye – happy holocaust![4]
>
> (Bion, 1991, p. 577)

Bion has not left us clear technical tools to deal with his new conception of integration. It is left to us to pick up this task. I thus return to Mark briefly to show the journey from meaningless pain to a pain that breaks the heart. Around six months after the sore neck without-a-meaning, as I was finishing an earlier version of this chapter, and we were about to separate for a break, Mark had a dream in the session. *In the dream he saw a coffin and a body lying in it as in a bed. At the feet, curled up was another person.* He had an image of the death of the Pharaohs who were buried with their courtesans. It did not require an interpretation.

Notes

1 Has it been worthwhile to take such elaborate measures over the text of the Project? Freud himself would very probably have said 'no.' He dashed it off in two or three weeks, left it unfinished, and criticized it severely at the time of writing it. Later in life he seems to have forgotten it or at least never to have referred to it. And when in his old age he was presented with it afresh, he did his best to destroy it (Strachey, 1954, p. 290).

2 As an aside and because this is a burning matter. I see racism emerging from a specialized basic assumption of pairing. Namely, the assumption that same race couples will save the humanity by preserving the purity of the breed.

3 Freud's beginnings were also first based on the body and physical symptoms. His ego-precursor lay in the peripheral nervous system as he stated in the Project (1895).

4 "Bye-bye – happy holocaust!" gets the reader's attention. While invoking horrific historic events, Bion's use of *holocaust* here can be read as destruction on a mass scale.

This speaks to the seeming impossibility of *integration*, of bridging the caesura between parts of the self in discord – especially body and mind – as well as warring elements of humanity. A *holocaust* may involve the killing of the bodies of (O)thers in an effort to do away with projected, hated aspects of one's own internal world. And it may also describe hostile and destructive body–mind relations in psychosomatic disease.

References

Aulagnier, P. (2001). *The violence of interpretation: From pictogram to statement.* Brunner-Routledge.

Aulagnier, P. (2015). Birth of a body, origin of a history. *The International Journal of Psychoanalysis, 96*(5), 1371–1401.

Bion, W.R. (1957). Differentiation of the psychotic from the non-psychotic personalities. *The International Journal of Psychoanalysis, 38*:266–275.

Bion, W.R. (1961). *Experiences in groups.* Tavistock Publications.

Bion, W.R. (1963). *Elements of psycho-Analysis.* Butterworth-Heinemann.

Bion, W.R. (1991). *A memoir of the future.* Karnac Books.

Bion, W.R. (1992). Note dated August 10 159. In: *Cogitations* (p. 64). Karnac Books.

Freud, S. (1913). Totem and taboo: some points of agreement between the mental lives of savages and neurotics. In J. Strachey (Ed. and Trans.), *The standard edition of the complete psychological works of Sigmund Freud* (Vol. 13, pp. vii–162). Hogarth Press.

Freud, S. (1914). On narcissism: An introduction. In J. Strachey (Ed. and Trans.), *The standard edition of the complete psychological works of Sigmund Freud* (Vol. 14, pp. 67–102). Hogarth Press.

Freud, S. (1918). From the history of an infantile neurosis. In J. Strachey (Ed. and Trans.), *The standard edition of the complete psychological works of Sigmund Freud* (Vol. 17, pp. 1–124). Hogarth Press.

Freud, S. (1923). The ego and the id. In J. Strachey (Ed. and Trans.), *The standard edition of the complete psychological works of Sigmund Freud* (Vol. 19, pp. 1–66). Hogarth Press.

Freud, S. (1950[1895]). Project for a scientific psychology. In J. Strachey (Ed. and Trans.), *The standard edition of the complete psychological works of Sigmund Freud* (Vol. 1, pp. 281–391). Hogarth Press.

Isaacs, S. (1948). The nature and function of phantasy. *The International Journal of Psychoanalysis, 29*:73–97.

Klein, M. (1961). Narrative of a child analysis: The conduct of the psycho-analysis of children as seen in the treatment of a ten-year-old boy. *The International Psycho-Analytical Library, 55*:1–536.

Marty, P. & de M'uzan, M. (1978). Das operative denken ("pensée opératoire"). *Psyche – Zeitschrift für Psychoanalyse, 32*(10):974–984.

McDougall, J. (1993). Of sleep and dream: A psychoanalytic essay. *International Forum of Psychoanalysis, 2*(4):204–218.

Meltzer, D. (1967). *The psycho-analytical process.* Karnac Books.

Nemiah, J. & Sifneos, P. (1970). Affect and fantasy in patients with psychosomatic disorders. In O. Hill (Ed.) *Modern trends in psychosomatic medicine* (Vol. 2, pp. 26–34). Butterworths.

Strachey, J. (1954). Editor's introduction to "Project for a scientific psychology". In J. Strachey (Ed. and Trans.), *The standard edition of the complete psychological works of Sigmund Freud*, (Vol. 1, p. 290). Hogarth Press.

Winnicott, D.W. (1965). *The maturational processes and the facilitating environment: Studies in the theory of emotional development.* The Hogarth Press and the Institute of Psycho-Analysis.

Part II
Oneiric body

4 Introduction

Caron Harrang, Drew Tillotson, and Nancy C. Winters

Both of the following chapters ("Body as dream space" by Judy Eekhoff and "Dreaming into death" by Rikki Ricard and Adrian Jarreau) present accounts of the oneiric (dreaming) body and its communicative potential, but do so with very divergent narrative styles.

Drawing on a phrase from McDougall (1989), Judy Eekhoff begins her chapter asserting that "body is a dream space" where sensory and emotional experience is transformed into personal meaning. At the same time, she notes sensory overwhelm can obliterate an individual's capacity for thinking (Bion, 1962a), resulting paradoxically in a hyper focus on the body, yet devoid of space for dreaming. "Somatic experience used defensively," Eekhoff says, "interferes with the body's capacity for making meaning from experience. Somatic responses can replace dreaming rather than aiding a person to dream."

Employing Bion's (1962a) connection between the use of the senses and the development of a capacity for thinking, Eekhoff believes that in health, "the place where thoughts first appear is in the body." How then does the psychoanalyst approach working with individuals who use sensory experience as a barricade against unbearable aloneness and nameless dread? Elaborating on this dilemma, Eekhoff notes that patients alienated from their own lived experience often cannot sense the analyst's embodied presence. The resulting situation for both analyst and patient may become one of "total isolation and terror in the face of immense need and vulnerability."

Eekhoff's central thesis is that thoughts arise in the body and require a container/contained relationship with an embodied object for thinking and dreaming to evolve. In the analytic situation, this necessitates the analyst being able to enter into (and later awaken from) the patient's nightmare of nameless dread and somatic overwhelm; an experience she insists precedes the efficacy of verbal interpretation of this horror. Implications of this approach aimed at fostering a new experience of the body as dream space are explored in a detailed clinical vignette with Ada, who sums up her initial dread of embodied existence saying, "When my despair and terror destroy my conscious will [to live], my body goes on. I feel at those times that my body betrays me. It just keeps going on."

One of the vitalizing aspects of Eekhoff's approach is how she implicitly invites the reader to join her in struggling with difficult clinical experiences.

DOI: 10.4324/9781003195559-4

For example, after describing the aforementioned group of patients who have trouble using their bodies as a dream space for organizing and generating experience she writes, "I used to think such patients maintained a delusional denial of otherness. Today I believe such individuals have an internal place where they deny *their own existence* via a representation of a blank place (Green, 1999)." Then, in anticipation of the reader's surprise, she acknowledges the "delusion of not existing is paradoxical," especially in light of the individual's obsessive focus on the concrete aspects of bodily experience. How this contradiction plays out for Ada, and how the analyst 'learns on the job' to differentiate somatic delusion from embodied aliveness will leave readers with an unsaturated sense of what 'dreaming in body' means in the analytic encounter.

"Dreaming into death" by Ricard and Jarreau is an experiential piece about the couple's inspiring journey as they faced Jarreau's approaching death with "as much consciousness and openness" as they could. In his Foreword, Jeffrey Eaton queries "how often have you been invited into a significant conversation, one that challenges you to think, feel, reflect, question, and imagine?" Ricard and Jarreau invite us into just such a conversation in which their awareness of Jarreau's approaching death allows them to be more fully alive. As Eaton observes, they are learning from experience not just about the concept of death, but the reality of death. This distinction is reminiscent of Bion's (1965) notion of transformations in O (shared emotional truth), which he conceived as growth in *becoming*, not *knowing*.

But what of the dreaming body, the theme of this chapter? During the couple's vacation before Jarreau knew he was ill, he had two dreams depicting his death. Soon afterwards he learned he was terminally ill. Ricard and Jarreau hypothesize in the form of a question, "is it possible that the body 'communicates' with the unconscious in such a way that information is passed on to us about what the body is experiencing?" Such a possibility suggests the body knows itself to be ill and creates the dream—an intermediary—as a message to the mind.

The body dreaming of its death raises interesting theoretical issues about lasting imprints of the bodily origins of unconscious life. In her well-known paper on the infantile origins of unconscious phantasy Isaacs (1948) sees no dichotomy between mind and body, only a "single, undifferentiated experience of sucking and phantasying" (p. 86). Relevant to Ricard and Jarreau's chapter Isaacs notes, "the world of phantasy shows the same protean and kaleidoscopic changes as the contents of a dream" (p. 82). One might hypothesize the body's sensing something is not quite right evokes death anxiety and phantasies of annihilation that *become* the contents of a dream.

More recently, Fonagy and Target (2007) return psychoanalysis (and attachment theory) to its rootedness in the body. The earliest physical gestures and bodily experience form the nonconscious structure of primary process and metaphoric thought. They call attention to the way "style in speech, thought, and relationships may be determined by an underlying, unifying coding system of embodied images or procedural memories of experiences rooted in bodily experience" (p. 446). Ricard and Jarreau's theme of the dreaming body as messenger has a place with these and other theoretical progenitors.

This intimate account invites the reader into Ricard and Jarreau's shared process of 'dreaming into death.' Here dreaming is not only the body's nocturnal dream as messenger of its somatic state but also conscious dreaming in the Bionian sense, opening each of them to the reality of death and the emotional truth of the aliveness remaining. The reader will be grateful for the opportunity to learn from their searching, painful, and ultimately enlivening journey.

References

Bion, W.R. (1962a). A psycho-analytic study of thinking. *International Journal of Psycho-Analysis, 43*:306–310.

Bion, W.R. (1965). *Transformations.* Karnac Books.

Fonagy, P. & Target, M. (2007). The rooting of the mind in the body: New links between attachment theory and psychoanalytic thought. *Journal of the American Psychoanalytic Association, 55*(2):411–457.

Green, A. (1999) *The work of the negative,* Andrew Weller, translator. Free Association Books.

Isaacs, S. (1948). The nature and function of phantasy. *International Journal of Psychoanalysis, 29*:73–97.

McDougall, J. (1989). *Theaters of the body: A psychoanalytic approach to psychosomatic illness.* W.W. Norton.

5 Body as dream space

Judy K. Eekhoff

In his paper "A Theory of Thinking," Bion (1962a, p. 306) states "…thinking has to be called into existence to cope with thoughts." He goes on to admit that this is not the typical way to conceptualize the process of thinking and highlights that most people assume the opposite. Bion's notion of "thoughts without a thinker" has fascinated me for some time. Where, I have asked myself, do these original thoughts come from? And how do we discover them? Furthermore, how do we create a space in psychoanalysis for thoughts to appear and a thinking mind to develop, especially if the person we are with has used their mind to defend against a terror of being alive?

When I combine this idea with another of Bion's (1962b) namely that somatic overwhelm attacks and destroys our capacity to think, I am reminded of the difficulty I experience when working with patients whose capacity to think has seemingly been destroyed and whose focus of attention is on the somatic. Although focused on the somatic, these patients are unable to be embodied or to use their bodies as a 'dream space.' Their capacity to think has been conscripted and redirected toward the more urgent task of dealing with the unbearable awareness of being alive and alone. Being alive includes an infinite array of somatic responses that are coupled with an emotional experience of aloneness, isolation, and dependency (Ogden, 1991).

Body as background object

The body in health is a background object, much like Winnicott's environmental mother or Freud and Bollas' shadow of the object. The body in health is also a space essential for the growth and development of the mind. Just as Winnicott claims there is no such thing as a baby without a mother, I am saying there is no such thing as a mind without a body. Aside from the obvious, the mind needs the body in order to dream. The body is a dream space where sensory and emotional experience is transformed into representations that can be used to make personal meaning (Eekhoff, 2019). Psychic meaning-making involves bringing two things together to make a 'third' or that which can be symbolized. Representations in the body evolve into symbolization in the mind. Symbolization evolves in union with the body, just as the body concretely evolves after the union of egg

DOI: 10.4324/9781003195559-5

and sperm. The 'third,' physically and psychically, emerges from the body of the mother and through the name of the father (Lacan, 1966).

The physical and psychic body is a space that enables a sense of going-on-being (Winnicott, 1949, 1960, 1963; Ogden 1986, 1989a, 1989b, 1991). A sense of going-on-being is necessary for psychic existence, psychic functioning, psychic elaboration, and creativity. Impingement (Winnicott, 1974) in infancy, or reality coming in too soon (Tustin, 1986), can be traumatic, interfering with going-on-being. Initially going-on-being occurs as a very subtle sense of a self that is bounded by tactile experience (Bick, 1968, 1986).

In addition to being a psychic space for a sense of going-on-being, the body also marks time, moving us continuously into the future. Of course, this is true concretely as the process of aging from birth to death changes our psychic awareness of time. Marking time also occurs psychically via the body's processing of sensory experience in a cumulative manner. Accumulative experience involves memory and representation. For example, when a bodily experience is linked to an emotional experience and remembered, such as the smell of lilacs in Berlin, the present is linked to the past. This is more than a cognitive event; it involves a somatic link to an emotion that links with an unconscious phantasy. To mark psychic time and space effectively, the body communicates to the mind and to others who will listen. Such communication includes information of well-being as well as of pain and suffering, of pleasure and displeasure. Among other things, communication from the self to the self informs one where in time and space one is. When traumatized, the mind attempts to foreclose future experience and distorts time, trapping one in the distressing moment or what Scarfone (2015) calls "the unpast."

Psychic equilibrium depends upon the integration of mind and body so that experience can be interpreted and creative transformation of experience can happen. When this occurs, new experience can be generated from the old, creating a structure that holds and evolves. New experience always disrupts psychic equilibrium, but if the body holds a sense of going-on-being this experience can be integrated with past experience. The body does all this, as well as maintaining life. Most of this bodily communication is unconscious, but nonetheless informs and helps us find personal meaning via a dream process Bion (1962b) terms "alpha functioning." Our nighttime dreams do the same, linking body and mind.

If we accept that the body is a dream space, we have to ask ourselves, who is the dreamer who dreams the dream (Grotstein, 2000) and what actually is the process of dreaming? Why should dreaming require an actual space and how is the concrete body essential for such a creative process to occur? How could such a space become both the container and the contained so as to make dreaming possible? Dreaming is a process of making meaning of experience by representing it. The process of representation evolves from the sensorium. Pictograms and images evolve from the sensorium and their information is essential for the act of figurability (Aulagnier, 2001; Botella & Botella, 2015; Eekhoff, 2019). Figurability is a process of representation, which evolves out of bodymind experience.

In this manner, the body is a continual generator of experience and the source of subjectivity. Ogden (1988) has named the earliest relationship between subject and object as the autistic contiguous position and recognizes the body as the foundation of all experience. Ogden (1989b, p. 129) says,

> Sensory experience in an autistic-contiguous mode has a quality of rhythmicity that is becoming continuity of being; it has boundedness that is the beginning of the experience of a place where one feels, thinks and lives; it has shape, hardness, coldness, warmth, texture, etc. that are the beginnings of the qualities of who one is.

Sensory experience is an aspect of relationship with both internal and external objects. Like the paranoid schizoid and the depression positions, the autistic contiguous position is present throughout life. The body is essential for all three positions, for the organization of emotional experience, and for the development of the mind. The body provides a "sensation matrix" for the mind (Ogden, 1991).

I have used Joyce McDougall's (1989) words "the body as dream space" because I believe the body is more than a storehouse for "memories in feelings" (Klein, 1961, 1975). Additionally, the body serves as a container for "memories in sensorium" (Eekhoff, 2019). Memories in sensorium are memories that recall earliest prenatal and postnatal experience, such as sensations, smells, or sounds that evoke feelings of well-being or even feelings of terror. Sometimes we view the word memory as static. Alternatively, I am using the word memory to describe a fluid process involved in making meaning out of experience. Memories in sensorium and memories in feelings are transformed in an elemental form of dreaming which begins in the body. By dreaming, I am describing a process, delineated by Bion (1967, 1970), where sensate and perceptual experience is used by the mind to create personal meaning.

Think for a moment of your own experience of dreaming. Typically, what we call a dream is a story we recall upon waking and tell ourselves or someone else. This story is a transformation of the actual dreaming process. A nighttime dream begins when the body is still and perceptual awareness remains active. Tactile awareness during sleep—of the temperature of the air, the weight of the blankets on our skin, the ambient sound sensations, the sensations of our partner's presence—link with unconscious emotional associations to form new connections that further elaborate our waking lives. The sensorium's output evolves into pictograms or visual images that evolve into linked images forming 'movies' in the mind. These movies are then transformed into emotional narratives that include language so as to be memorable. This whole process, which Bion (1962b, 1970) calls "alpha function," goes on whether we are awake or asleep.

Such somatic emotional dreaming enables the person to find relationship and passionate connection to both self and other. I suggest this process is enhanced and deepened when shared with another. Moreover, the intersubjective elaboration of dream thought begins at or before birth and continues for a lifetime. The body and the proximity of the other (Eekhoff, 2017) is a major container for the

creative elaboration of meaning. Bion (1962b, 1965) describes this relational connection within and between others as Love, Hate, and Knowledge. These links,
even when they are attacked (Bion, 1959), represent uniquely personal emotional
thoughts that are simultaneously relational and universal. These individual and
universal passions reflect the personal process of representation and symbolization. Somatic and perceptual experience is infinite, taking in immeasurable
information. Thinking is called into existence to cope with the infinite. A thinker
is called into existence to make use of thoughts.

Body as defense

Some patients defend against overwhelming awarenesses by shutting down psychic space and attending to the concrete necessities of life. Rather than using
their somatic, emotional experiences as communication, they use them as autistic defenses against overwhelming terror and persecution. I surmise that for
these patients uncontained experience occurred first in utero or in the first few
months after birth. In the absence of the containing reverie of their mothers,
they have turned to their own bodies as mother substitutes. A patient told me his
mother did not know she was pregnant with him until she arrived at the hospital
emergency room in pain. His mother denied her pregnancy with him, believing
then that she was having an appendicitis attack. He often felt terrified and had
repeated experiences of nameless dread, accompanied by panic attacks. He frequently had no experience of my presence with him, stating he could *see* me but
could not *feel* me as with him. He always felt alone. To compensate, he turned to
alcohol, telling me the feeling of being inebriated was one of being accompanied.
When he drank, he no longer felt alone. I imagine that inebriated states recalled
his prenatal hazy experience in the womb. I further imagine that his mother's
psychic abortion or denial of his existence was repeated in his difficulty feeling
me in the room.

Healthy sensuality is necessary for well-being; however, the sensual can also
be a defense. The use of the sensual as a defense is difficult to notice in analysis
because it is often silent (Eekhoff, 2015). When used defensively, sensuality is
perceived as concrete and denies the separateness and reality of the other while
simultaneously using the other in support of a delusion of oneness. The patient
appears to be thinking, speaking, and relating to the analyst as a separate object,
yet is using the experience to adhere to the analyst in a sensual way. Only when
the analyst becomes aware of this fixation and the intoxication it brings to both
parties can this *psychosensual impasse* be addressed via language so that growth
may resume.

The use of somatic responses to internal and external stimuli seems to serve as
a distraction from a terrifying awareness of aloneness. It is more than aloneness,
however; it is also an awareness of infinity and its unbounded and uncontained
nature. Somatic experience used defensively interferes with the body's capacity
for making meaning from experience. Somatic responses can replace dreaming
rather than aiding a person to dream. For example, this happens when an analyst

and a patient get caught up in the concrete meaning of language, ignoring the emotional and unconscious function it serves. Some patients are attached to the sound and rhythm of speech, rather than to symbolic meaning. Links between mind and body are compromised when somatic responses are the sole focus of attention. Focusing on the sensory, when used defensively, enables one to deny the gaps inherent in all relationships. Denying a gap forecloses the necessity of making a link. Without adequate linking, the mind's capacity to dream is also severely inhibited. Along with this difficulty, patients who use their body's re-sponses defensively are unable to make use of their objects or sometimes even to relate to them (Winnicott, 1969).

Paradoxically, individuals who use their sensory experience defensively lack the capacity to accurately reflect upon and interpret bodily experience. They are often somatically overwhelmed and hypersensitive to sight, sound, and touch. They seem to use one sensation to block out others. In this way, although they retreat to the sensory, they do not experience themselves as embodied whole persons.

Out of these observations, I have come to believe that *the place where thoughts first appear is in the body*. In health, the body links us to the infinite experience of being human. In an analysis with primitive states, transformation occurs first in the body before it reaches the mind as an emotional experience (Damasio, 1999). This process of transformation or change, when it occurs in analysis, is evoked primarily but not exclusively via physical proximity to the analyst (Eekhoff, 2017).

Patients who have suffered early infantile traumas have difficulty using their bodies as a dream space for organizing and generating experience. Instead, they have turned to their bodies as a substitute for containment provided in health by the other. Such patients reveal an awareness of an early uncontained and unme-diated experience of being overwhelmed, while feeling all alone. Their memories of being overwhelmed are held in their sensorium. The overwhelming experi-ence while feeling alone was impossible to bear in infancy and is now, when re-experienced in the transference, quite awful for both analyst and patient to bear.

Patients who have suffered early traumas feel alone and unfortunately are una-ble to experience the embodied presence of the analyst. The analyst may also feel alone and unable to reach the patient even though feeling present for them. The experience for both is of total isolation and terror in the face of immense need and vulnerability. In spite of being largely unmentalized, the competing needs and terrors are held in the body as implicit memories. A background ambience of blankness evolves as both a potential that was not realized and as a defense against overwhelming experience.

I used to think such patients maintained a delusional denial of otherness. Today I believe such individuals have an internal place where they deny *their own existence* via a representation of a blank place (Green, 1999). Without a sub-jective experience of self, otherness is not a relevant experience. The loss of a subjective sense of self is relevant. This blank place or delusion of not existing is nonverbal and preverbal. It is experienced primarily somatically rather than psychically. Although the blank place may become represented (Green, 1999), the representation of an absence becomes a background object of pain (Eekhoff, 2018a, 2018b; Bion, 1962b). I have described this elsewhere as present with patients whose mothers suffered trauma and passed the trauma unknowingly onto their children via their psychic absence and preoccupation with their own pain. Infants and young children internalize their suffering mothers and unconsciously identify with it. Identifying with a 'pain mother' is corporeal and experienced as psychosomatic symptoms or as a void.

The delusion of not existing is paradoxical. One would expect that excessive attention to the somatic would confirm one's existence. One would also expect that a memory held in the body would counter the delusion of nonexistence rather than supporting it. However, paradoxical reversals and negative hallucinations are part of the delusional denial of otherness and the delusional denial of self. These reversals and negative hallucinations, that is, the perception that sensory experiences are *not* happening, contribute to the difficulty in uncovering and treating this delusion.

Some individuals have access to early traumatic experiences because their psyche is called into existence too soon (Tustin, 1986) in order to cope with physical and psychic overwhelm. Awareness comes before repression is possible, before splitting and projection are sufficiently in place to deal with the intensity of the perceptual field. The awareness, which is clearly a mental activity, is held not in the mind so it can be thought, but in the bodymind, where it cannot be repressed or forgotten. Ada, the patient whose story I will later relate, describes it thus: "When my despair and terror destroy my conscious will, my body goes on. I feel at those times that my body betrays me. It just keeps going on." It is at such times that the thought of suicide or the idea of not being comforts her.

Perhaps for this reason most of us have long ago repressed our awareness of such early experiences. Our own development of thoughts from early sensations as well as the continuing development of our thoughts from somatic experience, in other words our personification and individuation, makes joining with patients at this primitive level disturbing. To go there with our patients requires a great deal of us. We have to be able to access and tolerate our own experience of nothingness, meaninglessness, and the black hole (Grotstein, 1990). Unless we can do this, our patients won't be able to bring these experiences to us.

When the analyst speaks from her own bodily awareness it can form a bridge for clarification of a patient's relationship with his or her own body, thereby differentiating somatic delusion or symptom from somatic communication. This action of the analyst fosters development in the patient of a deeper and lasting connection to him or herself and to others. Also, development in the somatic process may occur both moment to moment and over time. Body relations (Bleger, 1967) and object relations develop simultaneously in health. Our patients' relationship to their bodies changes considerably in analytic treatment, as does their capacity to tolerate affect and relationship to self and other.

Patients who use their bodies to defend against their emotional experiences deny relationship with others. Denial of emotional relationship with another may make discovering the transferential relationship to the analyst difficult. I have elsewhere referred to this phenomenon as a "silent transference" (Eekhoff, 2015). Psychosensual processes within their own body and in relation to the analyst's body become a substitute for the emotional transferential relationship, that is at once concrete and representational.

The analyst's attention to somatic phenomena and painstaking efforts to recognize and name these processes over time provides the patient with a new experience of relatedness between two physically and psychologically separate persons. A new relationship to the body, namely, an integrated psychosomatic embodiment that normally would be accomplished between a mother and her infant, may be achieved in the analysis. It is not that an old experience is recovered. Rather, a *new experience of embodied relatedness* is realized. After much time, patience, and constancy, the experience of being contained and held in body and in mind, or bodymind, is internalized. This enables what Cassrola (2018) calls "dreams for two." Dreams for two require two people who are psychically separate, not fused as Ada was with me initially. As no two patients are alike and no patient is the same from day to day or from moment to moment, this process involves much trial and error.

A small number of patients are unable to dream. It is not only that they do not recall their dreams. Their concrete attachment to the sensorial bodily experience leaves no gap to be filled with processing the meaning of their sensations. Without this gap, there is no psychic space between patient and analyst. Without space internally, there can be no dreams for two. They project weakly or their projections themselves are not communications, but are evacuations that contribute to this primitive blank place.

In the case of Ada, who frequently said to me, "There is no there, there…," beneath her projections lay a more difficult non-projective defense; that is, a negative hallucination that fed the delusion that *she herself did not exist*. When her delusion of not existing, of nothingness inside, surfaced to awareness she went from feeling empty to a feeling of fullness. The fullness felt terrible and terrifying. It made her feel claustrophobic in relation to her own presence. It was not a welcome change and she again retreated from her own aliveness, creating an oscillation between full and empty, empty and full. Somatically, these experiences were expressed in various ways. A common one was through her breath and her pattern of breathing. Other physical symptoms such as difficulty swallowing, upset stomach, and feeling cold sent her again and again to her physician. She could not imagine these physical symptoms were psychologically meaningful communications from her bodymind.

Before this oscillation and rhythm between empty and full is established inside the patient's bodymind, there may be reference to nothingness or talk of a void or a black hole. After the somatic defenses and mental use of the body and sensation are made conscious, a beginning experience of a self may evolve experienced as nothing but pain. This is not identification with a pain mother. The nothing-but-pain experience is a lifting of the psychosensual defense and a coming alive.

Coming alive includes feeling emotional pain. For me, with Ada and patients like her, this is the most difficult juncture in the analytic journey. It is the point when patients cry out, and Ada in particular said to me, "All I am is pain!" "Why?" "Why did you take me here?" "What good is it to know this?" At such moments, the analyst needs to hold onto her own separateness, her own faith in the power of the life force and effectiveness of the psychoanalytic method. If not, the risk is of being drawn into an enactment that destroys separateness and hinders development instead of viewing pain as communicating a specific need in the present moment.

Put another way, at this crucial juncture in the analytic process the hidden delusions of no self, no other, no time, and of no space or infinite space may give way. Slowly, the reality of something beyond the concrete—of meaning in emotional relatedness to somatic and psychic self as well as to bodily and mental otherness—can finally be experienced. When this occurs, healthy projection and introjection becomes possible. The embodied process of dreaming becomes possible. In Bionian terms, somatic beta experience is transformed into alpha experience. However, initially any emotional contact with self or other may be felt as unbearable and defended against by a process that makes relationship concrete or sensate and superficial at best. Often the most ravaging and painful moments come after a momentary experience of emotional contact between analyst and patient. This is because concrete experience is, like an iceberg, breaking up. There has been an experience of somatic and psychic separateness in the lived emotional experience between patient and analyst that is terrifying. And, this experience implies space and time and an unknown and unknowable future.

Patients who do not experience themselves existing are difficult to treat and feel at times that they are untreatable. Yet, I believe they are treatable. I hypothesize that those who heal are able to do so because they possess an innate capacity for unconsciously experiencing a container/contained relationship within their own bodies and in psychical proximity (Eekhoff, 2017) to the analyst's body and to the analytic setting. In my view, this capacity is an expression of the life instinct and of the patient's capacity for utilizing "thoughts without a thinker" necessary for learning to relate more fully to multi-dimensional life. This capacity for utilizing an embodied relationship may also emanate from the universal experience of being contained physically and psychically in the womb during gestation. This universal physical experience is present even when the mother's reverie has been inconsistent or hostile.

The capacity for making use of sensory experience has been described by Bion as alpha function. Cassorla (2018, p. 67) describes this ability as making up the

> … mental representation of emotional experience, acquiring the quality of 'thinkability' without yet actually taking the form of thoughts. This stimulates the formation of an 'apparatus' for thinking them, which causes dream-thoughts, unconscious waking thinking, dreams, memories, ideas, and more complex thoughts.

I am adding that the somatic experience of both the mother and the infant, as well as the analyst and the patient, is the foundation of the emotional link between body and mind.

Clinical vignette: Ada

I have written about Ada previously (Eekhoff, 2019). She was 33 years old when I met her, and is the middle of three children. She came from an upper middle-class family with two working parents. She reported an unremarkable childhood. Purportedly, Ada was neither abused nor deprived physically, although she believes her parents were indifferent to her emotional needs. Reportedly, her mother was depressed both before and after her birth. Via construction using the transference relationship, I came to believe her mother was not only indifferent, but perhaps was repelled by Ada's infantile demands. Ada says her mother told her she never wanted children. She felt herself to be an unwelcome child (Ferenczi, 1929). When with her, I frequently had an image of a dying baby. Initially, I experienced her constant talking and angry demeanor as intrusive, leaving me little room for thinking and no space for dreaming. I contributed to the problem by my own attempts to speak. In speaking, I was contributing sound and action without the aid of reverie to find or make meaning. Ada herself reported no nighttime dreams for the first three years of her analysis.

Her problems presented in the first few sessions were:

"I'm in a new relationship and will need support when it fails."
"I am actively suicidal ten to twelve days a month."
"I think I have a borderline eating disorder, as I binge and then think I am fat, so I starve myself."
"I grew up in a House of Horrors."
"I'm panicked at work all the time, and I feel intruded upon if anyone talks to me."

What I am interested in describing in this vignette are the somatic expressions in Ada's analysis that mark internal empty places, a somatopsychic no-place, along with a no-thing or a no-object or a no-self. I agree with Tustin, Meltzer, Bick, Bleger, Mitrani, Ogden, Grotstein, Lopez-Corvo, and D. Rosenfeld that these internal states of mind are pre-thought experiences as well as pre-splitting and pre-projecting states of being.

In other words, these selfless and objectless states exist in a time and space before the paranoid schizoid and depressive positions. Bleger (1967) calls this symbiotic state of normal undifferentiation the glischro-caric position. Ogden (1988, 1989b) calls it an autistic contiguous position that he views as non-pathological and part of our experience throughout life. However, these positions can become fixed (López-Corvo, 2006, 2014) and part of a pathological organization. Meltzer (1975a, 1975b) has described somatic dismantling used as defense during post-autistic or post-psychotic states. Dismantling, the separation of one sense from another, is an attempt to stop overwhelming emotional experiences.

Ada told me that nothing could accumulate inside of her because her skin didn't hold her. She experienced herself as a sieve, whose contents were leaking out. As a result, she felt often there was nothing inside of her; that she was a two-dimensional cartoon character. She also experienced me as not having an inside and being two-dimensional. This meant we were both sieves. Consequently, she could not rely on me or anyone else to contain her.

Perhaps her feeling of not existing and having nothing inside her was felt by me in the first session as evidenced by my speaking more than usual. She expected answers from me and then interrupted my attempts to speak, foreclosing the possibility of containing her. She herded me again and again toward her preconceived notions and attempted to get me to agree with her. For example, when I wondered if she might leave her boyfriend rather than be left by him, she ignored me. She was certain he would leave her. She seemed to have all the answers. If she needed anything from me, it was as a filler of space. My experience was that the two of us conspired to fill the space with sound, leaving no room for emotions or dreaming to arise.

In that first session Ada avoided eye contact. For her to look at me would have been to acknowledge our separateness. As she healed, eye contact increased until she reached a point of being able to tolerate not seeing me, thus benefitting from using the couch. As the analytic work deepened, the visual depravation when using the couch became unbearable and she once again needed to sit up so that she could see me. At first, she needed to "keep an eye on me" fearing I might hit her when she wasn't looking. I came to understand through somatic countertransference that for Ada sitting up and seeing me involved a primitive experience of the danger of the other. To deny this, Ada looked at me, and in looking unconsciously became me. While lying down, she could in phantasy be inside of me thus reducing her fear of myself as a separate other. She went up and down on the couch, preferring to sit up and see me when experiencing the greatest anxiety.

Ada's world as she described it to me was two-dimensional, consisting mostly of surfaces or sensations experienced concretely and devoid of symbolic significance. For symbols to form, for words to have meaning, there needed to be a recognition of my separateness from her, of a gap between us. She could not tolerate such a gap. She lacked a psychic space for dreaming. I did not at first recognize this. Ada was articulate and highly verbal. She had been in treatment for ten years before coming to me. She knew how to speak about herself, without being truly reflective. She could speak about feelings without having any. I erroneously assumed that Ada's words had the same emotional meaning for her as they did for me. They did not.

Ada had an uncanny capacity to mimic me. She took my words and fed them back to me. For example, she believed I was telling her what to do and how to feel and act. At first, I thought this meant she was internalizing our work. I was impressed with how quickly she was changing. Later, with horror, I recognized her mimicry and experienced her as nowhere to be found psychically in our work together. She was present physically along with the sound of her words, but not psychically. She repeated this pattern in all of her relationships; matching herself to others, leaving no difference, bumps or protrusions that would interfere with what I came to understand as her desire for perfect fusion.

This transference/countertransference situation was also evident in how she related to her own body. I initially attempted to interpret a transference relationship that was silent (Eekhoff, 2015). In hindsight, it would have been better if I had been able to speak to her bodily experience. Eventually I was able to shift in how I spoke to Ada and in what I offered in the way of verbal interventions.

This shift in how I spoke to Ada was helpful to her gradually forming a relationship with her own body. For example, prior to analysis, Ada had no way of knowing when she was hungry or tired. She did not feel a need to urinate or defecate. She sought medical treatment fearing various aches and pains indicated a lethal illness. Her sensory world, which kept me out of contact with her in the transference, did keep her unconsciously in contact with her own life force as it evolved in utero and in relationship with her mother and with me. Her obsessive use of exercise, while serving an evacuative function, simultaneously gave her an experience of her beating heart.

Ada severely restricted her food intake, but forced herself to eat so she did not become anorexic. Hers was a pre-pubescent body and she prided herself on wearing the same size clothing when I met her as she had worn in junior high school. Whenever she felt stressed by contact between us, she perceived herself as fat, looking into the mirror and actually seeing a fat torso. As her ability to tolerate fullness and dimensionality increased, she has come to feel herself to be and to look womanly.

Ada's sensory experience was initially used primarily as a defense against psychic overwhelm. Interestingly, her experience was that her sensory world provided a relational connection. Moreover, it felt to her like the only contact she had with her own or others' humanness. At the same time, her attempt to control and distort her body was a way of denying her own life force and her need of others. Still, her bodily connection to me kept her in the treatment when her mind was against it. That is, the sensorial aspects of the treatment served to bind her to me. At the same time, her mind was continually devising ways to rid herself of what I was saying and of me. She constantly stripped meaning from my words and emotion from my well-intentioned interactions. For example, she continually told me that she was quitting analysis. At the same time, she in fact did keep coming. She stuck to me in a most elemental way, adhesively via mimicry (Meltzer, 1974), trapped by her own sensate needs, while denying any emotional relationship with me.

First and foremost, Ada developed an attachment to the frame. The constancy of her analytic hours became important to her. This attachment included the physical space of my office; its sight and smell and the texture of the room, the softness of the couch, the quality of the light coming through my windows, and the changing colors of the leaves on the trees she could see outside. Also included in the frame was the rhythm and sound of my voice. These are the things she clung to, while ignoring the content of my words and consciously denying my value. While she was telling me that I was useless, even bad for her, and I feared she would flee analysis at any moment, she was unconsciously burrowing in and hanging on to me for dear life. When I was feeling most battered, beaten, hopeless, and useless, she was physically relating to me.

Whereas my awareness of what was happening in the analysis evolved over-time, I will try to demonstrate through her words how these clues came to me. I recognize the limitations of words to describe what I believe are a deeply unconscious and nonverbal continuous sensual experience that operates primarily at a somatic level.

Eventually Ada began to understand how she was relating imitatively or 'going through the motions.' She described a man whom she loved as "looking like a boyfriend, smelling like a boyfriend, feeling like a boyfriend and acting like a boyfriend, but [for her] not a boyfriend." A few weeks later she said the same about herself; that she was looking like, acting like, talking like a person but had been for many years not a person. She was horrified at realizing how she had in many respects not existed as a person. She simply wasn't home. Her words and actions were mostly mimicry.

How does one notice the presence of an absence? After years of analysis, Ada told me she sensed it in her body. She said she has "always known something was missing," or "It's comforting, I don't exist at all." Later she described a place seemingly at the cusp of this no-place that was quite horrific. "I feel devastated," she said, "like after the atom bomb, there is nothing left to experience. Is there? Nothing is left." She wondered if her experience was like what happens when matter and anti-matter come together. Poof! Nothing.

Toward the end of her analysis Ada said,

> I am getting used to my body and to myself. Bodies have a cadence. I was always pushing other people, but I was pushingmyself too. Now I am listening to my body, resting when I'm tired, eating when I'm hungry. Can you believe that I never knew until recently what it felt like to be hungry?

Discussion

In *Elements* Bion (1963) describes the use of the senses as a necessary component of thinking. He elaborates his description of the thinking process by linking the domain of the senses with the domains of myth and passion. He provides evidence of the body as a dream space. Ada came to me unable to dream in either her body or her mind. The work we did together required us both to experience our perceptual identities, the physical responses of our bodies as they responded to the proximity (Eekhoff, 2017) of each other. Proximity leads to primary identification via the psychosomatic resonance and reverberation between analyst and patient. Eventually these sensory experiences could be noticed with Ada and named. Eventually her early experience that she had not registered could be experienced somatically and emotionally within the analytic hour.

The *motion of the senses* is essential to the development of the mind. Ada's rigidity and fear of any experience she could not control caused her to shut off awareness of her body's responses. She preferred stasis to movement. In so doing she limited her emotional life and restricted her capacity to think. She was shut off and shut down. At the same time Ada used her mind to tell her when it was necessary to urinate or defecate, eat or drink, sleep or waken. Her body's natural rhythms were lost to her. Lost too were any feelings of sensual pleasure or sexual desire.

Ada did not experience her own body as a container of her sense of self. Because her primary experiences had not been represented first in her body and then in her mind, she was caught in agitation, irritation, and extreme anxiety that left her suicidal. She was hypervigilant and hyper stimulated. In spite of this, she felt she did not exist. Ada did not repress because "It is not possible to repress something that has not yet been represented through some mental process" (Bergstein, 2019, p. 14). In Ada's case the process of representation and mentalization was short-circuited by unconscious restrictions she placed on her somatic experience. Before her body could dream, sensually creating the sensate experience of her skin as a container and her eyes as the image-maker that could become movies in her mind, Ada shut down. In such a deadened state, psychic elaboration or the process of figurability (Botella & Botella, 2015) could not flourish. What I concluded as my own understanding evolved is that Ada's sensory experiences functioned as an umbilical connection to me and as a second skin (Bick, 1968, 1986).

As painful and tumultuous as her analysis was, it awakened her body so she could experience herself as existing in the real world. Only then was she able to embody her experience and dream so as to develop her mind. Transformation replaced repetition and re-presenting. Finally, thus embodied, she was able to marry and have a child and experience her own body and mind as existing.

Conclusion

An analytic space is typically envisioned as a space within the symbolic order. Openness enables a space for dreaming, which brings primitive sensory and emotional representations into the symbolic order. As analysts, we are privileged to encounter patients wherever they are in the body's dream space and process of dreaming. When early experience is traumatic and the infant and child have not been contained by the mother's reverie, analytic work is more difficult, since language itself may be imitated or borrowed rather than generated. Differentiating that which was beginning to form but was attacked from within or without (Bion, 1959) from that which has never been realized is the task of a receptive and containing analyst. The difficulty of this distinction is, in my view, influenced by the internal make-up of both analyst and patient. The way in which the analyst matches and meets the flesh and blood person in the consulting room and the way in which the analysand processes information and feels understood, misunderstood, or not understood can contribute to or ameliorate this difficulty.

Separating mental from bodily processes at this primordial level is purely an intellectual exercise. The emotional interaction of two people in continuous oscillation between container and contained involves body and mind or, more accurately, bodymind. The oscillation is movement and movement is a function of the dream.

Transformations in the bodymind of both analyst and analysand enable psychic transformations, some of which become symbolized. The psychic transformations happen via dreaming or alpha function. In my view, only a tiny minority of these transformations becomes organized into language. Most remain in the body as background and are present but not recognized. In either case, emotional transformations require a thinker to cope with them (Bion, 1970).

Some people with seemingly benign upbringing nevertheless struggle enormously with somatic transformations. To bear their experiences, they must alter and distort them. Others with horrific reports from their childhoods manage to hold and contain and examine their experiences without excessively attacking themselves or the analyst in the transference. They are somehow able to experience themselves without excessive distortion as happens in the case of massive intrusive or evacuative projective identification.

Dreaming is a process of transformation that enables psychic growth and change. The analyst's maternal function and attention to the body as well as to the primitive bodymind states of the patient allow dreaming and change to occur outside of conscious awareness, outside of remembered dreaming, and in the body itself through a sensorial experience of the emotional contact. In analysis, both analyst and patient are involved in organizing these unconscious transformations. The analyst's experience of emotional and perceptual contact, or lack of it in the here and now of the session, makes it possible to differentiate somatic delusion from somatic holding and the integrative or nonintegrative use of the body as a dream space.

Just as I believe it is the mother's responsibility to do all that is humanly possible to prevent reality from coming into the infant's awareness prematurely, so too it is the analyst's responsibility to notice and protect patients from sensorial and psychic overwhelm to ensure a space for dreaming. In this way, experience that was once unable to be dreamt can be slowly brought into the analytic relationship and into the symbolic order.

References

Aulagnier, P. (2001 [1975]). *The violence of interpretation: From pictogram to statement*, trans. A Sheridan. Routledge.

Bergstein, A. (2019). *Bion and Meltzer's expeditions into unmapped mental life: Beyond the spectrum in psychoanalysis*. Routledge.

Bick, E. (1968). The experience of skin in early object relations. *International Journal of Psycho-Analysis*, *49*: 484–486.

Bick, E. (1986). Further considerations on the function of the skin in early object relations. *British Journal of Psychotherapy*, *2*(4): 292–299.

Bion, W.R. (1959). Attacks on linking. *International Journal of Psychoanalysis*, 40:308–315.

Bion, W.R. (1962a). The psycho-analytic study of thinking. *International Journal of Psycho-Analysis*, 43:306–310.

Bion, W.R. (1962b). *Learning from experience*. Karnac Books.

Bion, W.R. (1963). *Elements of psycho-analysis*. Heinemann.

Bion, W.R. (1965). *Transformations*. Karnac Books.

Bion, W.R. (1967). *Second thoughts: Selected papers on psychoanalysis*. Jason Aronson.

Bion, W.R. (1970). *Attention and interpretation*. Tavistock.

Bleger, J. (2013 [1967]). *Symbiosis and ambiguity: A psychoanalytic study*. Editors, J. Churcher & L. Bleger; Translators, S. Rogers, L. Bleger, & J. Churcher. Routledge.

Botella, C. & Botella, S. (2015). *The work of psychic figurability: Mental states without representation*, trans. A. Weller with the collaboration of M. Zerbib. Routledge.

Cassorla, R.M.S. (2018). *The psychoanalyst, the theatre of dreams and the clinic of enactment*. Routledge.

Damasio, A.R. (1999). *The feeling of what happens: Body and emotion in the making of consciousness*. Harcourt Brace.

Eekhoff, J.K. (2015). The silent transference: Clinical reflections on Ferenczi, Klein, and Bion. *Canadian Journal of Psychoanalysis*, 23(1)57–73.

Eekhoff, J.K. (2017). Finding a center of gravity via proximity to the analyst. In H. Levine & D. Powers (Eds.), *Engaging primitive anxieties of the emerging self* (pp. 1–20). Karnac Books.

Eekhoff, J.K. (2018a). Somatic countertransference as evidence of adhesive identification in a severely traumatized woman. *American Journal of Psychoanalysis*, 78(1):63–73.

Eekhoff, J.K. (2018b). Terrified by suffering, tormented by pain. *American Journal of Psychoanalysis*, 78(4): 350–369.

Eekhoff, J.K. (2019). *Trauma and primitive mental states: An object relations perspective*. Routledge.

Ferenczi, S. (1955 [1929]). The unwelcome child and his death-instinct. In Balint, M. (Ed.), *Final contributions to the problems and methods of psycho-analysis* (pp. 102–107). Basic Books.

Green, A. (1999). *The work of the negative*, trans. Andrew Weller. Free Association Books.

Grotstein, J.S. (1990). Nothingness, meaninglessness, chaos, and the "black hole". *Contemporary Psychoanalysis*, 26(3): 257–290.

Grotstein, J.S. (2000). *Who is the dreamer who dreams the dream? A study of psychic presences*. The Analytic Press.

Klein, M. (1961). Narrative of a child analysis. *The International Psycho-Analytical Library*, 55:1–536. The Hogarth Press and the Institute of Psycho-Analysis.

Klein, M. (1975). Envy and gratitude and other works 1946–1963. In M. Masud R. Khan (Ed.), *The International Psycho-Analytical Library*, 104:1–346. The Hogarth Press and the Institute of Psycho-Analysis.

Lacan, J. (1977 [1966]). *Écrits: A selection*, trans. Alan Sheridan. W.W. Norton.

López-Corvo, R. (2006). *Wild thoughts searching for a thinker: A clinical application of W.R. Bion's theories*. Karnac Books.

López-Corvo, R. (2014). *Traumatised & non-traumatised states of the personality: A clinical understanding using Bion's approach*. Karnac Books.

McDougall, J. (1989). *Theaters of the body: A psychoanalytic approach to psychosomatic illness*. W.W. Norton.

Meltzer, D. (1994 [1974]). Adhesive identification. In Hahn, A. (Ed.), *Sincerity and other works: The collected papers of Donald Meltzer* (pp. 335–35). Karnac Books.

Meltzer, D., with Bremner, J., Hoxter, S., Weddell, D., & Wittenberg, I. (1975a). *Explorations in autism: A psychoanalytic study*. Clunie Press.

Meltzer, D. (1975b). The psychology of autistic states and of post-autistic mentality. In D. Meltzer (Ed.) J. Bremner, S. Hoxter, D. Weddell, & L. Wittenberg, *Explorations in autism*: (pp. 6–29). Clunie Press.

Ogden, T.H. (1986). *The matrix of the mind: Object relations and the psychoanalytic dialogue*. Jason Aronson.

Ogden, T.H. (1988). On the dialectical structure of experience—Some clinical and theoretical implications. *Contemporary Psychoanalysis, 24*(1):17–45.

Ogden, T.H. (1989a). *The Primitive Edge of Experience*. Jason Aronson.

Ogden, T.H. (1989b). On the concept of an autistic-contiguous position. *The International Journal of Psychoanalysis, 70*(1): 127–140.

Ogden, T.H. (1991). Some theoretical comments on personal isolation. *Psychoanalytic Dialogues, 1*(3): 377–390.

Scarfone, D. (2015). *The unpast: The actual unconscious*, D. Bonnigal-Katz (Trans.) with J. House (Contrib.). Unconscious in Translation.

Tustin, F. (1986). *Autistic barriers in neurotic patients*. Yale University Press.

Winnicott, D.W. (1949). Mind and its relation to the psyche-soma. *British Journal of Medical Psychology, 27*:201–209.

Winnicott, D.W. (1960). Ego distortion in terms of true and false self, In *Maturational Processes and the Facilitating Environment*, (pp. 140–152). International Universities Press, 1965.

Winnicott, D.W. (1963). Communicating and not communicating leading to a study of certain opposites. In *The Maturational Processes and the Facilitating Environment*, (pp. 179–192). International Universities Press, 1974

Winnicott, D.W. (1969). The use of an object. *International Journal of Psychoanalysis, 50*:711–716.

Winnicott, D.W. (1974). Fear of breakdown. *International Review of Psychoanalysis, 1*:103–107.

6 Foreword to "Dreaming into death"

Welcoming death

Jeffrey L. Eaton

Analysts are not usually very open about their intimate personal journeys. Maybe such reticence can be a barrier to learning from experience. Psychoanalysis is not only about a clinical situation. It is about human experience, the human mind, and human emotions. It is about existential facts of life, like birth, aging, violence, loss, and death. How do we help a patient get more deeply in touch with his or her own experience? How deeply can we touch our own hopes, fears, desires, and doubts? A patient's picture of the world is not just a product of unconscious phantasy. It is an attempt to represent the significance of experience and often a window into all the internal and external obstacles toward making sustained meaning of life's joyful and traumatic moments.

How often have you been invited into a significant conversation, one that challenges you to think, feel, reflect, question, and imagine? A conversation that pushes the boundaries of what you will ordinarily tolerate paying attention to? A psychoanalytic session can sponsor a space for thinking, feeling, and transformation. Writing and conversing can also open such spaces. We need to help each other develop and sustain the capacity to talk about pain, to face it, open to it, and learn from it. Rikki and Adrian have opened a conversation about the reality of dying, not the concept of dying. We must stretch to open to such intimacy. We need each other to face a task like investigating the pain of the reality of death.

As Ernest Becker described so well, ours is a culture that denies death in many ways. Very few people prepare for death in a mindful intentional way. The vitality of the body wanes, and it becomes harder to deny vulnerability and dependence as we age. Older people acknowledge it more because they begin to outlive some of their friends and relatives. Some people have a sense of humor about it, others are more resigned. Few people accept aging and death as a natural part of life, "a game that must be lost", as Adrian Stokes described it (1973).

One of the ways that some people unconsciously deny death is by living outside of the body. Many people are partially or almost completely disembodied, living only in their minds and intellects. Recent advances in technology accelerate the flight from the body into "screen time". Where are you when you are interacting on social media? I have seen many teens who tell me about "friends" who they have never actually met in person but who they spend hours playing with remotely. They may know very few details about that kid but feel a strong

DOI: 10.4324/9781003195559-6

connection to him because of hours spent interacting in the virtual space of a multi-player online game. The boundaries between what I call real and what a younger generation consider real have shifted greatly.

Virtual selves don't die. At the same time, people become so deeply attached to their "devices" and the experiences they sponsor that they feel them to be elements of self. To lose access or connection to the various social networks that capture people's attention is like losing a part of the body, and it feels like dying! Now it is a phantom body that carries the libidinal and affective investment of a person's life. Pornography is a vivid literalized example. Pornography has become as common as the daily newspaper once was.

It matters how people live in the world. An analyst has no upper hand in living a wise ethical life. Choices matter. What kinds of experience put us more in touch with the fabric and texture of life? Death is woven into this fabric. Death must be a part of every person's picture of the world if that picture connects deeply to reality. How many courses did your institute offer in dealing with the reality of death?

I remember a conversation with a teacher (Debbane, 2002, personal communication) who told me that his mentor, Clifford Scott, was curious about how people pictured their own death-scene. What would a good death look like or be like? How did one imagine dying? How did one desire to die? It is an important thought experiment that can be performed at any phase in life. It is not unlike a Buddhist practice of preparing for death even while one is healthy.

The time of death is uncertain. It is a comforting delusion to believe that we will live to wake to a next day and a next and a next. At some point, that sequence stops. Buddhists call facing the uncertainty of the time of death an awareness of impermanence. Focusing on impermanence is a practice that points one toward reality.

The confrontation with death brings you suddenly "now-here". Time and space become suddenly present rather than elsewhere. You're back in your body. We reach a limit we cannot deny or transcend. Oddly, facing this fact makes us feel more alive.

Rikki and Adrian's chapter requires a personal response from every reader. That is also what Death requires. There is no preformed way to face death or to grieve the loss of a loved one. Adrian pictured his death in two remarkable dreams.

When I was a very small boy, I had a dream that terrified me. In the dream I was standing at a beach on the Puget Sound near our house. I was watching a small boat sail toward me. I somehow knew that if the boat reached me, I would be asked to get on. If boarded the boat, I knew, somehow, I would sail to my death. I was, of course, too young to understand the concept of death. But I had a preconception that terrified me, and I spoke with anguish for months afterward about "the boatman coming".

This dream was probably my unconscious symbolization of the fact of death. I think it was influenced by my father's father dying just weeks before I was born, and my father's mother dying when I was about two years old. My mother's father died when she was just a girl and I carry his name forward as my own. In many families, the reality is endured but the significance of that reality cannot be spoken about. To get in touch with the significance of experience requires time and conversation to process.

Many years ago, in a small bookstore in Munich, I discovered a simple small book depicting 41 woodcuts by the artist Hans Holbein who lived from 1497 to 1543. In his "Picture-Book of Death" (1965) he depicted the way death accompanies everyone in daily life. Death is personified visiting every role in the village. From the richest to the poorest, from the oldest to the youngest, from the wisest to the most foolish, from the powerful to the helpless, death is always already walking by their sides. The Latin notion of *Memento mori* means "Remember that you too will die". This is the spirit of Holbein's slim volume. It is also the message of Rikki and Adrian's chapter. The impact of Holbein's images now joins Rikki and Adrian's testimony. I hope their message supports more waking from the trance of distraction that threatens daily life and sponsors connection and conversation about the blessings of being alive together.

References

Holbein, H. (1965). *Bilder des todes.* J. Bohn & Sohn.
Stokes, A. (1973). *A game that must be lost: Collected papers.* Carcanet Press.

7   Dreaming into death

Rikki Ricard and Adrian Jarreau[†]

Although informed by theory, this is not a theoretical chapter. This is a chapter infused with experience. My late husband, Adrian Jarreau and I were inspired to write this chapter based on our experience of facing into his death together with as much consciousness and openness as we could. The process was so meaningful to Adrian and I, and so inspiring to our work, that we felt it might have meaning and inspiration to our colleagues and to our work with others. Death is not a topic that enters any of our worlds easily. Most of us are conditioned to look away from the certainty of death. We deal with it when confronted with it. Yes, Adrian and I were confronted with it but we also made the choice to open to it emotionally and face into the unknown together in a way that I believe will inform my life and my work moving forward, without him. This chapter invites you to join with us on the journey we made together. A journey that is full of questions and very few answers. We began the process of writing this chapter together but Adrian died much earlier than we anticipated and so I have chosen to complete this chapter alone.

When Adrian and I began thinking about this, we came to realize that the notion of death and certainly the death of the body is experienced by all of us throughout our lives. The connection between the body and the unconscious was dominant in Adrian's and my thinking. Is it possible that the body "communicates" with the unconscious in such a way that information is passed on to us about what the body is experiencing? We were faced with the ending of an embodied experience and we found we needed to bring as much analytic thinking and exploring as we could to this encounter. I wondered if in some very significant way our lives are shaped, albeit mostly unconsciously, by an awareness in the body—an awareness that it will die.

All of us who work with patients realize how many deaths we encounter throughout our work no matter what the presenting problem or issue. Helping our patients grieve seems essential to this process. What we both were to discover is what an intense bodily experience grief can be. The body is the container of all these feelings and often works in conjunction with the unconscious to communicate to our conscious minds the enormity of what needs to find containment.

The journey I am sharing actually began with two dreams. In the early winter of 2017, Adrian and I were on vacation in Mexico. In the course of one night my

[†] The author is deceased.

DOI: 10.4324/9781003195559-7

husband had two dreams in which he died. In the first he was snorkeling and decided to dive. As he came up to the surface, his snorkel filled with water, and in an attempt to blow the water out of the snorkel, he swallowed the water and drowned. It was so startling he woke me and we processed the dream in our usual way—through questions and associations and metaphor. Later the same night, he had another dream in which a bee flew into his mouth. In the dream, his thought was that the best remedy was to swallow the bee. In the process of doing so, the bee stung his throat many times; it swelled up and he suffocated. Again, this seemed like a dream to wonder into—what needed to die? What needed to be swallowed? As I now reflect back on this, I am somewhat amazed and inspired by the question of what aspect of Adrian was communicating to him through these dreams. He had no idea at this point that there was anything going on in his body and certainly no sense that death was a year away.

Upon returning from this trip, Adrian began to encounter back and shoulder pain. Being 71 years old, this was not an uncommon experience and the usual ways of working with such pain were employed—stretching, icing, yoga, building core strength, massage, and visits to his chiropractor. On one of these visits, a series of X-rays were taken and a mass showed up on his right lung. Healthy man that he was, there was initially not much concern about this. Soon, however, we were meeting with an oncologist who informed us that this was stage 4 non-smoker's lung cancer that had metastasized in his bones, thus explaining the back and shoulder pain. This defined the course of our lives, our minds, and our relationship over the next ten months; and in many ways, for me, the rest of my life.

When coming up against the reality of the loss of the body, how do we face into that level of uncertainty, that degree of fear, with consciousness? And what is the nature of the consciousness required to do so? Freud stated in *The Ego and the Id* that the first ego is a body ego and I would now propose that the last encounter with ego is through the experience of the body, the dying body. We know that the body dies. Does the ego die? Is there a spirit, a soul, a mind that also dies? As we reflected back together on the dreams that Adrian had in Mexico, we were awed as we wondered what aspect of Adrian was communicating something in these dreams. Was there a knowingness in the body that came through in the unconscious communication of two dreams of death in one night? What we did know was that we were up against an experience that was certainly not metaphorical in relation to death but actual and extremely frightening.

I propose that when faced with the reality of this most significant of losses, people are brought back to the primal mind in such an intense way that it can be compared to an infantile state of mind—unable to "think", and often even unable to "feel"—at least in the way we had come to understand feeling in our adult lives. The mind that we have come to know and depend on doesn't know what to do with such high-level uncertainty. I thought that in some way this is possibly the most intense encounter with what Bion came to call "O" that one can experience in a lifetime. O as ultimate reality. Death as ultimate reality.

We did find the primitive mechanisms of splitting and denial to be very useful during this experience. To continue to live and work and proceed with the necessities of life, we absolutely needed to be able to deny the reality of death and split off the fears and frustrations accompanying that reality in order to continue to move through our lives.

Through the sharing of this journey into such raw and emotional waters, we hope to bring you the reader up against your own concepts of death and to encourage you to travel there with as much awareness as possible. How does one bring consciousness to this level of uncertainty? Possibly the greatest help for both of us as we faced into this mental chaos was the body. It was paradoxically the body—that which was dying—that was the most constant, vital touchstone for us as we came up against the fragmentation of our minds and the storm of our emotions. When thought and feeling overwhelmed us, we could come back to our bodies as "dreaming spaces" that allowed us to reconnect to ourselves and to each other. I say "dreaming spaces" because we needed to depend on a quality of mind that I believe to be most accessible to us in dreams. In this way, we were attempting a kind of "lucid" dreaming, a way to allow the mind to travel to places it did not want to go. In fact, our conscious minds often tried to pull us away from this level of exploration. Again, we were reminded of the dreams that Adrian had in Mexico. Maybe there was a way of trusting the unconscious connection to the body to be a holder of a truth—the truth of his potential death—that felt at best uncertain, and at worst, devastating.

As we often encounter in the work we do with our patients, there are indeed times that the mind sends out warning signals. Conscious or unconscious warnings not to travel any deeper into the issues being presented. When we tried to realistically face into what seemed to be the reality of Adrian's passing, the mind would often try to prevent us from any further exploration into this possibility. However, we realized that in order to find the deepest truth of our experiences, we had to ignore these red flags and continue to push into the emotional storms evoked by the need to encounter such an intense degree of loss.

Often a pulling away was necessary. As the poet T.S. Eliot reminded us, we humans cannot bear too much reality. It was the body that continued to inform us and call for our attention. And dreaming into the body that allowed us to continue to move forward.

After the diagnosis, we were shocked. We were afraid. We were intensely committed to bringing as much consciousness and feeling to this awe(ful) experience as we could. Death has been an aspect of our lives since we could remember. Our dear friend, who introduced us 30 years ago was diagnosed with cancer one year after this introduction and died after a two-year illness. We cared for him in the final weeks of his life and were with him when he took his last breath. He was also committed to a conscious death. However, even up until the very end, he was confronted with the question of whether he was dying or healing. His breathing in the final day of his life was very reminiscent of one in labor—it seemed as if he was trying to birth something. The breath was often full of pain but then would subside into shallow breaths that were easy and fluid. We talked with him about his fears, his dreams, and the pain of all that would be lost to him. He was 43 years old with two small boys, a loving wife and a successful career. It was a shocking, humbling experience.

Following our dear friend's death, Adrian and I traveled in India for six months. During this time, 28 years ago, we read aloud to each other from *The Tibetan Book of Living and Dying*, by Sogyal Rinpoche. His encouragement to incorporate the reality of death into one's daily life became an inspiration to us in the years to come. We often spoke to each other of our hope that we might die a conscious death. Easier said than done. We had no idea what we were really asking for, of course, as such an encounter is one thing when done abstractly and quite another when the pressing reality of death is in front of one's face and mind and heart.

We moved forward into this space of encounter holding onto each other and those who loved us and facing into the questions, the uncertainty, the fears— overwhelming at times—into the love and the ultimate loss. I began what is known as a CaringBridge Site and soon discovered that I needed this "blog" site to find the words, when I could, to try to make sense of the enormity of the intensity of experience we were having. When trying to find one's mind while up against so much unknown, we found the poetic expression, the world of metaphor, was the closest we could come to a kind of truthfulness of experience. What I mean by this is that the most accessible mind was so filled with confusion and future fantasy that we needed to drop down into the body, into the breathing and feeling space, into the informing unconscious to find the voice of the poet that could assimilate the intensity and use the symbolic voice to contain the concrete fear.

In order to share some of the immediacy of this experience, I include some of the passages from CaringBridge written by me and my husband during the ten months of his life with cancer. A month after Adrian's diagnosis I wrote:

> Life will never be the same. We are doing a lot of the same things we've always done—working, eating, going for walks, seeing friends and family, lawn bowling, watching our TV shows, etc.—but it's all very different. For one thing we do it much slower. But most significantly, there are these large hovering questions that follow us, guide us, bring us to our knees—how much time do we have left?
>
> It's haunting. If it's years then we can just let it hover lightly, still inform-ing but not threatening. If its months, then what is important? Are there things we MUST do, places we MUST see, people we MUST talk to? We are brought up against priorities daily and they mostly land on love, grat-itude and honesty. I am not suffering fools easily these days. Life changes completely in one moment. If we could only know this before we HAVE to know this.

Later that same month:

> This may seem so obvious but coming up against the reality of the loss of the body experience is devastating. During our amazing regular evening chats, my husband starts to cry and asks me how it will be possible to feel the awesome love he has for me when he is no longer in his body? For both of us?
>
> I am thrown up against that wall of loss. Yes. How?

I have felt so sad that I am the one being left. But I will be left with a body. A body that can feel—feel the grief, the love, the fear, the rage. Then the enormity of HIS loss hit me hard. We feel through the body and he will no longer have one. How will he feel? Is that even a question one can ask?

During this time period, we were reading aloud to each other from Steven Levine's book, *A Year to Live* (1997, p. 180). He writes:

> It was a question that reminded me to stay open to any possibility. And in that willingness to understand there arose one day an interesting thesis, an answer not necessarily the answer. If on another plane someone were in that dream level experiencing him—or herself meeting us again and speaking to us, might not their extraordinary concentration and strong attachment project them through into this one? Perhaps their experience of using another world becomes our experience of them in this world? Do we meet in the dream that each dreams of the other, living with the consequences of love?

"The dream that each dreams of the other". The experience of the mysteriousness of the unconscious and how it truly communicates to us and thus relationally to each other, was a territory we found ourselves smack dab in the middle of. Following the dreams of Mexico, and now encountering the "dream" state of facing into the death of a beloved, accompanied by a body that is dying, made us question so many assumptions we had held onto in the past. What is the nature of unconscious communication? What role does the body have in this communication? What do we trust? What is reality and what is phantasy?

During this time, we came upon a number of authors and poets that were amazingly helpful to us as we faced into these questions. I have chosen to include a couple of longer quotes from two of them to share with you. In this first quote from Nina Coltart's book, *Slouching towards Bethlehem* (2000), she is addressing a particular phase of analytic work. What we found so inspiring in this was how poignantly significant it was to the space we were trying to find with ourselves and each other as we attempted to look directly into the face of death. Coltart says in reference to analysis:

> After a preliminary work there comes a time which is exhilarating, when the pace quickens and the gears change. Paradoxically again, this is often the time when darkness begins to close in, but it is a darkness having that special quality of the unknown which is moving towards being known. Freud was speaking of a time like this, I imagine, when he said that sometimes he had to blind himself in order to focus on the light in one dark spot. ... During phases like this in analysis, it is true to say that one does not *think* at all during some sessions, at least not in the ordinary cognitive use of that word ... This switch into fifth gear cannot exactly be legislated for, although Bion's advice that we should rigorously practice for it is relevant, and it does not by any means always happen ... In the fifth gear phase, when the act of faith is

most fully deployed, when our listening ear seems to be directly connected with our tongue and speech, interpretative dialogue is not a process which I would regard as being under everyday conscious control.

(p. 8)

Our ongoing work with our patients was inspiring our personal journey together and vice versa. Adrian continued to see patients up until a month before he died and I imagine it was some of the best work he ever did. We were continually grateful for the work we had done in our analytic training and our ongoing endeavor in our work with patients to listen for and to the unconscious and its intimate connection to the body. After six months of living in this world of cancer and keeping this intended chapter in mind, my husband wrote:

Why does the mind gravitate so much toward the negative? IT HAS TO KNOW! It can't tolerate uncertainty at times. It latches onto things that seem to help it "know" something and those things are almost always negative and troubling. I guess it's a kind of survival mechanism. "Latch onto the negative, know something, and then act on that." FOLLY. What I truly want is to let go of the need to know. To give it over to something I really don't know, except in the body. Perhaps religion was founded on this premise that when one is fearful, that fear could be given over to a god without the obsessive mind having to know. For those of us who are not religious, we have to find a way to be able to dismiss the strong tendency to know something in order to avoid the vulnerable, more quiet state of uncertainty.

We did find helpful inspiration from a number of spiritual writers. Pema Chodron in her book *When Things Fall Apart* (2002) writes:

All anxiety, all dissatisfaction, all the reasons for hoping that our experience could be different are rooted in the fear of death. Fear of death is always in the background. As the Zen master, Shunryu Suzuki Roshi said, life is like getting into a boat that's about to sail out to sea and sink. But it's very hard—no matter how much we hear about it—to believe in one's own death. Many spiritual practices try to encourage us to take our own death seriously, but it's amazing how difficult it is to allow it to hit home. The one thing in life we can really count on is incredibly remote for all of us.

(p. 55)

Adrian and I, both alone and together, wrestled with this awareness constantly. For the first month following the diagnosis, we found ourselves in an amazing dream space that allowed us to encounter the notion of death in a real and focused way. However, as time moved on and splitting and denial ensued, we moved away from this direct encounter with death and into an amazingly time-altered sense of the present. Days felt like weeks and weeks like months. Time no longer meant what it had for most of our lives. As the cancer progressed and the treatment continued to fail, we again needed to look into the reality of Adrian's dying. Re-entering that space became more difficult than the initial gift, in that first month, of a kind of imaginative possibility.

During a time when the pain had returned and the hope for years together was declining, Adrian wrote on the CaringBridge Site:

> Two nights ago Rikki and I started talking about how my self-care seemed to be taking up an excessive amount of time. Perhaps it had become obsessive. If this were true then it had taken on a defensive measure. What was I defending against? I proceeded to defend my self-care, of course. At a certain point Rikki intervened. She prepared me by saying I might not want to hear what she was going to say. I braced myself. She said, "Maybe you're dying." I didn't respond right away. But I knew what she had said might be true. I had been having similar thoughts that I dismissed right away because I have been too scared of the enormity of the loss. So there was no way I was seriously going to consider this. But this night was different. I couldn't continue to dismiss this possibility if I was interested in the truth. So for the first time in a long time I opened up to that possibility. Of course, a lot of grief came up and I wept. I could no longer hold onto the notion that if I come up with the right treatment I would be cured. I was fighting with my disease and I didn't really want to get caught up in that. After all, as Rikki said, it is a part of me. The cancer is a part of me in a physical and psychic way. Fighting it doesn't make sense. Furthermore, I've seen very clearly the amazing effects the disease has had on me. Sometimes when I see this I'm blown away by what an awesome process of opening this has been for me and I'm grateful ... I could die soon, like in the next six months. I realized I had to face this possibility and as we talked I began to see how liberating that could be. Perhaps I didn't have to be so afraid of dying.

The following quote, again from Pema Chodron's "When Things Fall Apart" (2002), is too appropriate not to share:

> Underneath our ordinary lives, underneath all the talking we do, all the moving we do, all the thoughts in our minds, there's a fundamental groundlessness. It's there bubbling along all the time. We experience it as restlessness and edginess. We experience it as fear. It motivates passion, aggression, ignorance, jealousy, and pride, but we never get down to the essence of it.
>
> Refraining is the method of getting to know the nature of this restlessness and fear. It's a method of settling into groundlessness. If we immediately entertain ourselves by talking, by acting, by thinking—if there's never any pause—we will never be able to relax. We will always be speeding through our lives. We'll always be stuck with what my grandfather called a good case of the jitters. Refraining is a way of making friends with ourselves at the most profound level possible. We can begin to relate with what's underneath all the bubbles and burps and farts, all the stuff that comes out and expresses

itself as uptight, controlling, manipulative behavior, or whatever it is. Underneath all that, there's something very soft, very tender, that we experience as fear.

(p. 44)

About three weeks before my husband died I entered the following on our CaringBridge Site:

> It's late at night. My darling struggled his way up to bed. I am using this site to get to the depths of my experience. I guess I'm asking for indulgence. Some will by ok with this and I know some will react. So be it. This place of aloneness seems so important for me to make contact with right now. Isn't that what I'm helping so many of my patients with so much of the time? Finding a relationship with that deepest place of solitude. It's not an easy thing. We all begin as babes, crying in the middle of the night, expecting or not, hoping or not, that someone will respond to our cries. And then we find out it ultimately needs to be us that responds—not without relational help—but us, alone with our selves.

And then three days before he died I wrote:

> Getting old might not be for sissies, but it has nothing on this dying thing. It feels like I am midwifing a birth that has some serious complications. My dearest is not going gently. He is definitely in his last days. No food for some-time and a small amount of fluids. He is in and out of consciousness and when in, it's very reminiscent of being in a dream state. Once in a while I get very direct contact with him in a present way. This morning after a very rough nite, he looked at me very clearly and asked, "Rik, why are you crying so much?"
>
> I am wracked with grief but I'm also wanting this "birth" to happen. This bird needs to fly. I need strength to stay in my compassionate attention. It's hard to love this much.

Adrian died three days later surrounded by family and finally at rest. The desire to stay in the body was an incredible event to witness. This amazing body, this locater of experience. This container of life and relationship and all the meaning we give to everything we experience. I feel committed to encouraging this conversation about death and dying and facing into them with as much consciousness as possible. The body is indeed a primal psychoanalytic object. My mind returns to the mysterious dreams Adrian had before he consciously had any idea he was dying or was even aware that he had cancer. What is the communication path between the unconscious and the body? Does the body have a "knowing" that it relies on the unconscious to communicate? This internal listening seems like such a significant task to undertake, especially when faced with all the intensities of uncertainty and confusion that can accompany so much of our life, and most particularly in this case, of our death.

References

Chodron, P. (2002). *When things fall apart*. Shambala Publications.
Coltart, N. (2000). *Slouching towards Bethlehem*. Other Press.
Levine, S. (1997). *A year to live*: How to live this year as if it were your last. Three Rivers Press.

Part III

Nascent body in early object relations

8   Introduction

Caron Harrang, Drew Tillotson, and Nancy C. Winters

In "Clinical impasse: the infant body and gathering of a soul" by David Brooks and Patricia Antin, and "The environment within: On the fetus' capacity to differentiate self from other" by Dana Blue, the authors consider the experiences and capacities of both the pre- and postnatal mind. While their treatises differ substantially, both chapters convey the significance of close attunement to 'primordial' embodied communication in countertransference and transference phenomena.

In "Clinical impasse: The infant body and gathering of a soul," David Brooks and Patricia Antin examine the relationship between body and soul in infancy and in psychoanalytic treatment with adults. Informed by infant observation studies and the work of Winnicott and Bion, Brooks and Antin see clinical impasse originating from primordial affective experience when it overwhelms the patient's insufficiently established ego. These moments of psychosensory overwhelm evoke defensive reactions such as schizoid withdrawal, envy, reversible perspective, and some forms of perversion. Not infrequently, the patient's efforts to defend against catastrophic anxieties (e.g. 'nameless dread' and primitive fears of bodily dissolution) are viewed as destructive attacks on the well-intentioned efforts of the analyst. For Brooks and Antin, verbal interpretations along these lines are one of the causes of clinical impasse.

Through their own painstaking encounters with impasse in the analyses of adults, Brooks and Antin propose a principle for technique: the analyst must "turn [herself] over in the countertransference to receive the silent signals of breakdown emanating from the transference-countertransference nexus." It is the analyst's responsibility, they contend, to establish a proper communication channel for the analytic dyad through which the patient's nascent sense of self can emerge. When this occurs, phenomena mistakenly attributed to the death instinct or to an excess of destructiveness naturally abates.

Infant observation is widely recognized as a crucial component of psychoanalytic training, allowing analysts-in-training to develop skills such as negative capability, highly relevant to analytic work with children and adults. However, it is rare for this connection to be so clearly shown as it is here by Brooks and Antin. They propose infants are "born in bits, so to speak" and must be "gathered up in a way that realizes [their] innate capacity for authentic object relatedness." This

DOI: 10.4324/9781003195559-8

"gathering of a soul" is the foundation for all subsequent forms of verbal and nonverbal communication. Vignettes from infant observation illustrate moments of gathering through maternal containment and reverie. For example, ten-day-old Sasha's momentary expression of distress while sleeping (scrunching her face, crying, kicking her legs) is noticed by Mom who watches and waits. Brooks and Antin describe Sasha's settling coupled with Mom's attentive waiting without prematurely acting, as a "healthy psychosomatic partnership" allowing for moments of un-integration and integration.

Applying this perspective to analysis with adults, Brooks and Antin offer clinical vignettes illustrating the analyst's ability to hold the patient through cycles of disintegration, un-integration, and integration required to develop an embodied sense of self. Courageously, they offer a final vignette illustrating a moment of impasse when a transference interpretation precipitates the patient feeling he's being held in "an interpretation choke hold." Rather than tightening the interpretive grip, the analyst is able to identify with the patient's dissolution-into-despair and remains open. This shift from interpretation to what Brooks and Antin call "visceral receptive observation" allows for reestablishment of an embodied communication channel between analyst and patient. Recognition of the vulnerability that underlies impasse, accessed through the analyst's counter-transference, provides an avenue for restoration of healthy psychosomatic partnership and ongoing lived experience.

Dana Blue's "The environment within: on the fetus' capacity to differentiate self from other" emerged from her experience as a doula and a psychoanalyst working with adults. As a doula, she provided emotional support and guidance to many expectant parents and attended the delivery of their babies. One birth she attended (described here) led to her central thesis: the pre-natal mind has a capacity not only to differentiate self from other, but also to communicate through projective identification its nameless dread and death anxiety. A profound somatic countertransference with an adult analysand led her to further speculate these primitive anxieties may re-emerge later in psychoanalysis, lodged in the analyst's body.

Blue draws inspiration for her conjectures from Bion's "Evidence" (1976), in which he imagines the fetus in the womb, aware of a disturbance going on— loud noises between mother and father, or the mother's digestive system: "Then the foetus might omnipotently turn in hostility towards these disturbing feelings, proto-ideas, proto-feelings, at a very early stage, and split them up, destroy them, fragment them, try to evacuate them..." (p. 134).

Blue then considers Winnicott's famous statement, "There is no such thing as a baby" (1975, p. 99). While she agrees with Winnicott about the enormity of mother's influence on the baby, Blue challenges Winnicott's assertion of the uni-directional flow of influence from mother to baby, positing "currents of influence between mother and fetus flow both ways."

Blue's clinical vignettes convey the power of hypothesized somatic projections of fetal death anxiety. During the delivery of Louise, who died shortly after birth due to a previously unidentified anomaly, Blue was gripped by an uncanny "pit of my stomach dread" of a magnitude she'd never experienced. She suggests she became the bodily container of Louise's death anxiety as birth (and, sadly, death) approached. Although the fetus' anxiety undoubtedly comingles with mother's terror so often present during the parturition process, Blue posits (in distinction to Winnicott) the fetus may at times be "sensitive to its separate self" and experience its own terror of annihilation.

Blue's second vignette details a session in the analysis of Paul, whose birth history was traumatic. During one session, Blue has a terrifying somatic countertransference reaction leading her to speculate her body has become the container for Paul's pre-natal death anxiety. She employs Lemma's idea (2015) that the analytic setting, especially for patients in symbiotic relation with the analyst, is experienced as "contained in the analyst's body." Blue also agrees with Lemma's emphasis on somatic countertransference as an important technical tool in understanding the state of symbiosis, and affects inaccessible to representational forms of communication.

Blue gives further evidence for extending object relations to fetal life in the work of Piontelli (1992), Maiello (1995), Robinson (2008) and Anderson (1995). Albeit conjectural, her bold theoretical proposal in this chapter encourages analysts to pay more attention to somatic reverie and somatic countertransference, which may contain otherwise inaccessible information about primitive anxieties stemming from fetal life. Bion (1976), quoted by Blue, should have the last word,

> We may be dealing with things which are so slight as to be virtually imperceptible, but which are so real that they could destroy us almost without our being aware of it. That is the kind of area into which we have to penetrate.
>
> (p. 135)

References

Anderson, M.K. (1995). "May I bring my newborn baby to my analytic hour?": One analyst's experience with this request. *Psychoanalytic Inquiry*, *15*(3): 358–368.

Bion, W.R. (1976). Evidence. In C. Mawson (Ed.), *The complete works of W.R. Bion* (Vol. 10, pp. 133–135). Karnac Books.

Lemma, A. (2015). *Minding the body: The body in psychoanalysis and beyond*. Routledge.

Maiello, S. (1995). The Sound object: A hypothesis about prenatal auditory experience and memory. *Journal of Child Psychotherapy*, *21*(1): 23–41.

Piontelli, A. (1992). *From fetus to child: An observational and psychoanalytic study*. Routledge.

Robinson, M. (2008). Catastrophic change and emergence—A turbulent journey out of encapsulation [Paper presentation] The 2008 International Evolving British Object Relations Conference, Seattle, WA.

Winnicott, D.W. (1975). *Through paediatrics to psycho-analysis*. Hogarth Press and the Institute of Psychoanalysis.

9 Clinical impasse

The infant body and gathering of a soul

David M. Brooks and Patricia K. Antin

> There is nothing so real as a child's cry, a rabbit's may be wilder but it has no soul.
>
> Sylvia Plath (2010, p. 72)

> When two personalities meet, an emotional storm is created. If they make sufficient contact to be aware of each other or even sufficient to be unaware of each other, an emotional state is produced by the conjunction of these two individuals…
>
> W.R. Bion (1979, p. 136)

Was "nameless dread" (Bion, 1962) always nameless? Was it a dread that became nameless? Did Bion have a more specific dread in mind but language it this way to emphasize a threat so violent it is refused signification? Oddly, the first stanza of "Rock-a-bye baby" (*The Real Mother Goose*, 1994/1916) ends with poetic imagery of catastrophic collapse and fall into what Houzel calls "precipitating anxiety" (1989). It's an intensifying despair of pending death without words; we can imagine a "vanished last scream" (Eshel, 2019) depending on the frequency.

> Rock-a-bye baby, on the treetops
> When the wind blows, the cradle will rock
> When the bough breaks, the cradle will fall
> And down will come baby, cradle and all

The remaining stanzas counter this catastrophic drop down a hole of annihilating despair with images of primary maternal preoccupation to secure or restore and inspire hope:

> Baby is drowsing, cozy and fair
> Mother sits near in her rocking chair
> Forward and back, the cradle she swings
> Though baby sleeps, he hears what she sings

> Rock-a-bye baby, know not you fear
> Never mind, baby, mother is near

DOI: 10.4324/9781003195559-9

Wee little fingers, eyes are shut tight
Now sound asleep until morning light

Before responding to separateness, one has to feel sturdy enough in one's existence as an 'I' with durability, continuity, and extension apart from the excess of emotion stirred inside the self. Clinical impasses occur when primordial affective experience cannot be allowed to exist because there is no durable enough an 'I' yet to register experience, let alone transform such proto-mental agonies into verbal shape for communication and thought. To prevent annihilation into a void where a durable psychic base should be, the false self deploys a kind of Maginot Line, a barricade of schizoid withdrawal, reversible perspective, envy, and perversity against live contact. For if the scope, depth, and intensity of infinite despair emerged to be named, it would threaten all that has come to be taken as one's world with catastrophic result (like approaching the Twin Towers on 9/11 from the cockpit of one of the planes moments before impact). Such extraordinary survival measures have been mistakenly cast as the result of a putative 'death instinct.' As one patient described it, "I'm inside an iron maiden"; that is, trapped inside a *security system* that kills. Like parents who try as best they can, the analyst may miss the struggle, unbearable pain, and anxiety at these earliest layers or be unable to receive them, naively assuming that if expressed with good intentions, interpretations will be received as such.

Through our efforts to resolve clinical impasses we have come to articulate a principle for technique: one needs to *turn oneself over in the countertransference* to receive silent signals of breakdown emanating from the transference–countertransference nexus. Inspired by infant observation and the late work of Bion and Winnicott, we find mute pain occupying the place where a nascent, embodied 'I' might be gathered and emerge as the nucleus from which an authentic emotional experience can be integrated and symbolized. In our view, it is the analyst's responsibility to establish a proper communication channel through which the unborn 'I' can emerge. When this happens phenomena often mistakenly attributed to an excess of destructiveness naturally abate. We put forward a second principle: unless the analyst has a clear grasp of aliveness in the transference–countertransference, s/he is in no position to feel confident discerning actual from apparent destructiveness.

Proper embodiment

Tausk (1933, p. 530) describes the heartbreaking situation of a schizophrenic's progressively dismantled experience of her body and mind:

> The outstanding fact about the [influencing] machine is that it is being manipulated by someone in a certain manner, and everything that occurs to it happens to her. When someone strikes this machine, she feels the blow in the corresponding part of her own body.... Those who handle the machine produce a slimy substance in her nose, disgusting smells, dreams, thoughts,

[and] feelings [that] disturb her while she is thinking, reading or writing. At an earlier stage, sexual sensations were produced in her through manipulation of the genitalia of the machine; but now the machine no longer possesses any genitalia, though why or how they disappeared she cannot tell. Ever since the machine lost its genitalia, the patient has ceased to experience sexual sensations.

Tausk used the earliest infantile experiences of struggling with embodiment for figuratively cohering both the positive and negative symptoms of schizophrenia. He pioneered imagining the earliest happenings in pre- and post-natal life when psyche first comes online and encounters endogenous forces: the lights, sounds, pressures, temperatures, pains, and pleasures of being embodied.

The [influencing machine as a] projection of one's body may, then, be traced back to the developmental stage in which one's own body is the goal of the object finding. This must be the time when the infant is discovering his body, part by part, as [if it were] the outer world, and is still groping for his hands and feet as though they were foreign object[s]. At this time, everything that "happens" to him emanates from his own body; his psyche is the object of stimuli arising in his own body but acted upon as if produced by outer objects. These disjecta membra are later on pieced together and systematized into a unified whole under the supervision of a psychic unity that receives all pleasure and pain from these separate parts. This process takes place by means of identification with one's own body. The ego, thus discovered, is cathected with the available libido; in accordance with the psychic nature of the ego, narcissism develops; and, in accordance with the function of the individual organs as sources of pleasure, autoeroticism results.

(1933, p. 542)

Tausk's cites man's unending experience of being "compelled to find and recognize himself anew" (p. 544), or "narcissistic libido," as the endogenous source of the infantile ego's integrative capacities. For us, both "innate narcissism" required for basic proper bodily inhabitation and subsequent "acquired narcissism" of the autoerotic phase require maternal gathering, receptivity, and mirroring. We emphasize maternal holding and mirroring to gather the infant's undeveloped integrative capacities necessary for experiencing itself as an embodied being.

Following the Kleinian tradition, Alvarez (2006) feels most babies are born with some rudimentary cohesive ego capacity, rather than this primary cohesion being entirely supplied through maternal or environmental provision. We are indebted to Klein's pioneering work without which we would not be aware of or have the means to explore the internal world of adults, children, and pre- and post-natal infants. We do not dispute that babies have constitutional instincts that from an adult perspective may be viewed as expressing aggression, love, and meaning making. However, we disagree with notions of primary envy and any more than nascent object relations capacity from birth.

Fairbairn (1952), Winnicott (1945, 1960) and Guntrip (1962, 1968) called for a reorientation of analytic theory in the direction of understanding ego development that begins with it lacking essential structure and cohesion to an extent not previously appreciated.

We hope to extend Klein's theorizing in this direction, drawing upon the work of other British object relations analysts and certain concepts from neuroscience and attachment research (e.g. Kumin, 1996; Malloch & Trevarthan, 2009). Drawing on Bick (1986) and others, we believe infants are born in bits, so to speak, and must be gathered up in a way that realizes the infant's innate capacity for authentic object relatedness and object usage and provides a foundation for all forms of verbal and nonverbal communication. As Enid Balint (1963) wrote regarding her successful treatment of a schizophrenic woman, these early experiences occur prior to the onset of Klein's paranoid-schizoid position since they involve emergence prior to the full development of projective and introjective processes:

> …. I have stressed that aspect of a good relationship where the mother is stimulated by her baby so that her reactions will be felt by her child as an echo or a proper feedback…. Because of this lack of feed-back Sarah felt that she was unrecognized, that she was empty of herself, that she had to live in a void.
>
> (p. 479)

Alternatively, we believe infants are born in a state of un-integration and their capacities for integration are facilitated by the gathering actions of the caregiver. Holding and receiving provides needed feedback or psychosomatic resonance for infant's emerging existence (Balint, 1963). Once sufficient integration is established through the back and forth rhythms of integration and un-integration, a solid foundational self begins to form which gives the infant to feel embodied and 'real.' Haag termed this development "verticalization" (1991). It begins with the mother's capacity to catch the meaning of her infant's experience in the back of her mind, return it properly, and thereby catalyze the infant's proto-ego identity. The mother uses properly attuned maternal instinct *to affectively shape herself into baby's emergent self-in-experience* as it takes shape out of the "normal fusion (normal projective and adhesive identification) that is in fact the only way to establish the feeling that a solid base and boundaries exist" (Haag, 1997, p. 189).

Rather than assuming each person has a single experience of coming into being, Winnicott believes the origin of one's sense of self is the sum of many beginnings. The mother's physical and emotional holding facilitates ego-relatedness and the achievement of an embodied unitary ego and sense of self around one year to eighteen months (the 'I am' stage). This unitary identity is not an end in itself; "it is a position from which life can be lived" (1989). Authentically traversing the depressive position or what Winnicott (1963) calls "the stage of concern," the oedipal stage, latency, and adulthood are all built upon this base.

Winnicott's (1971) notion of the mother's mirroring role emphasizes that facilitative and pathogenic feedback is expressed bodily and the quality of her gaze has profound implications for the extent to which the baby (or adult analysand) can have foundational experiences of a real self, at-one-with and at-home-in one's body, safely able to emerge spontaneously in a receptive and responsive world.

> What does the baby see when he or she looks at the mother's face?… ordinarily, what the baby sees is himself or herself…the mother is looking at the baby and what she looks like is related to what she sees there…. Many babies, however, have to have a long experience of not getting back what they are giving…. their own creative capacity begins to atrophy…. perception takes the place of apperception…. beyond this in the direction of pathology is predictability, which is precarious, and which strains the baby to the limits of his or her capacity to allow for events. This brings the threat of chaos, and the baby will organize withdrawal, or will not look except to perceive, as a defense…. If the mother's face is unresponsive, then a mirror is a thing to be looked at but not into."

(pp. 151–152)

Our notions of time, experience, and "the sense of Real" (Winnicott 1990/1984) are likewise achievements of maturational processes in the context of proper holding and mirroring. What is real for the baby comes through the mother's experience. At the same time, an authentic experience of nascent 'I-ness' requires a sense of the real for development of an embodied self capable of inhabiting lived-time and lived-space. Lived-time begins with an elemental and differentiated sense of *before* and *after*. Similarly, lived-space begins with an embodied sense and distinction between *here* and *there* with the nascent ego as the implicit reference point. In this way, health, time, and space are imbued through primary omnipotence and proper maternal mirroring of the baby's experience. Being-in-time is an aesthetic experience, both personally meaningful and life affirming, not just a thing-that-happens; or worse yet, lived-time and space experienced as a demand for perpetual compliance. When a baby is gathered, held, and properly mirrored by his mother the early ego has a platform for development as states of experiencing fold into each other and a continuity of "going-on-being" is established.

A unitary sense of self is the result of the ego's integrative tendencies reflected in a process of embodying personal history that in health is stitched together and grasped through language (Aulagnier, 2015). If this secure base of self is not established, the earliest form of despair is interwoven into the experience of any need and life possibility. Hence, our clinical research compels us to view *primal despair as that which accompanies all nameless dreads.* Thus, emotional contact with the analyst threatens to unleash infinite and overwhelming primal despair. In this scenario, the false self takes over to arrest the threat of dissolution from within by preventing contact with the analyst as a means of survival (Brooks, 2019).

In infancy, it is the mother's capacity for dreaming her baby's existential dilemmas that provides a basis for communicative attunement and realization of the nascent embodied 'I.' This basis for proper attunement is temporarily missing when there are impasses in analytic treatment and threatens the nascent 'I' with annihilation by dissolution. In our view, it is the analyst's responsibility to locate and open a pathway for the emergence of the patient's authentic 'I.'

Infant observation: receptivity, negative capability, and addressing impasse

Infant observation provides a model for the prerequisite receptivity essential to negative capability. In this vignette, the observer captures a moment when a receptive and responsive mother is able to allow her baby to use its innate capacities to experience healthy un-integration. An early moment of integration as a *oneness-as-a-whole-of-bits* develops.

> Ten-day-old Sasha is sleeping for a long time snuggled in her blanket. After a while she moved her arms almost straight out to her sides with one hand. Fingers completely open on that one hand while, the on other hand her fingers are slightly curled. She moved her open hand to her face and put it gently on her chin and cheek while still lying motionless and sleeping. All at once baby scrunched her eyes tightly, cried a bit, kicked her legs and moved her arms before settling again. Mom was able to be there but, to wait and see if baby woke before picking her up or disturbing her in any way.

Sasha's "settling again" coupled with mom's attentive waiting attests to early life moments when the environment facilitates a healthy psychosomatic partnership. The environmental mother holds space and time wherein the infant's natural integrative tendencies can operate, building up an authentic embodied 'I.' This nascent self—a tenuous assemblage of islands of 'I' psychosomatic experiences—can and must at times disintegrate. With proper reception and mirroring, a foundational floor forms upon which baby can reintegrate and continue making use of these unintegrated-to-integrated or disintegrated-to-reintegrated experiences throughout life.

The next vignette illustrates emotional work around bathing for a three-week-old baby. We see a "rhythm of safety" (Tustin, 1986) emerge as mother empties herself of her own emotional stuff (memory and desire) enough to receive baby's turbulent experience, identify with it, and feed it back properly during a moment of unavoidable upset. The mother establishes a channel for communication by unconsciously attuning to her baby. She gathers baby's bits, allowing him to experience an island of healthy un-integration before falling asleep.

> The entire family, mom, dad, [baby], and sister (age 2 ½) convene in the bathroom. Dad has placed an infant car-seat like bathing apparatus into the bathtub. He is in the tub with the seat and the baby, while mom sits on the side of the tub with sister next to her. [Baby] is splashed with some water and he scrunches up his eyes and mouth…. [Baby] seems to try and fend

off the water with his arm/hands, moving them in the direction the water is coming from. Both mom and dad continue to wash [baby] despite his mild appearances of protest with his bodily movements. When done, dad has some trouble picking [baby] up and out of the seat, which heightens his displeasure; he begins to cry and becomes inconsolable; mom takes him. She quickly covers him in a hoodie towel, holding him against her chest. He quiets immediately as mom speaks to him soothingly. Once calmed mom takes him to the changing table; she puts him down he is upset and begins to cry with some ferocity.

[Sister] mimes baby's cries. Mom helps [sister] to use her words to talk with baby about how upset she is that he feels so distressed, experiencing his bath and changing as such an unpleasant ordeal. Mom picks [baby] up to comfort him …. She is speaking to him, telling him that she knows it's hard for him as she diapers him. She speaks in a sensitive, soft, soothing tone throughout this whole experience. Mom puts him down once more to clothe him and he is quite unhappy, crying intensely again and thrashing about with his arms and legs. Mom picks him up again and wraps him while holding him in a blanket and continues to rock him gently until he falls asleep in her arms.

Mother's capacity to be turned inside out, so to speak, by her baby's aggression and distress while remaining attuned is what allows him to survive the as yet nameless experience of shocking external and painful heterogenous internal sensations. Mom's holding allows her baby to develop a crucial layer of early integration and 'I'-ness.

Rustin (2005) succinctly describes the direct link between infant observation and its clinical utility.

> The observer as the analyst cannot register or record her data without being stirred by the mental activity and states she is exposed to. [Infant] Observation provides obvious links to the transference and counter-transference…. The 'frame' of watching, waiting and seeing which we learn from observation can be … transferred to our reception of our patients' communications in our consulting rooms.

'Infant' is from the Latin *infans* which means "unable to speak." As in infant observation, receiving the unable-to-speak communications from our patients requires negative capability and turning oneself over to the countertransference. This requires faith in blind psychic perception or intuition to find our way in the dark. It is often difficult to discern during the clinical hour what triggers the analyst's countertransference, particularly at a somatic level. One must patiently watch, wait, and listen without using memory and desire precipitously for immediate understanding. Formulaic lines of interpreting often signal defensiveness by the analyst against preverbal communications of mute excruciating protomental experience, an example of the analyst's vulnerability to transformation in hallucinosis (Brooks, 2018). Parallel to a mother's failure to attune to her baby, when the analyst misperceives or fails to recognize the unable-to-speak aspects of experience, the patient may fall into black holes of despair containing previous experiences never received or seen by anyone.

Clinical illustrations: receiving and gathering the patient's emerging 'I'

Rosenfeld (2001, p. 58, emphasis added) notes, "The analyst needs to be able to *fuse intimately* with the patient and, at the same time, withdraw; he must temporarily abandon his own way of thinking in order to follow the journeys of the patient's mind."

We understand "fusing intimately with the patient" to express the requisite receptivity Bion called "becoming O" of the patient (Bion 1965, 1970). Likewise, the infant observer must abandon their own conscious mental activity in order to become at one with the infant's experience. The observer temporarily fuses with baby's experience, described by Winnicott (1958a, p. 185) as "primary maternal preoccupation." It is an introjective approach to empathy and interpretation, as compared to a projective view—'putting oneself in the other's shoes'—described by Etchegoyen (Ahumada, 1997). The introjective approach is described by Mitrani (2001) as 'taking the transference.'

Psychoanalytic comprehension and conjecture allow the analyst to dream the pain from where the unable-to-speak lives, just as the mother does in the previously described vignettes. Theodore Reik first described the introjective basis of psychoanalytic understanding:

> Comprehension is preceded by a reproduction of what goes on in the other person's mind; it is an unconscious sharing of emotion, seized upon by endopsychic perception...
>
> The special form in which the ego is transformed by taking another person into itself for a moment can only be called an introjection.... followed by projection, whereby the transformed ego is thrown outwards and perceived as a psychological object. This sequence—the incorporation of a psychological Thou into the ego and its ejection—are conditions as essential to psychological investigation and the observation of other minds as the intaking and outgoing of breath are to the organism. They constitute the primary psychological conditions of the comprehension of other people's unconscious processes.
>
> (2014/1936, p. 199)

The following illustrates Rosenfeld's approach to the analyst's introjective identification with the patient's experience. The sixth chapter of *Rosenfeld's Italian Seminars* (2001) provides a detailed supervision working through an impasse involving transference psychosis. The patient's proto-ego is in a struggle wherein to exist and integrate extreme need and pain in an internal situation where her proto-object-mother is experienced as a persecutory force (not quite an object):

> When the patient was 5 years old, she dreamed of her [psychotic] mother as a kind of ghost who moved and had a human appearance, but whose mouth was completely missing. I believe this dream to be hugely significant.... Try to imagine what it is like to have a persecutory figure who moves around you, who does all kinds of things, but who does not speak. Imagine how one must feel; it must be terrifying. In this situation the patient has many "things" that talk to her, but this is not the case with the most persecutory figure of all who does not speak.... It is thus essential to understand what it means when she does not talk, or when there are silences. I would put a red circle around this point.
>
> (2001, pp. 124–125)

Rosenfeld insists analysts need to use words at any given moment that give shape to what the patient is experiencing. That is, using the patient's innermost situation as the context for interpreting the patient's communications, not the analyst's experience of what is being done to the analyst by the patient from a besieged-breast point of view, so to speak. Too often, the analyst resorts to negative transference interpretations rather than using their countertransference to transiently fuse with the patient's proto-mental experience. Rosenfeld addresses this iatrogenic way of missing the patient:

> The patient very clearly states that with his death she not only lost her father, she lost the protection from her crazy [psychotic] mother, and she found that she had to tackle the situation alone because there was no one else around to help her. This is why the patient did not have space: she was taken over by the fear, by this anxiety, by the situation.... Then she says: "I'm not finding out a thing here..." This is an expression of her lack of faith in being protected [by the analyst]; she doesn't know what to do, and she asks: "Please, help me get over my father's death, try to understand what it meant to me, how defenseless I felt, how much difficulty and anxious..." She cannot succeed in establishing even a partially stable emotional situation.
>
> But when the analyst offers his interpretation on her father's death and how she couldn't cope with it, she expresses the desire to have an analyst who not only understands her but feels what she experienced in order to help her tackle the deeper meaning of these experiences.... This is why she gets angry; because the analyst does not seem to acknowledge what she has gone through. The analyst persists in emphasizing the whole negative transference when he says: "In the same way as you think your father..."
>
> (2001, pp. 158–159)

We think Rosenfeld emphasizes "reaching the patient" as a superordinate priority over positive and negative transference interpretations because impasse occurs when an analytic unconscious to unconscious communicative link is absent. Establishing this link requires contact before or beneath the object-relating level wherein the analyst is at-one with the experience of a nascent 'I.' Transference interpretations generally emphasize the differentiated object-mother as the focal point, dislocating the fragile incipient 'I' from the primary task of gathering and identifying with its endogenous experience; as such, transference interpretations risk impinging upon the formation of "the capacity to be alone" (Winnicott, 1958b), which is essential for authentic self-development. Reaching the patient at this level means holding the patient through cycles of disintegration, un-integration, and integration required to develop a unit-status ego that can experience feelings in the presence of an attuned background other. The patient is constantly seeking an echo of herself through the analyst; an echo shaped through gathering unorganized and unspeakable emotions which allows organization of experience into a self-in-time who feels real and alive; where internal spontaneous changes, pushes and pulls of emotion and impulse, and shifting vectors of pain and pleasure happen all the time.

In an under-appreciated contribution, Elenora Fé D'ostiani (1980) follows a similar route to reach autistic children and psychotic adults. Like Rosenfeld, D'ostiani invites us to identify with the existential plight of the tenuous ego as a way of becoming oriented and attuned to the proper communicative situation. Through her writing it is clear D'ostiani first turns herself over to the countertransference to (1) gather bits of proto-mental affective experience within herself before being able to (2) dream her patient's plight so that she can (3) establish the proper basis for communication which catalyzes ego emergence and growth (p. 91):

> As the session with Peitro clearly shows, the process of descent into the inferno of the child's psychosis is not complete unless we succeed in transferring our point of view, in seeing "through the child's eyes". The room, the session, and our own efforts look very different from the way we see them from our own point of view.... The therapist becomes, in a certain sense, the child himself and feels what the child feels, sees the world as the child sees it and, in being dropped emotionally to the place the child is, must be able to integrate the same feelings of fear, anger, hatred, desperation, discomfort and loss of hope. Because the child could not bear them and [had no one] to bear them for him until he was strong enough to do so, these overwhelming feelings have caused an arrest or deprivation of development—if the psychotic child is to arrive at "psychological birth"
>
> (Tustin, 1977)

In turning oneself over to one's countertransference, the analyst surrenders to psychotic experience and risks transient ego disintegration (un-integration) in order to assimilate and integrate the patient's experience within oneself. Only then can the analyst find embodied language and the proper demeanor to say what needs to be said to the patient and begin transforming impasse into ego emergence. Aulagnier (2001) refers to this process as maternal "word bearing."

This model for resolving clinical impasse has transformed how we think about and receive our patients. It gives us space and authorization to observe in silence without interpretive intervention until such time as we can *feel* the experience we are living in the present moment, with this particular patient, and speak to it as it is unconsciously communicated to us.

Clinical example: the analyst's receptivity and resolving impasse

In his Italian Seminars (1977), Bion offers a story which makes clear that a patient's "depths of depression and despair" can be a defense against the terror of confronting an even more primal despair in the face of the final disappearance of a life-line object.

> To make the point clearer using a pictorial image: a party of some five people were survivors from a shipwreck. The rest had died of starvation or had been swept overboard.... They experienced no fear whatsoever—but became terrified when they thought a ship was coming near. The possibility of rescue, and the even greater possibility that their presence would not be noticed on the surface of the ocean, led them to be terrified. Previously the terror had been sunk, so to speak, in the overwhelming depths of depression and despair.
>
> (p. 119)

Where impasses emerge, we posit that the pathological organization removes the possibility of real contact in a misguided effort to protect the unborn ego from exposure to raw despair emanating from annihilating attachment to an unreliable, "tantalizing object" (Fairbairn, 1952). Like shipwreck survivors, psychic survivors of early trauma often experience contact with a good object as signaling hope; hope that's become unbearable because it is welded to the threat of absolute despair. A psychic tourniquet is needed to stop the bleeding, until or unless the analyst can demonstrate she is able to adequately receive and metabolize the threat of unbearable hope and associated absolute despair. As Guntrip (1968, p. 213) wrote, "Psychotherapy and the internal bad-objects world represent rival policies for saving the ego."

Like so many primitively traumatized patients, the analysand in the material below had no words to express that he felt misunderstood and un-received. He could only rage and reject; hardening himself in an autistic defense against the terror of dissolution in feeling dropped by the analyst's misunderstanding. Analysts have previously tended to think of this contact barricade as an attack on the analyst or on the analysis. We offer this material followed by our understanding of how to work with impasse in a way that does not pathologize the patient's hatred and aggression.

PATIENT: I was listening to my favorite news show on the way here and the newscaster said she was reviewing a book written by this woman who just won the

Pulitzer Prize for journalistic [sic]. Did you know that they're people who our government has been paying to shoot plutonium into them? Isn't that just the most evil, horrific thing you've ever heard? I'm just horrified, I can't even imagine that we can and do... do something like that in this country and no one is even stopping it.

ANALYST: I think you also feel shocked and amazed about discovering how much poison you feel you've been shooting into your own mind as well as worried about what you may have done to me and my mind.

PATIENT: Well yeah but I just keep thinking about what they were saying, it's so amazing to me, our country does the most evil, heinous things and it's just unbelievable...

[The patient escalates into one of his rants where he appears to be getting lost in the content of his story, voice escalating, so I interrupt him before he gets too far away.]

ANALYST: It seems really hard to think right now about what I just said and how it may relate more directly to what you are feeling about me and your work here.

PATIENT: [After a longish pause] That just really pisses me off. You just totally interrupted me and my association. I was telling you what I thought; and I don't think I'm evil; I don't know what you want from me; whatever I say I can't do it right. I was trying to respond to what you say but no, it's never good enough for you, everything that comes out of my mouth is about me and my pathology and everything about me is pathological and sick according to you, you didn't even let me finish.

[long pause]

ANALYST: You're so angry and feel so criticized by me.

[This did calm him for a moment, however, he went on in a huff and his rant continues]

PATIENT: [Furious, with indignation in his voice] It's like I'm in an interpretation choke hold here! You're trying to control my mind.

ANALYST: You feel like I'm shooting plutonium into you.

PATIENT: I do. You just told me I'm crazy and pathological and sick and that I don't even know what I'm saying. I knew there was symbolism in what I was saying but no, you have to shove what you think down my throat and never allow any room for me. I can't even have a thought on my own.

ANALYST: [Feeling frustrated and provoked yet working hard to hold onto myself] So that's interesting. It occurs to me that it was in fact my having introduced a new and different, separate idea than one that you thought of, a new direction that feels so poisonous and offensive to you.

PATIENT: [Long pause and then in a venomous voice] I know that concept but that's not what happened here. I can't let go of what I was trying to do and that you interrupted me.... No, I can't, I can't let this go, I just can't. So maybe I can't look at this today, but I don't think that the reason.

[He says this with a tone of intense distain and blame; he was fine before and I did this to him]

ANALYST: So perhaps you're right, you can't look at this today, as we do have to stop for today.

[The patient leaves in silent fury without making eye contact.]

Here, the patient is like a baby who needs to be changed and the analyst/mother with an agenda to feed, who assumes her good intentions should be experienced by the infant as such. Like most people, analysts are susceptible to an erroneous assumption that our subjectively experienced intentions, rather than the patient's subjectively experienced reception of our interventions, define the truth of a communicative situation. Often lost in a sea of despair and uncertainty, it was difficult to learn through consultation and experience that becoming O of the session requires one's entire being to viscerally register what seeks reception from the depths of the patient's body–mind that is typically refused signification.

One outcome of this transformative work is learning to differentiate apparent destructiveness from actual destructiveness as categories of experience in the heat of the analytic moment. This involves realizing that the patient's primitive defensive organization and relentless attacks may at times be the only way of surviving a deeply disorganized, chaotic, proto-self-in-bits. They are not attacks on the analyst or the analysis or indications of the patient's innate life-hating aggressiveness. In the following material we see how the analyst is able to shift and become more receptive to the patient's experience in a way that transforms a moment of impasse into an opportunity for growth.

Opening the waiting room door, the patient glances at me suspiciously as if doing something forbidden as he enters. He smiles tightly, lays down and sounds alarmed. I wonder if he's just seen an accident or something horrible judging from his tone and escalating tears.

PATIENT: I feel like I'm about to have a panic attack. I can't believe what I just witnessed. I had extra time so I was sitting across a park reading before my appointment. I'm already anxious about going to New York and then I started thinking about dying and who would know if we all died in a plane crash together. Who does these things or figures them out, and who would let me know if you died or how would anyone know who to notify if you died. I got myself so worked up that I actually made a list of things to do. I looked up and across the street [and] there was this squirrel and he was pulling this smaller dead squirrel. He dragged it up over the whole fence and down the other side, I've never seen anything like it and didn't know what to do [crying intensely]. I had such a difficult night. I was horrid, horrible to be with and live with, angry and mean. I don't even know what's good. I'm all poison [yelling, his tone turning caustic and sarcastic]. I guess the squirrel is my fear my anger is killing someone off, [killing] you off. I'm so mean to you, and I guess it's obvious a day away from you is hard on me.

ANALYST: This dead aspect that lives deep inside you is difficult and burden-some to carry with you constantly; the only way you manage to move around with it is to become, as you say, mean and horrid. This gives you some dis-tance from all this despair.

[His tears intensify and he cries deeply. Then his tears abate some and he seems to calm a little. I feel the shift in his mood as he seems to have taken in what I said and use my words to calm himself.]

PATIENT: That must be right [with genuine laughter and lightness in his voice]. The other day Mom was showing me this picture in National Geographic, and there was this tiger and his cub; he prevented his cub from dropping sixty feet from a branch he was precariously perched on and someone man-aged to shoot this picture.

ANALYST: Much like you feel like I caught you, so that right now you feel a bit more grounded than you did when you walked in.

[He is silent for a minute and then reverts quickly, without warning, to a ranting tone.]

PATIENT: It's all hard to hold onto. I do feel calmer for a moment and then my mind starts raging and racing again in that mean, angry way, asking you challenging questions that I know are just ways of distancing myself from all this despair, but the thoughts are here nonetheless. I keep hearing a voice in-side saying to you, what makes you think you are telling me anything new? If all this is true and I am still so fucked up after all this work, what's the point? I'm hopeless. So, if that doesn't prove how impenetrable I am and not worth it and you should just give up on me, I don't know what does.

ANALYST: So much pain, so much despair.

[He cries deeply and intensely until I say we have to stop for today. He leaves as he arrived, walking quickly, not looking at me, not saying goodbye.]

For the analytic pair depicted in these vignettes, the growth and transformation in the analyst allow the patient to feel received and gathered in ways he has never felt before. A psychic transformation has occurred. The patient no longer yells endlessly, or melts-down in stormy ways. When he feels criticized or missed he has faith that he can reconstruct his experience in ways the analyst will be receptive to ensuring the analytic work can continue. He has grown parts of his mind that previously only carried deadness held by a container of hatred and attack.

Despite these improvements, the patient's silent scurry from the consulting room avoiding contact suggests he felt preoccupied by the defensive pull of in-ternal sadomasochistic object relations (attacks and counter attacks), which he struggled with during the session vis-a-vis the analyst. In separating from the analyst, his haywire security system resurges. To paraphrase Guntrip (1968), analysis and internal bad-objects represent rival policies for ego survival.

The patient can only be open to as much pain as the analyst is able to achieve at-one-ment within herself. This principle, which seems so obvious when stated and is easily derived from infant observation, nevertheless seems to be underutilized when teaching the essential analytic priority of following the patient, meaning less interpreting, more visceral receptive observation, silence, and waiting before offering verbal interpretations. In our view, this stance requires a great deal of psychic effort and patience on the part of the analyst.

Conclusion

Meltzer (2008, p. xvi) states the analyst must be able to lose him or herself in the patient's experience and also be able to "surface" and understand what has happened in this state of immersion. We can imagine Winnicott might agree with Meltzer's view when he observes, "Changes come in an analysis when the traumatic factors enter the psycho-analytic material in the patient's own way, and within the patient's own omnipotence" (1960, p. 21). Our notion of the analyst internally gathering all of the bits of the patient's experience through turning oneself over in the countertransference—particularly to the viscerally experienced aspects—is a way to operationalize Winnicott's recommendation and a means of unwinding clinical impasses.

Impasse represents a point in the analytic process where a psychic tourniquet is needed to save the patient's insufficiently structured ego from unbearable dissolution-into-despair in the face of aesthetic conflict; unable to simultaneously bear so much need and love and pain (primitive heartbreak) that it is walled off or encapsulated *for survival* in a "psychotic island" (Rosenfeld, as cited in De Masi, 2001). We believe the aforementioned description of impasse is relevant whether the patient has an overall neurotic, borderline, or psychotic structure. Impasse occurs when the basis for communication between infant/mother or patient/analyst breaks down, is lost, or was never securely established in the first place. In this circumstance, it is the analyst's responsibility to establish a solid basis for communication with the unable-to-speak aspects of the patient as he struggles to exist and, under the proper conditions, integrate new emotional experiences. It is essential that the analyst differentiates experientially between apparent destructiveness (e.g. envious attacks) and actual destructiveness to unwind impasses as illustrated in our clinical vignette.

References

Ahumada, J. L. (1997). Empathy in clinical practice. In *The perverse transference and other matters: Essays in honor of R. Horacio Etchegoyen,* (pp. 115–133). Jason Aronson.

Alvarez, A. (2006). Some questions concerning states of fragmentation: un-integration, under- integration, disintegration, and the nature of early integrations. *Journal of Child Psychotherapy, 32*(2):158–180.

Aulagnier, P. (2001). *The violence of interpretation.* Bruner-Routledge.

Aulagnier, P. (2015). Birth of a body, origin of a history. *The International Journal of Psychoanalysis, 96*(5):1371–1401.

Balint, E. (1963). On being empty of oneself. *The International Journal of Psychoanalysis, 44:* 470–480.

Bick, E. (1986). Further considerations on the function of the skin in early object relations: Findings from infant observation integrated into child and adult analysis. *British Journal of Psychotherapy*, 2:292–299.

Bion, W.R. (2014 [1962]). Learning from experience. In C. Mawson (Ed.), *The complete works of W. R. Bion*, (Vol. 4, pp. 261–365). Karnac Books.

Bion, W.R. (2014 [1965]). Transformations. In C. Mawson (Ed.), *The complete works of W. R. Bion*, (Vol. 5, pp. 121–280). Karnac Books.

Bion, W.R. (2014 [1970]). Attention and interpretation. In C. Mawson (Ed.), *The complete works of W. R. Bion*, (Vol. 6, pp. 221–330). Karnac Books.

Bion, W.R. (2014 [1977]). The Italian seminars. In C. Mawson (Ed.), *The complete works of W. R. Bion*, (Vol. 9, pp. 99–194). Karnac Books.

Bion, W.R. (2014 [1979]). Making the best of a bad job. In Mawson, C. (Ed.), *The complete works of W. R. Bion*, (Vol. 10, pp. 136–145). Karnac Books.

Brooks, D. (2018). The barbed-wire hole of despair: Retreat from aesthetic conflict. In M. Harris Williams (Ed.), *Aesthetic conflict and its clinical application*, (pp. 189–203). The Harris Meltzer Trust.

Brooks, D. (2019). *Anhedonia or the will-in-despair?: Despair in three clinical keys*. [Paper Presentation] Duquesne University Simon Silverman Phenomenology Center, Pittsburgh, PA.

De Masi, F. (2001). *Herbert Rosenfeld at work: The Italian seminars*. Karnac Books.

D'ostiani, E.F. (1980). An individual approach to psychotherapy with psychotic patients. *Journal of Child Psychotherapy*, 6(1):81–92.

Eshel, O. (2019). The vanished last scream: Winnicott and Bion. *The Psychoanalytic Quarterly*, 88(1):111–140.

Fairbairn, W.R.D. (1994 [1952]). *Psychoanalytic studies of the personality*. Routledge.

Guntrip, H. (1962). The manic-depressive problem in light of the schizoid process. *International Journal of Psychoanalysis*, 43:98–112.

Guntrip, H. (1968). *Schizoid phenomena, object relations and the self*. Karnac Books.

Haag, G. (1991). Some reflections on body ego development through psychotherapeutic work with an infant. In R. Szur & S. Miller (Eds.), *Extending horizons: Psychoanalytic psychotherapy with children, adolescents, and families*, (pp. 135–147). Karnac Books.

Haag, G. (1997). Psychosis and autism: schizophrenic, perverse and manic-depressive states during psychotherapy. In M. Rustin, M. Rhode, A. Dubinsky, & H. Dubinsky (Eds.), *Psychotic states in children*, (pp. 189–211). Routledge.

Houzel, D. (1989). Precipitation anxiety and the dawn of aesthetic feelings. *Journal of Child Psychotherapy*, 15(2):103–114.

Kumin, I. (1996). *Pre-object relatedness: Early attachment and the psychoanalytic situation*. Guilford Press.

Malloch, S. & Trevarthan, C. (2009). *Communicative musicality: Exploring the basis of human companionship*. Oxford University Press.

Meltzer, D. (2008). *The Psycho-Analytical Process*. Karnac Books.

Mitrani, J.L. (2001). 'Taking the transference': Some technical implications in three papers by Bion. *International Journal of Psychoanalysis*, 82(6):1085–1104.

Plath, S. (2010). *Ariel*. Faber and Faber.

Reik, T. (2014). The instinctive basis of psychological conjecture. In *Surprise and the psychoanalyst*, (pp. 191–205). Routledge. (Original work published in 1936).

Rustin, M. (2005). *The relevance of infant observation for clinical work with children, adolescents, and adults: Some reflections*. [Paper Presentation] Infant Observation Conference, The Psychoanalytic Center of California, Los Angeles, CA.

Tausk, V. (1933). On the origin of the "influencing machine" in schizophrenia. *Psychoanalytic Quarterly*, 2:519–556.

Tustin, F. (1977). *Roman seminars*. [Lecture Series] Istituto di Neuropsichiatria Infantile, University of Rome, October 19, 20, 21, 1977.

Tustin, F. (1986). *Autistic barriers in neurotic patients*. Karnac Books.

The real mother goose. (1994). Scholastic Inc. (Original work published in 1916).

Winnicott, D.W. (2016 [1945]). Primitive emotional development. In L. Caldwell & H. Taylor Robinson (Eds.). *The collected works of D. W. Winnicott*, (Vol. 2, pp. 357–368). Oxford University Press.

Winnicott, D.W. (2016 [1958a]). Primary maternal preoccupation [1956]. In L. Caldwell & H. Taylor Robinson (Eds.). *The collected works of D. W. Winnicott*, (Vol. 5, pp. 183–188). Oxford University Press.

Winnicott, D.W. (2016 [1958b]). The capacity to be alone. In L. Caldwell & H. Taylor Robinson (Eds.). *The collected works of D. W. Winnicott*, (Vol. 5, pp. 241–248). Oxford University Press.

Winnicott, D.W. (2016 [1960]). The theory of the parent-infant relationship. In L. Caldwell & H. Taylor Robinson (Eds.). *The collected works of D. W. Winnicott*, (Vo. 6, pp. 141–158). Oxford University Press.

Winnicott, D.W. (2016 [1963]). The development of the capacity for concern. In L. Caldwell & H. Taylor Robinson (Eds.). *The collected works of D. W. Winnicott*, (Vol. 6, pp. 351–358). Oxford University Press.

Winnicott, D.W. (1971). *Playing and reality*. Tavistock Publications.

Winnicott, D.W. (1989). Character types: The foolhardy and the cautious: On *funfairs, thrills and regressions* by Michael Balint. In C. Winnicott, R. Shepherd, & M. Davis (Eds.), *Psychoanalytic explorations*, (pp. 433–437). Karnac Books.

Winnicott, D.W. (1990). Varieties of psychotherapy. In C. Winnicott, R. Shepherd, & M. Davis (Eds.), *Deprivation and delinquency*, (pp. 232–240). Routledge. (Original work published in 1984).

10 The environment within

On the fetus's capacity to differentiate self from other

Dana M. Blue

Introduction

Using Bion's idea of imaginative conjecture into prenatal realms as a starting place, in this chapter I delve into a study of 'primary fusion' and 'primary differentiation', potential states of the fetal mind that might indicate in the first instance "we are one", and in the second "we are separate". I provide a detailed clinical vignette which led me to wonder if the fetus may projectively impact the mother at a somatic level, which opens space for speculation of a fetal state of separate-mindedness from within the womb. Following Alessandra Lemma (2015), in a second vignette I consider that elements of the analytic setting might be lodged in the analyst's body for some analysands who are in a state of merger with the analyst. I link an intense somatic countertransference experience in a psychoanalytic encounter with my reverie of an adult patient's early conviction of his power to kill his mother by becoming separate. I then follow tracks of this primal terror over time as it evolved in our work.

I emphasize the prominence of the fear of death in the perinatal period. Considering that the fetus's death instinct or death anxiety before birth might have a somatic representation in the fetus's mind, I further speculate that this representation could be projected into the mind of mother, and that such early death anxiety could re-emerge later in the analytic work. This more complex view of the mind of the fetus in interaction with the mind of the mother opens space for thoughts about life and death drives, especially in the birth process, and how in the adult they may be embodied by the analytic couple.

The infancy of thought

From Bion's paper "Evidence":

> Let us take flight into fantasy, a kind of infancy of our own thought. I can imagine a situation in which a nearly full-term foetus could be aware of extremely unpleasant oscillations in the amniotic fluid medium before transferring to a gaseous medium—in other words, getting born. I can imagine that there is some disturbance going on—the parents on bad terms, or something

DOI: 10.4324/9781003195559-10

of that sort. I can further imagine loud noises being made between the mother and the father—or even loud noises made by the digestive system inside the mother. Suppose this foetus is also aware of the pressures of what will one day turn into a character or a personality, aware of things like fear, hate, crude emotions of that sort. Then the foetus might omnipotently turn in hostility towards these disturbing feelings, proto-ideas, proto-feelings, at a very early stage, and split them up, destroy them, fragment them, and try to evacuate them…

I have invented terms for my own private purposes like, 'sub-thalamic fear', meaning the kind of fear that one would have if no check on it at all was produced by the higher levels of the mind. A patient may in fact be subject to tremendous feelings of fear…

Supposing we are in fact always dealing with some kind of psychosomatic condition. Is it any good talking to a highly articulate person in highly articulate terms? Is it possible that, if feelings of intense fear, self-hatred, can seep up into a state of mind in which they can be translated into action, the reverse is true? Is it possible to talk to the soma in such a way that the psychosis is able to understand, or vice versa?

It would be useful if we could formulate our own impressions about this before giving them an airing. It is important to recognize that there is a world in which it is impossible to see what a psychoanalyst can see, although it may be possible for some of those who come for analysis to realize that we see certain things which the rest of the world doesn't see. We are investigating the unknown which may not oblige us by conforming to behaviour within the grasp of our feeble mentalities, our feeble capacities for rational thought. We may be dealing with things which are so slight as to be virtually imperceptible, but which are so real that they could destroy us almost without our being aware of it. That is the kind of area into which we have to penetrate.

Bion (2014 [1976], pp. 133–135)
Quoted by Nicola Abel-Hirsch (2018) Regional Bion Symposium

Much work has been done on the merged emotional states of mother and fetus in pregnancy and early postpartum. As Winnicott's famous dictum says, "There is no such thing as a baby",[1] and with this phrase he opened the discussion of the enormity of the mother's influence on the developing child. He amplified this idea by naming mother "environment". Mother is the elemental chamber of forces that shapes us.

Drawing on Bion's invitation to conjecture in the quote above, I suggest that the currents of influence between mother and fetus might flow both ways and will offer clinical vignettes that illustrate how I have reached this supposition. Of special interest here is a technical contribution put forward by Alessandra Lemma, who proposes that there may be an element of the setting that is contained in the analyst's body, particularly for patients who may be in a state of merger with the analyst (2015, pp. 111–127). Like Lemma, I find attention to somatic countertransference an invaluable aid for considering this state of merger, which I understand as relating to the perinatal 'time-before-time'. Working in this early and emotionally primitive terrain, attention to the body/mind register and its early origins can be of particular usefulness, as I hope to illustrate with three clinical examples, to follow.

The theory of object relations, and the whole of unconscious phantasy life, always involves at least three elements: a subject, object, and a relationship. Sandler (1990, p. 866) says:

> We can take the view that object relations always involve an interaction between self and object. So in memory and in thought, in conscious and unconscious fantasies and wishes, we do not get self- and object representations in isolation, but in interaction.

In Winnicott's 1965 paper, "The Maturational Processes and the Facilitating Environment: Studies in the Theory of Emotional Development" this original trinity was described in developmental terms:

> The infant and the maternal care together form a unit. Certainly, if one is to study the theory of the parent-infant relationship one must come to a decision about these matters, which concern the real meaning of the word dependence. It is not enough that it is acknowledged that the environment is important. If there is to be a discussion of the theory of the parent-infant relationship, then we are divided into two if there are some who do not allow that at the earliest stages the infant and maternal care belong to each other and cannot be disentangled. These two things, the infant and maternal care, disentangle and dissociate themselves in health; and health, which means many things, to some extent means a disentanglement of maternal care from something which we then call the infant or the beginnings of a growing child.
>
> (p. 39)

In psychoanalytic thinking today, if there is discussion of the matrix of this early land, the focus is most often on merger, the tangle, and its echoes in the transference situation. Salomonsson's (2018, p. 3) word here is "confluence". Findings from Kumin (1996), Mitrani (2008), Searles (1965), and others, suggest that mother and fetus might feel themselves at times to be indistinguishable one from the other. This line of thinking might be of clinical utility to the working analyst, to cultivate sensitivity to the way inadequate or incomplete psychic separation between mother and infant can crowd the mind of the adult patient and deform the analyst's capacity for emotionally integrated thinking.

The simultaneous and opposite view, that the infant mind might also be capable of differentiation, is less explored. From earliest pregnancy, while deeply and inextricably joined, mother and infant are never entirely the same. They are separate entities that for some while share a body, and possibly at times a mind/

body space. Pregnancy is not only a time of inchoate merger, but might also be a continual flow toward eventual separation—though sometimes the boundary (psychic and somatic) is only the width of a membrane.

In distinction to Winnicott, I'd like to suggest that there *is* such a thing as a baby, and from its initial psychological conception through fetal life it exerts a force that is both subtle and increasingly enormous. Here, Bion's (1970) model of container/contained seems to me very apt. There are two related and relating factors, one inside the other. There is somatic and psychic communication between them, a bi-directional current that transforms both. And the two elements, while of like kind, are not the same. One encompasses and enfolds the other. This size differential is increasingly important and, more speculatively, one might imagine it opens to a primitive awareness of generational difference.

Paul describes "the primordial sense of pain-to-extinction which the baby communicates in its scream to the mother post-natally" (1997, p. 86). This highlights the reality of death, and the awareness of death which, based on the clinical evidence I present, I locate in the fetus as well as in the maternal mind. This chapter, based on my work with many pregnant and formerly fetal patients, involves possible clinical evidence of the fetus's innate knowledge of death itself.

Primary narcissism or object related?

Winnicott felt that the developmental trajectory moves from a state of primary narcissism at birth, and only gradually becomes that of a subject relating to an object. It is the function of the ego in Winnicott's schema that integrates experiences into the personality. Winnicott refers to the ego that is based in the body and the ego that initiates object-relating:

> The ego is based on a body ego, but it is only when all goes well that the person of the baby starts to be linked with the body and the body-functions, with the skin as the limiting membrane. I have used the term personalization to describe this process ....
>
> (Winnicott, 1965, p. 59)

The handling the baby receives from the mother and others—all the multitude of aspects of bodily care—contributes to the infant's sense of himself as a person. By using the term "personalization" Winnicott highlights the converse of depersonalization—the psyche-soma split in the patient who has not experienced good-enough handling (Abram, 2007, pp. 149–150).

For Winnicott, integration into a "unit self" takes place within the environmental function of holding. The achievement of integration is the product of interaction.

> First comes 'I' which includes 'everything else is not me'. Then comes 'I am, I exist, I gather experiences and enrich myself and have an introjective and

projective interaction with the NOT-ME, the actual world of shared reality'. Add to this 'I am seen or understood to exist by someone'; and further, add to this: 'I get back (as a face seen in a mirror) the evidence I need that I have been recognized as a being.' In favorable circumstances the skin becomes the boundary between the me and the not-me. In other words, the psyche has come to live in the soma and an individual psycho-somatic life has been initiated.

(Winnicott, 1965, p. 61)

The fetal mind

For Winnicott, it is of theoretical significance that all of this happens after birth, and I will spell out the implications of this thought in a short while. With the benefit of modern technologies and the singular good fortune to have spent a great deal of time with pregnant people, I have come to disagree. Some might envision uterine life, from the baby's point of view, as life in a placid container, mother/womb holding baby at the optimal temperature, in the optimal state, until fetal maturity culminates in childbirth. In this view, the mother's main job is non-interference, to not (to use Winnicott's word) impinge on the growing child. However, recent discoveries suggest the system might be much more active than blissfully static. Some theorists have considered the possible existence of psychic objects in the mind of the developing fetus. Picking things up from the other side of the placenta, we might wonder what is a mother to a fetal mind?

Suzanne Maiello (1995) envisioned the formation of the object world by baby as originating in a soundscape; the low notes of bodily functions audible very early on; the higher notes of speech perceptible by four month's gestational age; silence and sound in overlapping and distinct pairing laying the tracks for relationship. Marianne Robinson (2008) amplified this theme in a paper entitled "Catastrophic Change and Emergence—A Turbulent Journey Out of Encapsulation", in her conceptualization of a very early 'sound' object, a line of thinking she has continued to develop through subsequent works.

Following Esther Bick (1968) and Didier Anzieu (1989), with their work on skin function and skin ego, respectively, it is possible to postulate a "touch" object, the 'me' and 'not me' of a hand sliding over a body surface. It must feel different, even under water, to stroke your own arm versus stroking a placenta. Even in the womb, it is possible for the fetus to 'get in touch' with the fact that the world is not only self. The kinesthetic sense, the movement of me and not me, is also operative here, though there is a radical reordering of experience at birth, when gravity reverses the terrain.

Salomonsson (2018, p. 14) speaking of pregnant parents, notes that regressive and progressive emotional trends help facilitate the movement from narcissism to object love for the child. I believe this action is also at work in the baby, prenatally and after birth. This back and forth action seems to me to be a description of growth, which is not a smooth linear curve but a series of cresting waves that rise over the beach of development.

It may be that there are several overlapping yet simultaneous psychic possibilities available, even for the fetus. Ogden writes: "The autistic-contiguous position has a period of primacy earlier than that of the two psychological organizations described by Klein and yet coexists dialectically with the paranoid-schizoid and depressive positions from the beginning of psychological life" (1989, p. 126).

Perhaps we have yet to determine where psychological life begins. In a series of intriguing case studies that begin in utero and extend into the early years, Alessandra Piontelli (1992) has noted the uncanny awarenesses some young children seem to carry from prenatal life.

That the fetus has an instinctual drive toward life is now taken as a given. I am grateful to Ken King, with whom many years ago I was watching a video clip on the capacities of the neonate. Left undisturbed in the first hour of life, the baby can crawl up the mother's body and latch itself to the breast. Noting that the newborn was using the scent of amniotic fluid on its fist as a navigational tool, Ken remarked "It's the first transference". There is no question that the baby arrives, aiming at life, and perhaps already attempting to reconcile loss.

However, what of death? I find I have arrived on the doorstep of one of the foundational Kleinian tenets, the existence of a death instinct, which finds a home in the early and savage superego. My Kleinian dictionary notes:

> In 1931 in The Psychoanalysis of Children, Klein adopts Freud's ideas about the life and death instincts but she disagrees with the idea that no fear of death exists in the unconscious; for her the fear of death is the primordial fear and she believes the newborn infant to be in danger of being flooded by this terrible anxiety.
>
> (Spillius et al., 2011)

Freud's view was of a death drive aimed at nullification, a kind of going to zero energy. In Klein's mind, based on her work with young children, the death instinct grew fangs, as it were. The death instinct is her name for indwelling destructiveness, ranging from the "wholesome sadism", to use Jim Gooch's phrase to describe the infant's healthy lust for life (Gooch, personal communication, 2008), the zeal to latch to the 'breast of life' so strongly the nipple might crack and bleed, to the sheer bloody mindedness, that just wants to break the place apart.

In the New Dictionary of Kleinian Thought, Spillius et al. (2011) note: "All of the following, for example, can be suggestive of the presence of the death instinct: a fear of falling apart and disintegrating, self-destructiveness, destructiveness, innate hostility to the outside world, envy, sadism, and strong and aggressive libidinal desires" (p. 298).

This view of the infant, with an inborn capacity to recognize and inflict damage, is as startling in its way as Freud's revolutionary ideas of infantile sexuality to the mores of Victorian society. It is at odds with the view of the newborn as a dewy stranger, suspended for the first months in the solitary capsule of primary narcissism. You can accept Freud's death drive, which is not absolutely object related, and maintain a belief in primary narcissism, but not so with Klein's, which requires an object.

If we look at Winnicott's view of the death instinct, we find yet another difference from the view I put forth in this chapter. It is not that Winnicott was unaware of primitive aggression, but as Dermen (2018, p. 5) explains

> The earliest manifestation of aggression is, for him, in the service of the life instinct, not the death instinct. He calls it "muscle erotism, the enjoyment of bodily movement, of activity, of seeking, basic pleasure in being alive at a psyche-soma level".

Winnicott (1965) who believed in neither object relatedness before birth (he struck camp alongside Freud with the concept of primary narcissism) nor a death instinct, noted that one implies the other:

> At this stage the word death has no possible application, and this makes the term death instinct unacceptable in describing the root of destructiveness. Death has no meaning until the arrival of hate and of the concept of the whole human person. When a whole human person can be hated, death has meaning, and close on this follows that which can be called maiming; the whole hated and loved person is kept alive by being castrated or otherwise maimed instead of killed. These ideas belong to a phase later than that characterized by dependence on the holding environment.
>
> (1965, p. 46)

Case illustrations

Two vivid experiences (Cases A and B) lead me to question Winnicott's formulations of the capacity for destructiveness and apperception of death in earliest life. Klein's view of the death instinct could be interpreted as leaving room for its presence in fetal life. In 1946, Klein wrote, "We know however, that the destructive instinct is directed against the organism itself and must therefore be regarded by the ego as a danger. I believe it is this danger which is felt by the individual as anxiety" (p. 4). Perhaps the place such unbearable anxiety might arise, in the most primitive communications from fetus to mother, is in the somatic receptivity of a containing other.

Case A: The first situation I describe took place decades ago, before I trained as a psychoanalyst and while I was working as a doula. For those who may not be familiar with the role, the doula is an emotional caregiver for childbearing women and families. The doula accompanies parents through childbirth and early postpartum, offering emotional presence and support during the unfamiliar and often terrifying tasks of parturition. The family I was with had had a dreadful previous childbearing experience. There had been a previous birth that went badly, and both parents were traumatized and terrorized at the inescapable birth of this second child. The onset of the labor was late, and it progressed very slowly. The mother was barely conscious during much of it, a situation she had chosen, a result of a combination of pain medicine, dissociation, and ordinary 'labor mind'. The father was more outside than within the birthing room. I became aware that I was swimming in anxiety; not the typical anxiety about all the unknowns of birth, but a powerful 'pit of my stomach dread', mixed with an intense experience of helplessness. Though I had participated in many previous births, this dread was of a magnitude that I had never experienced. I waited with this feeling for some hours, but it did not shift. Eventually, I felt so anxious that I spoke with the doctor, and she listened kindly, repeated all the vitals and confirmed that things were moving slowly but there was nothing physically wrong.

This reassurance did not reassure me as the feeling did not relent. I recall slumping in the corner of that hospital room while the mother dozed, feeling a paralyzing sense of doom. Louise was eventually born, sometime the next afternoon. After she slipped into life, it became clear that she had a severe anomaly that was incompatible with life outside the womb.

Louise lingered briefly and then died. Of course, the death of a newborn deeply touches everyone concerned. It was a tragedy for the family and an awful event for the rest of us. But that unthinkable feeling of doom—perhaps Bion's sub-thalamic fear—remained in my mind long after the grief had passed. It bothered me, and I didn't have any way to think about it. It stayed inside me, unprocessed, until my study of psychoanalysis could offer a new possibility. I have come to consider that being receptive and emotionally available I received a somato-psychic projection from Louise of her foreknowledge that her birth also meant her death. This is speculative, of course. It is possible that I was picking up on other anxieties, such as that of the mother, or father. However, the unavailability of the mother's mind, the relative receptivity of my own, and the intensity and primitivity of the feelings I encountered have led me to imagine the possibility that it was not only the parents' and my own anxiety, but that it was also Louise, to a greater extent than more elaborated personalities, signaling this unbearable distress.

This was a dramatic and very fortunately rare occurrence. Yet this experience may be instructive in understanding how the infant before and during the birth process might communicate its death anxiety. Ordinarily, according to Kleinian theory, the first anxiety, about death, is projected into the containing object *after* birth, and the familiar splitting into the good and bad breast/object/ mother begins.

Relevant to my supposition is Winnicott's description (1965, p. 46):

> Anxiety in these early stages of the parent-infant relationship relates to the threat of annihilation, and it is necessary to explain what is meant by this term.
>
> In this place which is characterized by the essential existence of a holding environment, the 'inherited potential' is becoming itself a 'continuity of being'. The alternative to being is reacting, and reacting interrupts being and annihilates. Being and annihilation are the two alternatives. The holding

environment therefore has as its main function the reduction to a minimum of impingements to which the infant must react with resultant annihilation of personal being. Under favourable conditions the infant establishes a continuity of existence and then begins to develop the sophistications which make it possible for impingements to be gathered into the area of omnipotence.

The register of being and annihilation that Winnicott points to is sometimes encountered in work with adult patients with infantile trauma, where the transference experience of the patient feels riddled with a primitive dread as if existence itself is at stake. I agree with Winnicott that the need to be in order to become is a fundamental task.

In distinction to Winnicott I believe the fetus to be at times, however fleeting and however dimly, sensitive to its separate self. This would seem a necessary precondition for the introjection of internal objects. If accurate, it would follow that there could be no initial post-birth state of primary narcissism before there is the perception of an external object. Might a fetus 'know' that death is a possible outcome, before it comes to life? I believe the *fetal* mind already contains an apprehension of death, and based on my experience with Louise, I surmise that a fetus might have a capacity to communicate this fear with a singular focus and intensity. Most often, the mother probably receives this terror, and it might comingle and be processed with her own life and death fears in the birthing phase, as mortality is a well-established thread in the weave of the maternal mind. Consider, for example, the dream of a young woman, pregnant for the first time, and a few weeks before birth: "I was in an ice cream shop, and there were all kinds of different, wild flavors. Most were good, but one was called 'graveyard'. I tasted it, but I didn't like it".

My second clinical vignette is of an adult psychoanalysis. The presence of a profound somatically experienced anxiety in the analyst offered another context in which to consider primal anxieties and destructive capacities that cluster in the perinatal period.

Case B: Paul presented for analytic treatment for a massive and disabling anxiety. From the first session he seemed to be in a merged transference with me. He was a young, unmarried man whose mother had nearly died in birthing him, a story that had been oft repeated. About nine months into the treatment, a few minutes into a session where Paul was talking about an exchange with his mother, whom he felt to be intolerant of separation and not well able to receive his emotional experiences, I felt a tiny pop in my head. At the time, I felt—not thought—that I had had a brain aneurysm. I began to feel panic, and could just barely remain focused on Paul. I told myself that if I was truly having an emergency, it would become more manifest over time. All I could do was to try to keep listening. It is hard to convey quite how real this somatic countertransference seemed, but I recall surreptitiously feeling in my ear to see if I was actually bleeding. Following this agonizingly long session, the 'symptoms' cleared, and I regained the thinking space to wonder about his primitive agony. It seemed to be a conviction that separation would kill his mother, like the original bodily separation almost had; in phantasy it *had* killed her. This was convincingly conveyed from his inside to my inside, in what I came to see as a somatic projective identification.

Some years later in the work with Paul, a related event transpired. Paul was a divorce attorney, working at times in highly contested and emotionally volatile situations. He had been working with a couple near finalization, and one partner was terrified of the impending separation. Paul developed a persistent and vivid fantasy that this person would come to the final meeting with a gun and shoot herself in the head, rather than accept the divorce. To me, this indicated significant change in Paul. In an evolution of his introjected capacity for containment, he now seemed to be able to represent this deadly terror, rather than communicating it via somatic projection. Like a punchline on a very long story, the second event, similar in shape to the first in the magnitude of the terror communicated to me somatically, deepened my conviction that the initial event had likely been a primitive communication from Paul relating to the earliest moments of his life.

Case C: The third case I will cite is from a published record of an analysis written by Maxine Anderson (1995). In it, the author relates her experience working with a pregnant analysand, and subsequently a mother and baby pair. This mother was filled with angry and hateful feelings toward her child. The baby at birth had wrapped the umbilical cord twice around her neck. As a very young child, she would tangle herself in strings and the like. As the mother, with her analyst's help, untangled and expressed her own feelings of resentment and hatred toward the child, this behavior subsided. Anderson notes:

> It is perhaps parenthetical but noteworthy that as the baby became mobile, she succeeded in putting cords and belts around her neck and behaved in ways that made her mother wish to strangle her (a haunting reminiscence of the cord wrapped around her neck at birth). Much analytic focus further revealed a close connection between my patient's intense negative feelings for her daughter (and herself) and the destructiveness her daughter seemed to evoke and attract. As my patient's feelings toward the feminine child in herself became more benign, the baby's tendency to put cords around her neck and to provoke hostile responses from others seemed to decrease. Both my patient and I wondered (with a bit of awe) whether the baby's response to sensing her mother's hostility by putting cords around her neck might have begun *in utero*. Less speculatively, as noted previously, we linked this intense hostility with my patient's perception of her own mother's hatred and rejection of her as a daughter.
>
> (p. 363)

Perhaps we might wonder with Anderson if this child could indeed perceive her mother's hatred antenatally and respond with movement toward self-annihilation. My hypothesis would be that such a thing does indeed seem possible, if we extend our model of object relations backward in time to fetal life.

Conclusions

In this chapter I have drawn from clinical experience to illustrate a hypothesis that alongside emotional merger, possibilities of separateness might be present in the fetal mind. In this chapter I have elaborated and extended the theories of Klein and Winnicott to explore the possibility of death anxiety in the fetus. I employ object relations theory, and contrast views postulated by Winnicott to trace implications from these possibilities, including the suggestion that fetal and neonatal persons may have capacities for projection and introjection, and that adult patients might also at times communicate these primordial anxieties, which might be apprehended somatically and made meaningful through psychoanalytic work.

Note

1 "I once said: 'There is no such thing as an infant', meaning, of course, that whenever one finds an infant one finds maternal care, and without maternal care there would be no infant" (Winnicott, Discussion at a Scientific Meeting of the British Psycho-Analytical Society, circa 1940).

References

Abel-Hirsch, N. (2019). From an unpublished paper at the Regional Bion Symposium, Los Angeles, CA. Used with permission of the author.

Abram, J. (2007). *The language of Winnicott: A dictionary and guide to understanding his work* (2nd ed.). Routledge.

Anderson, M.K. (1995). May I bring my newborn baby to my analytic hour? One analyst's experience with this request. *Psychoanalytic Inquiry*, *15*(3):358–368.

Anzieu, D. (1989). *The skin ego: A psychoanalytic approach to the self.* Yale University Press.

Bick, E. (1968). The experience of the skin in early object relations. *The International Journal of Psychoanalysis*, *49*:484–486.

Bion, W.R. (2014 [1970]). Attention and interpretation. In C. Mawson (Ed.), *The complete works of W. R. Bion* (Vol. 6, pp. 282–290). London: Karnac Books.

Bion, W.R. (2014 [1976]). Evidence. In C. Mawson (Ed.), *The complete works of W. R. Bion* (Vol. 10, pp. 133–135). Karnac Books.

Dermen, S. (2018). *Clinical Winnicott*. [Paper presentation] Regional Bion Symposium, Los Angeles, CA.

Klein, M. (1946 [1975]). Notes on some schizoid mechanisms. In *Envy and gratitude and other works,* (pp. 1–24). Melanie Klein Trust.

Kumin, I. (1996). *Pre-object relatedness: Early attachment and the psychoanalytic situation.* Guilford.

Lemma, A. (2015). *Minding the body: The body in psychoanalysis and beyond.* Routledge.

Maiello, S. (1995). The sound object: A hypothesis about prenatal auditory experience and memory. *Journal of Child Psychotherapy*, *21*(1):23–41.

Mitrani, J. (2008). *A framework for the imaginary: Clinical explorations in primitive states of being.* Karnac Books.

Ogden, T.H. (1989). On the concept of an autistic-contiguous position. *The International Journal of Psychoanalysis*, *70*:127–140.

Paul, M.I. (1997). *Before we were young: An exploration of primordial states of mind.* Esf Publishers.

Piontelli, A. (1992). *From fetus to child: An observational and psychoanalytic study.* Routledge.

Robinson, M. (2008). Catastrophic change and emergence—A turbulent journey out of encapsulation. [Paper presentation] The 2008 International Evolving British Object Relations Conference, Seattle WA.

Salomonsson, B. (2018). *Psychodynamic interventions in pregnancy and infancy: Clinical and theoretical perspectives.* Routledge.

Sandler, J. (1990). On internal object relations. *Journal of the American Psychoanalytic Association, 38*:859–879.

Searles, H. (1965). *Collected papers on schizophrenia.* Karnac Books.

Spillius, E., Milton, J., Garvey, P., Couve, C. & Steiner, D. (2011). *The new dictionary of Kleinian thought.* Routledge.

Winnicott, D.W. (1965). *The maturational process and the facilitating environment: Studies in the theory of emotional development.* Karnac Books.

Part IV

Body and psychosensory experience

11 Introduction

Caron Harrang, Drew Tillotson, and Nancy C. Winters

It is hard to imagine a better pairing of independently conceived chapters addressing body and shared psychosensory experience than what follows in Peter Goldberg's "Embodiment, dissociation, and the rhythm of life" and Caron Harrang's "River to rapids: speaking to the body in terms the body can understand."

In "Embodiment, dissociation, and the rhythm of life," Goldberg's overarching objective is to bring the somatic dimension of psychical life more fully into clinical theory, which he suggests requires saying what we mean by 'the body.' He offers three interrelated definitions including body as biological substrate (drives), as social-symbolic organization (unconscious phantasy, gender), and as sensory-somatic experience (beta function) embedded in the shared domain of communal perception or what he poetically calls the 'sensory commons.' Focusing on the third meaning, Goldberg's chapter extends an undeveloped implication in Winnicott's work that mental health lies in the body's capacity to lend vitality to psychical life, not the other way around. He challenges himself and readers to consider the actual body's "distinctive patterned existence" as opposed to the historical focus in psychoanalysis on what the mind does with the body (e.g. managing drives through repression or hysterical conversion).

Goldberg employs the polarity between embodiment and dis-embodiment to explore what being fully alive means and argues persuasively that psychoanalytic treatment requires attending to presentational (in addition to representational or symbolic) forms of communication including the pattern-language of movement, rhythm, sound-shape, color, light, etc. Moreover, he suggests psychoanalytic treatment with individuals who are dissociated requires the analyst's participation in "shared psycho-sensory experience" to engender embodied aliveness. This is more than technical advice for the practicing psychoanalyst or psychotherapist. Rather, Goldberg is challenging us to resist "the Cartesian impulse" of favoring mind and thought over body and intuitive feeling in order to fully appreciate the "semiotics of bodily being" inherent in immediate sensation—what is felt, heard, seen, and smelled—*as it happens*. Being embodied exposes both members of the analytic group to the richness and intensity of lived experience. At the same time—and this is one of the gems in Goldberg's chapter—he recognizes the increased sense of vulnerability to being overwhelmed or impinged

DOI: 10.4324/9781003195559-11

upon inherent in bodily aliveness and sees a role for moments of dissociation as part of health. Like projective identification, dissociation is problematic only when utilized excessively. The universality of dissociation as a self-regulatory mechanism places it "at the center of all clinical encounters." Goldberg's clinical vignette focuses on reclamation of aliveness with a markedly disembodied patient whose dissociation is used to enforce a rigid, unyielding structure of bodymind alienation. This leaves open the question of how the analyst approaches working with dissociative phenomena that is transitory and adaptive, part of what Bion calls the 'non-psychotic part of the personality.'

Like Goldberg, in "River to rapids: speaking to the body in terms the body can understand," Caron Harrang takes up embodiment and shared psychosensory experience but in a different direction. In her intriguing exploration of the body's role in analytic communication she addresses a question rarely, if at all, seen in psychoanalytic literature: "how to speak to the body in terms the body can understand." This inquiry has significant technical implications as typical analytic observations are *about* the body rather than *to* the body and are expressed verbally, focusing on lexical representation. Harrang acquaints us with the untapped and largely unrecognized potential of body-to-body communication, as well as communication emanating from bodily experiences (both individual and shared) of analyst and analysand. In four detailed clinical vignettes, Harrang illustrates the direct impact of verbal and nonverbal interventions on the analysand's body or *bodymind*, her preferred term for the unity of body and mind.

Harrang presents two theoretical concepts relevant to her inquiry, Winnicott's (1962, 1963) "direct communication" and Bion's (1965) "at-one-ment," making theoretical contributions to each. Winnicott's concept of "direct communication" posits a *unidirectional* transmission from baby to mother in her state of primary maternal preoccupation. Baby's needs are understood with no need for communication with mother, the subjective object. Harrang posits direct communication is *bidirectional* for mother and baby and the analytic couple, as they implicitly share psychosensory states in two-way communication. In contemporary psychoanalytic thinking where mother has become a subject, this model of bidirectional direct communication is a welcome contribution.

Harrang's vignette of Clara movingly illustrates the role of direct communication in speaking to the body in terms the body can understand. Clara sits with her tense body positioned at a distance while she fires a barrage of invective at her analyst. Instead of moving away, Harrang's body spontaneously 'leans in' toward Clara. Without conscious awareness, Harrang's *bodymind* understands Clara's need to be held closely in spite of her distancing maneuvers and rage. Clara's body reacts to Harrang leaning in with surprise and a softening of her anger. With Harrang's astute recognition of her body's leaning in and explication of how she and the analysand experienced this moment, she offers us an important tool and gives us permission to trust the wisdom of our bodies in responding to moments of intense affect.

Using the apt metaphor of "river to rapids" to convey the transit from calm to turbulent states of shared psychosensory experience, Harrang introduces Bion's notion of "at-one-ment" which enhances Winnicott's concept of direct communication and furthers an understanding of the "state of bodymind from which somatic interventions like 'leaning in' may arise." For Bion the analyst must be at-one with the analysand's psychic reality with the aim of *being* O of the session. Harrang finds the assumption that Bion considered at-one-ment an "intersubjective experience unrelated to bodily phenomena" incorrect; she argues Bion's nomenclature in the grid "suggests that sense impressions are the building blocks of consciousness, indivisible (except conceptually) from mental life." In her last vignette, "erection," Harrang and her analysand have clearly entered into the rapids when an instance of "at-one-ment with hallucinated somatopsychic reality" explodes a formerly taboo area of sexuality, opening a capacity for reflection and erotic aliveness in her analysand. Her other clinical vignettes are equally compelling.

Harrang leaves us with new insights about how the analyst speaks to bodily phenomena and *to* the body. She speaks of the river of silent moments of communion in shared psychosensory experience and other times when the analyst must "verbally narrate the body's contribution to analytic discourse." Discerning the difference, she tells us, is part of the art of psychoanalysis.

References

Bion, W. R. (2014 [1965]). Transformations. In C. Mawson (Ed.), *The complete works of W. R. Bion* (Vol. 4, pp. 115–280). Karnac Books.

Winnicott, D. W. (1962). Communication between individuals examined with reference to the development of a capacity for communication in the individual infant. A not final not complete unpublished manuscript presented to the San Francisco Psychoanalytic Society and Institute on October 8, 1962.

Winnicott, D.W. (2016 [1963]). Communicating and not communicating, leading to the studies of certain opposites - BPAS (not final version), 15 May 1963. In R. Adès (Ed.) *The collected works of D.W. Winnicott: Volume 12, appendices and bibliographies.* Oxford University Press.

12 Embodiment, dissociation, and the rhythm of life

Peter Goldberg

Introduction

There seems to be a growing interest in bringing somatic dimensions of psychical life more fully into clinical theory, and in giving the *actual* body its proper ontological role. Being embodied is, after all, essential to any actual experience of lived reality (Winnicott, 1960) – essential not only to sensing one's own existence, but also to the possibility of perceiving the reality of the world around us (Merleau-Ponty, 1962). Being embedded in our own bodies brings the world to life.

The question is, how may we think psychoanalytically about the body's own distinctive patterned existence? A reconsideration of the actual body, as opposed to what the mind does with the body (e.g. managing the drives through repression, or using the body for symbolic purposes, as in hysterical conversion symptoms), will require that we can imagine the psychic life of the body itself – the way somatic experience organizes itself along the lines of pattern-making, contiguity, rhythm, tone, texture, coloration, and so on.[1]

In exploring the psychical life of the actual body, I have found it indispensable to recognize the specific function of *body–mind dissociation*, which was first described by Winnicott (1949) in terms of the dissociation of *mind* from *psych-soma*. Recognition of this distinctive defensive function, much underappreciated in psychoanalytic clinical theory, forces us to consider what it is that we mean by the "body" in relation to the unconscious, the senses, and the soma. Recognition of body–mind dissociation also allows us to consider its clinical manifestations, and the importance of *shared psycho-sensory experience* in the clinical encounter with disembodied patients.

The body

The body in psychoanalysis

The body has had a rich and varied history in psychoanalysis, beginning with Freud's description of how the biological substrate crosses over into the psychical – his conception of the drives, and of the id. But for the purposes of understanding embodiment, it is Winnicott's (1949) contribution that I find most pertinent, with

DOI: 10.4324/9781003195559-12

his ground-breaking observations of the crucial importance in psychical life of the "indwelling" of mind in the psyche-soma (which is his term for the body). The term psyche-soma suggests that bodily experience lends its own significant qualities to the shaping of psychical life. Winnicott insists that only through the experience of living in the psyche-soma can a person feel alive and real; in fact, he views living too much in one's "mind" a kind of Cartesian symptom that arises when psyche-soma indwelling is interrupted. Accordingly, he increasingly downplays the role of interpretation and insight in his clinical approach, in favor of curating a facilitating environment in which the patient can regain a personal sense of embodied vitality. Here Winnicott poses a challenge to a basic assumption in psychoanalysis of the ascendancy of mind and of ego mastery. In asserting that the ongoing well-being of self depends upon the psyche's embeddedness in a living body, Winnicott implies that health and integration lies less in the mind's capacity to bestow meaning and order on an unruly body, and more in some capacity of the body to lend vitality and significance to psychical life. The ramifications of this idea remained undeveloped in Winnicott's own work, and psychoanalysis has yet to develop an adequate model of the value of somatic or bodily phenomena in and of themselves. But the idea of psyche-soma implies that the soma has psychical qualities of its own, its own way of ordering things, its own sensorial pattern language (Goldberg, 2012, pp. 791–812). In rethinking the place of the body, I would like to pursue the possibilities of this last idea about the psychical life of the soma.

What do we mean by the "body"?

In psychoanalysis today there is much renewed interest in the body, accompanied by a sense that it has somehow been taken too much for granted. But any discussion of this topic requires some clarification of what it is that we mean by the body. There is, in fact, no single viewing point from which we can see or define what the body is; it can only be grasped through multiple vertices. I will suggest three of these:

a   its existence as a biological substrate, which becomes the source of the drives in psychical life
b   its social-symbolic construction, central to individual sexual and identity formation, construed in manifold ways through the "mirror" of social discourses and through the lens of unconscious phantasmic constructions
c   its sensory-somatic existence, which connects the body to the world of objects in a sub-symbolic, pre-reflective pattern of contiguity, and shared psycho-sensory experience operating beyond the boundaries of the individual self, embedding the self in a shared domain of communal perception.[2]

My focus in this chapter is on the last of these, the way the actual body engages with the world through the senses in the context of shared communal sensoriality. This means that I will be less concerned with the ways in which the body has traditionally been addressed in psychoanalysis – that is, how the body is construed and represented in the mind (e.g. in terms of the phantasied body, or the body of hysterical conversion symptoms), or how the biological body is presented to the mind through the drives.

What are the possible transformations obtaining to these different "versions" of the body? We could say that the biological body has its own concrete reality, comprehended by medical science and the laws of physics, and like all biological organisms its mode of dependency on its environment can be observed and measured in stable and quantifiable terms. By contrast, the body as constituted through systems of representation (its social-symbolic, phantasmic, and specular versions) is plastic and quite incapable of being measured or pinned down at the individual level (big data and social psychology create measurable categories that nevertheless do not capture the experience of the individual). This socially constructed body is eminently capable of a makeover, of being shaped and structured by social signifiers, interpersonal identifications, and unconscious phantasy formations.

The sensory-somatic body differs from the biological and the social-symbolic dimension of the body insofar as it exists distinctly and *presents itself* exclusively in the sensory-somatic register (Scarfone's (2006) notion of "presentational affects" seems germane here). Two characteristics define the way in which the sensory-somatic body functions and presents itself:

a   It is found exclusively in the mode of presentation, in the pattern language of movement, texture, rhythm, sound-shape, color, and light. This means it relies not at all on systems of representation; in Bion's terms, it does not partake of alpha function transformation, and hence cannot be rendered unconscious (repression), nor can its functions be split-off and relocated through projection, denial, or disavowal.
b   The psycho-sensory body does not learn its "body language" in isolation. The embodied dimension of psychical life develops and evolves entirely in the shared sphere of perception, by means of sensing things together.

All the transmutations of the body wrought by social redefinition and imaginary identifications do not change the distinctive way the somatic body itself makes meaning, which is through the shared pattern language of sensoriality (mediated by what I call the *beta function*) – the movement of the body in relation to objects, its mode of attentiveness, the tempo and rhythm of its engagements, the textures of sensation and feeling that keep the body awake and responsive to the world. In those cases where this inherently shared "language" of the body has been interrupted, the most significant question is whether this distinctive non-verbal psycho-sensory pattern language of the body can be revived and shared.

The sensory-somatic body

The Cartesian impulse in psychoanalysis, the favoring of mind and thought over body and intuitive feeling, has tended to place its bets on the mind's ability to represent things, to symbolize, deploy language, and discriminate through thought, to replace impulse with idea. Under this assumption the body, since it cannot do any of these things, is equated with the primitive, mute, atavistic. But actual bodies are marvelously discriminating in their own way, and move and sense things in a complex pattern language. The semiotics of bodily being in the world do not partake of a representational system of signs and symbols, but find a pattern meaning in movement, texture, rhythm, tone, and other sensory qualities, which are experienced only and always in the form in which they are presented; in other words, the sense of self given through bodily experience is grasped and registered, not through the auspices of memory, idea, thought, or phantasy, but in the meaning given through immediate sensation, through what is heard, seen, and felt as it happens.

If the importance of the function of the soma has largely been obscured in psychoanalytic theory, retrieving it from this obscurity means emancipating the somatic aspect body from the shadow of the Id and the unconscious. We should not treat the body as if it is just a kind of heating system for the unconscious, producing the "drive derivatives" that propel the repression-based work of mental life. Certainly the body does present itself in this id-like way, but it is not simply and only a drive machine; it is, crucially, a conveyer of how it is to be in the world. In this respect, the soma-body is a maker and weaver of patterns of being in the world, connecting self to the object world while also serving as contact barrier with that world.[3]

Since the body is both the biological source of the drives and a somatic pattern-weaver, we can see that the work of dissociation is capable of divorcing from instinctual sources of desire and body vitality (as in Winnicott's (1960) "false-self organization"), but at the same time alienates us from somatic body's *patterning* capacities that weave us into the rich communal world of shared psycho-sensory perception. To be dissociated from the somatic body means becoming isolated, then, from the replenishing source of body language that exists in the sensory commons, and which gives us a sense of belonging in the world.

The important point here is that while the sensory-somatic dimension is obviously housed in an individual body, it is also a trans-individual and trans-subjective phenomenon: it is the way we meld with the world. In this regard, the body does not separate us from the world – it joins us to it. It is the mind, not the body, that separates things and separates us from things.

Because it is a product of the workings of the mind, the phantasied body and the socially constructed body are always to some extent molded by the work of repression, and its imaginary functions are capable of being valorized, split-off, projected, or evacuated. In other words, we can get rid of parts of our body, change its shape and function (Freud), confuse its functional properties (Meltzer). But the *actuality* of the sensory-somatic body is incapable of being repressed or split-off. In its corporeal reality, it stays put; the work of the senses cannot be stopped or abolished. The one thing we can do to change this reality is to dissociate ourselves from this actual body (and then replace it, as I have previously suggested, by a "fabricated," phantasmic, or symptom body).

The body and the unconscious

Clinical psychoanalysis took as its starting point the model of the unconscious as repository of the psychical derivatives of the body's unruly and incestuous passions, which by necessity must be kept under repression and transformed into more rule-bound forms of thought and feeling. This is a picture of an unconscious populated by images of what the instinctual body wants but the mind and society cannot let it have. To the extent that the entire method of clinical psychoanalysis was premised on finding access to the repressed unconscious (through dreams, parapraxes symptoms, transference, etc.), the instinctual body was always already implicated as the source of the prohibited derivatives.

In the modern era of psychoanalysis, attention turned to those many patients who suffer from maladies that are not born primarily from this conflict over repressed wishes, but from various types of *inability* to form coherent wishes, symptoms, and dream thoughts. This inability has been conceptualized in terms of failure of containment, impairment in thought, symbolization or mentalization, and inability to internalize or form attachments. Grappling with how to understand and treat these patients, modern psychoanalytic writers have proposed the existence of an *unstructured* or *un-repressed* unconscious (e.g. Matte-Blanco's (1988) "symmetrical," Bion's (1965) "dark and formless infinity," Donnel Stern's (2003) "unformulated experience," and the procedural unconscious of Beebe and others), something awaiting some kind of structuration in order to begin operating according to the more recognizable processes of repression, dream work, symptom formation, and transference neurosis. In Bion's (1962) formulation, for example, sensory elements can gain representation in the mind, and hence may be subject to repression, only once they have been transformed through alpha function into psychical qualities. In this formulation, the unconscious (system Ucs) comes into being through projective identification and the action of container/contained. Now the infinity of the unstructured unconscious takes on the familiar shape of the repressed unconscious. But Bion's paradigmatic insight into the mental mechanism that transforms sensory experience into thinkable psychical form nevertheless did not theorize the psychical reality of the body per se.

If clinical psychoanalysis at its inception took the existence of the unconscious for granted, it also assumed that we are naturally embodied – that we are psychically domiciled in the body. But today, we can no longer do so in light of what we recognize as body–mind dissociation. From our current perspective, we would have to say that *becoming embodied is a precondition* for the creation of the repressed unconscious; it is in response to living psychically in an actual body that repression becomes active and necessary, both to limit and to shape the effects of bodily needs and the emotions. When on the other hand mind becomes systematically dissociated from the living body, the repressed unconscious is disabled, or rather is rendered redundant. When we dissociate, there is no use for repression. Here the unconscious reverts to its unstructured forms, which leaves the psyche untethered and incapacitated with regard to feeling the vitality of the self and the world.

Disembodiment and mind–body dissociation

Embodiment

By embodiment, I mean perceiving self and world immediately through the senses, relatively unfettered by excessive mentation, hence giving generous scope for proprioception and for sensual apprehension of the world. This implies some tolerance for being in the experience of the world without yet comprehending or fully knowing the nature of what one is seeing or encountering. Being embodied, then, tends to entail more contiguity and unison with things and people, and hence a lesser degree of differentiation from the world of objects.[4]

In considering the significance for psychical life of being embodied, it is important to recognize its ambiguous, double-sided nature. Being embodied, by bringing psychical experience closer to sensory perception, exposes consciousness more directly to the rich intensity and complexity of the internal and external worlds, thus making the actuality of things more palpable and immediate. On the one hand, this heightened perception of self and world provides the sense of being real and alive in the world, and in this way underwrites the experience of viability of self that Winnicott (1971) called *going-on-being*. Only to the degree that we are embedded in the body, and hence perceive ourselves and the world from this location, is it possible to feel alive in the space/time dimensionality of the actual world.

But on the other hand, for the very same reasons, insofar as it makes more immediate the perception of self and world, being embodied also increases the sense of vulnerability to being overwhelmed or impinged-upon, heightening apprehension of the traumatizing potential of the world of objects. This makes living in the body a mixed blessing.

It is the mind's prerogative to guard the self from being overwhelmed by all that floods in from the body through the sensorium. We cannot remain too exclusively in the embodied domain; it is the function of the mental functions of representation and thought to render our lives self-consciously meaningful within a social-symbolic setting, and in so doing the mind constantly rearranges the locus of perception at some varying degrees of distance from the body.[5] This involves the ongoing work of the mechanism of body–mind dissociation. Endlessly inventive, and aided by culture in myriad ways, the mind is capable of construing the self's existence and its place in the world in ways that transcend the limitations of the actual body, so that it becomes possible for the self to seem timeless, even immortal; or to exist somewhere else, in a phantasy locale or an unchanging alter world (Goldberg, 2020) of fixed certainties, removed from the changeability, moodiness, and turbulence of actual bodies. The many socially constructed and phantasmic versions of the body provide a sense of freedom from corporeal limitation. By contrast, actual bodies are always tied to real time on earth, which invokes a sense of the limitations of mortal existence and of death anxiety and hence to intimations of mortality (Lombardi, 2017).

In light of the ambivalence inherent in living within the limits of the body, the tendency toward disembodiment – the continual adjustments in degree and style of embodiment – is an ever-present feature of psychical life. This is surely the reason why strategies for modifying states of embodiment, or escaping embodiment altogether, are so highly treasured at all times and in all cultures. If the shared psycho-sensory domain of culture provides ways for us to live in our bodies, it also – by the same token – constantly curates ways for us to alter our states of embodiment so as to temporarily take leave of its constraints.[6] While it is easy to see why the traumatizing potential of embodiment would be especially pronounced in the case of those who have indeed suffered excessive impingement and trauma, we all nevertheless have reason to titrate and adjust the degree to which we live in our bodies.

Body–mind dissociation

It is in this context that we may we recognize the particular importance and universality of the mechanism of mind–body dissociation, which specifically regulates the degree of psychical embodiment, both in everyday life and in pathological states. If the actuality of living in a body means exposure to its fragility and mortality, and to the potential of excessive emotional and physical pain, then dissociating mind from body provides a specialized and effective way to remove oneself from the immediate threat of a traumatizing excess.

Adapting Winnicott's (1949) model of mind–body detachment, first proposed in his paper *Mind and Its Relation to the Psyche-Soma* (1949), I propose a general model of body–mind dissociation as a distinctive and universal form of psychical defense and organization (operating alongside repression, splitting, and adhesion). The specific function of the dissociative mechanism is to titrate the degree of embodiment, that is, the degree to which we experience ourselves and the world from a locus of perception that is embedded in the body (Goldberg, 2020). Viewed this way – as a universal process in psychical life – dissociation can be understood as a mechanism that operates across a spectrum from normal to pathological. Transient dissociative states allow adjustments in the degree of embodiment and hence relief from everyday pains of emotional and physical life; the healthy function of dissociation is thus vital to everyday alterations in embodiment that help regulate states of attention, rest, relaxation, and anxiety. But the dissociative mechanism is also capable of being deployed more rigidly to rescue the self from the pathological effects of excessive trauma, which can result in regimes of extreme alienation of the body. Excessive deployment of body–mind dissociation leads to an array of pathologies of disembodiment that are worthy of our interest and attention. Especially in the case of these more pathological cases, dissociation carries with it the potential for depersonalization and loss of personal aliveness within oneself and in the world.

It is important to recognize certain distinctive characteristics of the dissociative mechanism and the processes subtended by it. The psychical action of dissociation is not carried out by means of phantasy processes or mental representations.

Instead, the mechanism of dissociation works at the level of alterations in attention and consciousness, carried out by means of hypnoid techniques including distraction, auto-hypnosis, auto-suggestion, and auto-stimulation, all of which affect shifts in states of consciousness. To me this is a crucial point: it means that the exploration of dreams and of transferences, which rely on the interpretation of symbolic meanings and associations, is rendered redundant by the dissociation. To make the point in a rather condensed way, where there is dissociation, the function of association is disabled. Nor can we count on the communicative properties of projective identification to afford a means of connection or linking in these cases.[7] This means that the therapeutic function of receptivity and introjective identification are much reduced in the treatment of dissociation.

Extreme threats of impingement or unrelenting psychic pain will activate the dissociative mechanism in a more far-reaching way, causing a more far-reaching and rigid detachment from the body and its catastrophic needs. If our minds take leave of the body too insistently and extensively, as is typically the case under persistently traumatic conditions, the threat of depersonalization becomes more severe, leading to more systematic difficulties in feeling alive and real in time and space (Lombardi, 2008). Time stands still, becomes stalled, or passes by too rapidly, and space stretches unbounded to infinity or collapses into confines so cramped that there is no room for anything to happen.

Under these more extreme circumstances, where ordinary transitory dissociative states have begun to mutate into fixed, intransigent structures of mind–body alienation, the personality starts to take on a pathological dissociative character, and there begins to occur far-reaching changes in both mind and body. Untethered to the realness of bodily based perception, the mind is prone to becoming lost in unanchored thoughts; sensuous thought is replaced by obsessional mentation, moralism, or vigilance. Unmoored from its realistic embodied context, without anchor in space and time, the mind tends to travel far afield from personal truth, becoming lost in abstractions, solipsism, and false distinctions (what Bion [1970, p. 97] called "lies"). More than being lost, when divorced from the body, the mind becomes the enemy of lived experience; it begins to build secondary defensive structure, becomes expert in disrupting the sense of existing in real time and space. In this way the mind might, as Bion (1962) said, begin to reject and hate reality.

On the other hand, if the mind is embodied, domiciled in the body, then the mind's ability to represent things and make meaningful distinctions will be grounded in the reality of actual bodily experience, which also then gives the sense of a temporal and spatial framework for being and living.

If extreme disturbance causes the mind to want to flee in order to escape the limits of embodied emotional and physical reality (leaving the psyche unanchored in sensual reality and prone to depersonalization anxiety and meaningless) then the body, for its part, also undergoes characteristic and unwelcome changes: it becomes a body alien to psychical life, unable to make use of the mind's verbal, conceptual, and imaginative capacities. Now the body is felt to be nothing other than a mass of undifferentiated *primitive* feelings and sensations, uncontained, and unarticulated. Consequently, either the body becomes a mute anarchic actor, seeking discharge for instinctual needs and proto-feelings arising within the organism, or the body is remade as a *symptom body* or what I have described as a *fabricated body*, colonized by the mind for the purposes of maintaining dissociative control over need and desire, and for the purposes of alleviating the threat of deadness and depersonalization by activating states of pseudovitality (Goldberg, 1995, 2004).

Clinical approaches to disembodiment

Psychical disembodiment means that it is possible for psychical life to proceed while alienated from the pattern language of the body. Recognition that the body, in its sensory-somatic dimension, has a psychical life of its own (i.e. that it partakes of pre-symbolic pattern language of rhythm, tone, texture, coloration, movement, shape), and that this sensory-somatic domain of meaning can become divorced from the mind, and has far-reaching implications for our understanding of psychopathology and for the way we approach things clinically.

The question of our clinical approach to the phenomenon of disembodiment goes beyond the specific challenge of working with post-traumatic personalities. The universal tendency toward self-regulation through body–mind dissociation places the actual body at the center of all clinical encounters. But I will limit my discussion here to the clinical challenges posed by more markedly disembodied patients, those who use dissociation to enforce a rigid and unyielding structure of body–mind alienation, rather than in a more transitory and adaptive way.

As I have suggested, body–mind dissociation makes transitions in states possible (e.g. the transition from mental alertness to relaxation and rest), thus playing an important role in the ordinary and necessary regulation of everyday psychical life. It is only when dissociative states lose their transitory and adaptive character that they begin to take on the form of systematic and unyielding structures of disembodiment that can become the dominant organizing feature of the personality. These rigid forms of mind–body dissociation are often well disguised and well organized, receiving much aid and support from current cultural and technological arrangements of everyday life. When successfully organized in this way, the dissociative personality operates along lines first described by Winnicott (1960) in terms of *false-self* illness, wherein the individual, while capable of an effective external adaptation to the social world, is nevertheless dislocated from the interior emotional life, and is typically troubled by emotional deadness, lack of sense of personal meaning and engagement in the world, and threat of depersonalization. In its culturally normalized version, which I have called "successful" dissociation, there is a shell of pseudo-normality and a functional pseudo-integration: the bodily self is dissociated but is also "colonized," that is, brought under control of and managed by the mind (Goldberg, 2004), which may take any number of forms, including, for example, the development of obsessional systems and compulsive food and exercise habits.

To the degree that a rigid structure of body–mind alienation (a pathological dissociative structure) has become established, it is necessary and even urgent to modify our clinical approach. In the face of disembodiment, it is futile – and can be counterproductive – to insist on the regular forms of analyzing unconscious conflict, transference, and resistance. Interpretations of intrapsychic and relational conflict depend on certain linking and symbolizing or *mentalizing* functions that are specifically unavailable in the dissociated patient, who will respond with a false-self accommodation and exacerbation of the dissociated state (or perhaps activation of a paranoid structure).

Writers who explore the trauma roots of dissociative states generally warn against premature interpretation and analysis of the transference. The traumatizing potential of the clinical encounter cannot be avoided with post-traumatic patients, as Ferenczi (1949) was the first to point out. And among the Relational school of analysts, for whom the task of reclaiming dissociated aspects of self is a guiding motif, it is above all the relational engagement of the analyst that serves as the means to the cure (Bromberg, 2010; Donnel Stern, 2003; See also Gurevich, 2015). But these important insights into the treatment of post-traumatic patients, which highlight the un-integrated self-states that arise from systematic trauma, do not address the broader dimension of disembodiment, which is after all central to all of psychical life.

Lombardi (2008), a psychoanalytic theorist who places the relation to the body at the center of his concerns, emphasizes the primacy of repairing the "vertical" mind–body link with all of his disturbed patients, including those with marked psychotic features. He insists that interpreting the relationship and the transference before securing a genuine mind–body connection will do no good and can even do harm. His clinical focus is on what he calls "cognitive reverie" (Lombardi, 2017, p. 898), the work of the analyst to structure and facilitate the connection to bodily experience. Lombardi (2008, 2017) does not eschew all kinds of interpretation. Instead, he makes the case for particular use of interpretation, highlighting its structuring effect; interpretation should serve first and foremost to stimulate the patient's attention toward embodied reality. In this context, interpretation is an active offering of the analyst's body–mind integration to the patient; it marks a momentary body–mind synthesis that the analyst has reached in himself in the context of the encounter with the patient, and as a result of the labor of subjective attention and notation of the experience of being with the patient in a focused way.

Beyond interpretation

A broader conception of the clinical approach to disembodiment must, I think, take us beyond interpretation, to the question of the analyst's engagement at the level of shared sensoriality or *sensory symbiosis* (Goldberg, 2012). This dimension of clinical work, which I have referred to as the *inductive dimension of the analyst-patient engagement*, involves a shift toward attending through the body. This aspect of the analyst's work takes place within a somatic matrix where perception is organized along the lines of the pattern language of the body, rather than through the hallucinatory or representational systems of the mind.

From this perspective, the essence of integrating the body into psychic life is not to be found in the mind's sophisticated ordering of the primitive urges into mental representations or structures. It lies instead in the somatic body's own capacities to participate in the shared psycho-sensory patterns of existence. Clinically, this entails establishing a therapeutic context within which the senses may be freed to perceive things from an embodied location, rather than being overridden by the intellect and by social discourses, so that perception continues to be held captive by the detached mind. It is to allow the rhythms of body time and the patterns of sensoriality to influence perception. Only then will it be possible for a fruitful interaction to occur between the presentational somatic "language" of the body and the representational (verbal-symbolic) systems of meaning in mental life.

It is only on the basis of sensing things together, which implies and requires participating in a shared domain of sensory perception, that any meaningful engagement with objects, ideas, and emotions can take place. Where shared perception does not exist, we must actively search for it.

Clinically, then, the starting point is in the domain of shared perception. This entails the analyst entering a pre-reflective state of psycho-sensory readiness, an openness to noticing things without reflecting or trying to assign either emotional or symbolic meaning to them. I have referred to this as the *inductive* dimension of the analyst's activity, in the sense that analyst and patient are constantly inducing states of embodiment in one another.

I have previously (Goldberg, 2004, 2012) advocated a deliberate effort to relinquish the interpretive state of mind, in favor of a mode of attention that allows one to notice things in their presentational form: the way things look, sound, and feel. This posture, which increases the scope of what may be called body-consciousness, involves what Marion Milner (1987) described as a "deliberate use of a wide rather than a narrow focus of attention" (p. 236), the cultivation of "direct psycho-physical non-symbolic awareness" (p. 237).

> What I mean by body attention or body concentration in the analyst is this: it is a state in which the direct proprioceptive body-self awareness, which I suppose is best called the body presentation, as distinct from the body representation or body image, becomes the foreground of one's consciousness rather than the pre-conscious background. As I see it, this kind of attention in the analyst differs from the free-floating kind that, when I first practiced as an analyst, was the only kind I thought appropriate and which most neurotics seemed able to manage with. It differs because it is not "in the air"; it deliberately attends to sinking itself down into a total internal body awareness, not seeking at all for correct interpretations, in fact not looking for ideas at all – although interpretations may emerge from this state spontaneously.

(pp. 239–249)

This active letting go of the search for meaning to some degree recapitulates Bion's (1970) extension of Freud's (1912) "evenly hovering attention," wherein Bion proposes that the analyst remains as free as possible of memory, desire, and understanding. But, whereas Bion hoped in this way to reach the level of the psychical by avoiding the sensuous world, I think that it is precisely the sensory-somatic dimension that must be reclaimed; this is how the actual body, which truly is the basis for all reality perception, is brought back into the center of self-experience.

What I add to Milner's invaluable description is in addressing the clinical situation, it is essential to keep in mind that psycho-sensory experience is always a matter of sensing things in common. The formation of soma-psychical life takes place beyond the boundaries of the individual self. Embodiment is foundationally a shared phenomenon, a factor not just of the interpersonal but the transpersonal and communal domain of perception. It is when the shared sensory-somatic domain atrophies or is seriously disrupted that the body, now isolated from its shared domain, becomes the fixed property of the individual. Here we see the emergence of pathological states of sensory isolation, where the biological and social body becomes something to be managed by the individual ego; it becomes, in effect, a false body (Goldberg, 2004), a body oriented toward serving as a barrier rather than a conduit to being in the world.

A marked feature of these dissociative personality organizations is the inability of the individual to make transitions from one state to another. Vigilance, omniscience, and obsessive-compulsive rituals are the visible manifestations of the need to remain in a fixed underlying state of disembodiment. These institutionalized dissociative states have the power of trapping the individual in alter worlds characterized by repetition, suspended time, devitalization, and aimlessness. Only if the analyst's presence and voice can be felt at the level of a *shared perceptual state* is it possible that the patient may be able to re-find a new basis for noticing things and being in the world, and hence be freed from the frozen state of isolation and repetition. It is not representation, symbolization, or interpretation that accomplishes this, but activation of the shared sensory-somatic patterns of bodily motion, rhythm, and texture, which brings the possibility of communal embodiment – and hence of being and belonging in the world – back to life.

In the next segment, I offer a brief clinical example of my efforts to engage a disembodied young man, with the caveat that one cannot approach these patients in a formulaic way. Above all, a distinctive and creative solution will have to be found for each individual case; the particulars of what I describe here are not generalizable.

Ken

Ken was an intelligent yet extremely reticent young man who blended unobtrusively into the social world, and interfaced with the world almost entirely electronically. It seemed the slightest contact with my symbolic therapist presence, most pointedly my way of speaking (my authority to address him as a subject), induced in him an immediate withdrawal. At first I assumed that his reticence was due to internal conflicts over aggression. Only gradually did I recognize the degree to which he subsisted in a chronic state of fugue-like semi-depersonalization, and how prone he was to falling quickly into a dissociative type of paralysis that could easily swallow not just a single session, but return him to a prolonged fugue-like state. I began to recognize the traumatizing effect of his encounter with me (and with others) could leave him in a practically out-of-body state for hours or days afterwards. Now, I could see how chronically removed he felt from his embodied self, causing him to teeter constantly on the edge of depersonalization, absence of embodied feeling, and lack of access to any shared affective connection with others. He was adept at the conceptual level, could emulate social discourses, but lacked any sense of the "communicative musicality" (Malloch and Trevarthan, 2009) of embodied human exchange. Signs of his chronic disembodiment became discernable: his inattention to signs of hunger and tiredness; indifference to weather conditions (he dressed in the same clothes irrespective of season); and his habit of rote masturbation without pleasure or desire. Above all was the strange feeling as he entered the office of no embodied response, no possibility of our noticing anything or resonating to anything together. I could see that, if left up to him, Ken would remain dissociated and isolated in perpetuity, that he needed to be grabbed out of his chronic semi-depersonalized state (here, Ann Alvarez's (1992) concept of reclamation comes to mind and seems apt). With time passing in desultory circles, the treatment losing traction while the patient emanated an impenetrable politeness, and affective sterility while a low-level eating disorder and other compulsive behaviors remained untouched, I began to consider my own level of engagement, my habit of resorting to symbolic communications and easy formulations, even though I sensed the futility of verbal interpretation. Seeking a different position within myself, I tried to shift my attention to how things got going – one might say the tempo and the initial tone of things – as we met in the waiting room. Seeking out new sources of data, and broadening my attention as best I could to take into account psycho-physical and sensory cues in the clinical field, I tried to wean myself of program-like responses and formulations, while seeking to attain a state of mind free of reliance upon familiar theoretical signposts. I specifically resolved to forego making explanatory interpretations of the patient's internal motivations or conflicts. My shifting into a kind of improvisational state of physical readiness at the beginning of the hours affected an experimental state of mind which seemed to start things a new direction.

Ken had had the habit of mumbling "how you doing" whenever I opened the door to the waiting room. Now, instead of ignoring or tepidly responding as before, I tried instead to concentrate on the physical act of stepping into the waiting room, to notice the feeling of it, and to let myself speak from a more embodied perspective, without much thought or concern about making sense. Because (due to the effort of concentration) I was at these times in a mild kind of trance state, it is difficult to give an accurate report of what I said,[8] but now when he mumbled "how you doing," I would say something like "awaiting expectantly," or "ready, but for what?" He barely seemed to notice, but in retrospect I can see how the exchange set up the beginning of an embodied exchange, something like the intonation and rhythm of a call and response. In due course, as he slumped into the chair, I extended my new way of engaging Ken, catching his attention with hand gestures as I spoke, and making descriptive comments about the state of things in the room ("feels like not much going on here," or "just noticed that crack in the wall"). Again, the therapist's speech here is significant not for its semantic but for its performative function: it serves the purpose of inducing a shared state of psycho-sensory and affective engagement.

The shift in my state toward a more embodied consciousness and locus of perception seemed to change the tone of things. Gradually, Ken began to show small signs of having a body in the sessions, showing an increasing interest in the office surroundings, the weather and light and plants outside the office. Low-key at first, this interest in the world, which he shared with me as if we were seeing it together, became a deep source of enlivenment and shared pleasure, forming the basis for what would emerge later: an awakening of curiosity about me, which grew into a game of spotting my flaws, ribbing me for my failings, satirizing the therapy situation with increasing muscularity and pleasure.

Yet, to the degree that he began to emerge from his autistic shell and experience states of aliveness through the shared embodiment of the clinical encounter, it became apparent that Ken needed help with the transition at the end of sessions. As the session drew to a close, I could see him returning to a disembodied state, to a default position of detachment and isolation, thus erasing the experience of a live connection to himself and the world around him. Clapping on the headphones as if in a fugue, he would stumble around trying to find which door to exit my office. So, gradually we developed a ritual of departure, carried out almost like a pantomime. I would point to the doors as if to say, "which is the way out?" Then as he stepped outside, he would pause for a moment at the doorway, perusing the office garden, taking note of what was happening out there. Over time, this transition ritual became more elaborate and playful, with a final gesture as he departed down the pathway: sometimes a bow, or a salute, or a dance move. In this way and in others, Ken found ways to retain the sense of embodiment that had eluded him.

Conclusion

Recognizing the psychical function of embodiment, its centrality to finding a rhythm of being alive in the world, and the accompanying recognition of body–mind dissociation as an ever-present self-regulatory process, has implications for our approach to dislocated and depersonalized patients in particular, but also clinical theory in general. The question of disembodiment is timely also because we increasingly live in a world where the options for living in dissociated states seem to be proliferating, enabled by certain aspects of contemporary culture, technology, and by the effects of social trauma and anxiety.

Dissociating mind from body offers a way out of the constraints and vulnerability that accompany life in an actual body living in the real world in real time. But there will always be a price to be paid for escaping the limitations of the actual body. To varying degrees, what is forfeited is a sense of authentic vitality and aliveness, and along with it the sense of being real, of meaningful engagement in the space and time of life, of being in the world. But accompanying the phenomenon of disembodiment is an inevitable failure of a sense of fundamental belonging, a loss of membership in the "sensory commons," the domain of shared psycho-sensoriality where our lived bodies are continually revitalized and re-shaped (Goldberg, 2012). For if a "pattern language" of the senses does exist in its own right, beyond verbal symbolic language and mental representation, then this psycho-sensory mode finds its originary shapes, textures, and rhythms not in the individual biological body, but in the affective encounter with the world of objects perceived in concert with others. The very possibility of fresh perception lies in participation in the shared domain of communal living through the senses, and it is this possibility of new experience in the world that is forfeited wherever the ego constructs an individualist dominion by establishing a fixed regime of disembodiment. Here, the body, having become the sole property of the individual, must somehow be re-inducted into the shared psycho-sensory domain from which it has been cut off and isolated. This is the challenge posed to psychotherapeutic work in the area of disembodiment.

Notes

1   As a way of conceptualizing this, I have postulated the existence of something like a *Beta Function* (Goldberg, 2017), a psychic mechanism that can be contrasted with Bion's concept of *alpha function*. The beta function operates in a psycho-sensory domain that makes no use of representational capacities or symbolization, functioning entirely in the mode of *presentation* in the sensorial field.
2   We may speak here of an erotics of shared embodiment, which contrasts with the sexual desire for the object.
3   In fact, the instinctual body only develops into a heat-source of erotic and aggressive *drives* demanding work from the mind – it is only capable of becoming the *wishful* body of psychoanalysis – once the mind has developed its representational processes, so that the ego is placed both *in contact* with and *at odds* with the Id.
4   Being embodied would seem to bring us closer to the experience of Bion's *O* rather than *K*, though Bion himself did not make this connection between at-one-ment (O) and being embodied. Indeed, he often took a seemingly opposite position: he felt our sensory involvement got in the way of reaching the experience of O.
5   A function of dreaming is to keep the representational capacities of mind connected with the language of the body.
6   Strategies for escaping embodiment more extensively or permanently have a special place in all cultures as well, occupying a frontier space where the work of culture caters to the individual psychical need to transcend the *actual*. Here, along this frontier, the pathological tendencies in both culture and individual psychology find opportunities to be expressed and realized.
7   Projective identification is a phantasy-based mode of inter-subjective communication whereby split-off aspects of self can be identified with in the mind of another. It is this dimension of phantasmic influence upon the other that is missing in these cases.
8   I doubt that the content of my comments was relevant, other than providing me with a means of maintaining my own functioning at the symbolic level.

References

Alvarez, A. (1992). *Live company*. Routledge.

Bion, W.R. (1962). *Learning from experience*. Tavistock.

Bion, W.R. (1965). *Transformations*. Tavistock.

Bion, W.R. (1970). *Attention and interpretation*. Tavistock.

Bromberg, P. (2010). Minding the dissociative gap. *Contemporary Psychoanalysis*, 46(1):19–31.

Ferenczi, S. (1949). Confusion of the tongues between the adults and the child—(The Language of Tenderness and of Passion). *The International Journal of Psychoanalysis*, *30*:225–230.

Freud, S. (1958 [1912]). Recommendations to physicians practicing psycho-analysis. In J. Strachey (Ed. And Trans.), *The standard edition of the complete psychological works of Sigmund Freud* (Vol. 12, pp. 109–120). Hogarth Press.

Goldberg, P. (1995). "Successful" dissociation, pseudovitality, and inauthentic use of the senses. *Psychoanalytic Dialogues*, 5(3):493–510.

Goldberg, P. (2004). Fabricated bodies: A model for the somatic false self. *The International Journal of Psychoanalysis*, *85*(4):823–840.

Goldberg, P. (2012). Active perception and the search for sensory symbiosis. *Journal of the American Psychoanalytic Association*, *60*(4):791–812.

Goldberg, P. (2017). Reconfiguring the frame as a dynamic structure. In A. Harris & I. Tylim (Eds.), *Reconsidering the moveable frame* (pp. 92–110). Routledge.

Goldberg, P. (2020). Body-mind dissociation, altered states and alter worlds. *Journal of the American Psychoanalytic Association*, *68*(5):769–806.

Gurevich, H. (2015). The language of absence and the language of tenderness. *Fort Da*, *21*(1):45–65.

Lombardi, R. (2003). Catalyzing the dialogue between the body and the mind in a psychotic analysand. *Psychoanalytic Quarterly*, *72*(4):1017–1041.

Lombardi, R. (2008). The body in the analytic session: Focusing on the body-mind link. *International Journal of Psychoanalysis*, *89*(1):89–109.

Lombardi, R. (2017). Entering one's own life as an aim of clinical psychoanalysis. *Journal of the American Psychoanalytic Association*, *66*(5):883–911.

Malloch, S. and Trevarthan, C. ed., (2009). *Communicative musicality: Exploring the basis of human companionship*. Oxford University Press.

Matte-Blanco, I. (1988). *Thinking, feeling, and being*. Routledge.

Merleau-Ponty, M. (1962). *Phenomenology of perception* (Trans. C. Smith). The Humanities Press.

Milner, M. (1987). *The suppressed madness of sane men*. Tavistock Publications.

Scarfone, D. (2006). A matter of time: Actual time and the production of the past. *Psychoanalytic Quarterly*, *75*(3):807–834.

Stern, D. (2003). *Unformulated experience*. Analytic Press.

Winnicott, D.W. (1949 [1958]). Mind in its relation to the psyche-soma. In *Through pediatrics to psychoanalysis* (pp. 243–254). Basic Books.

Winnicott, D.W. (1960 [1965]). Ego distortion in terms of true and false self. In *The maturational processes and the facilitating environment* (pp. 140–152). Karnac Books Ltd.

Winnicott, D.W. (1971). *Playing and Reality*. Tavistock Publications.

13 River to rapids

Speaking to the body in terms the body can understand

Caron Harrang

A generally recognized first principle in psychoanalysis is that mental life is rooted in bodily experience (the ego is first and foremost a body ego). At one level analytic dialog depends on the analysand's ability to verbalize thoughts and feelings and on the analyst's ability to offer meaningful verbal interpretations. Yet, increasingly the profession is both widening and intensifying the magnification of its collective lens to take account of preverbal, nonverbal, and unrepresented experience; protomental states and psychosensory experience expressed uniquely through the 'language' of the body. How then does the psychoanalyst apprehend and speak to these phenomena in terms the body can understand?

In this chapter I use the term *speaking* in two different ways. On the one hand, referring to nonlexical communication registered in the sensorium. For example, everything expressed by means of physical posture, breathing, gaze, scent, tone of voice, cadence of speech, and semi-autonomous movements such as yawning, sneezing, coughing, and so on. On the other, referring to lexical communication when it has the effect of bridging the caesura of body–mind. For example, when the analyst's words 'touch' or palpably impact the analysand's embodied sense of self. I'm thinking of moments when the analyst's words evoke a welling up of emotion expressed in unexpected tears or an audible gasp on the part of the analysand. Both meanings are employed in my clinical vignettes to illustrate when verbal interpretation elucidates the body's role in expressing what is occurring unconsciously in the analytic relationship as well as when talking tends to obfuscate or disrupt emerging psychosensory experience. By psychosensory, I'm referring to nascent sense impressions (beta elements) presented through the patterned language of the body, capable of being perceived and communicated with or without becoming represented lexically. In this realm, speaking to the body requires attention to nonlexical forms of communication.

The psychoanalytic literature reveals an increasing interest in the body in recent years (Abel-Hirsch, 2019; Blechner, 2011; Bronstein, 2014; Busch & Sandberg, 2014; Connolly, 2013; De Toffoli, 2011; Grubb, 2014; Küchenhoff, 2019; Levine, 2018; Lombardi, 2011; Martini, 2016; Miller, 2014; Sletvold, 2013; Tsolas & Anzieu-Premmereur, 2018; Willemsen, 2014). However, this understanding of the body's role in psychic development over the lifespan has yet to be integrated into our theory and clinical technique (Goldberg, 2019).

DOI: 10.4324/9781003195559-13

Levine et al. (2013, as cited in Godsil, 2018, p. 13) note there is not yet a shared technical approach to how we meet our analysand's primitive fusional needs even as it is generally recognized that early stages of psychic development involve the analyst's careful listening to her own inchoate somatopsychic responses. Where the body is addressed in the literature, the overwhelming emphasis is on how we *listen* and make meaning of nonverbal signifiers and rarely if ever on how we *speak* to our analysand's somatopsychic reality.

In drawing attention to this distinction, I suggest the analyst's verbal and non-verbal interventions have a direct impact on the analysand's body or, more accurately, bodymind.[1] Furthermore, the impact of these interventions can at times be observed and doing so carries important implications for clinical technique in relation to the body's role in analytic communication which is the central focus of this chapter.

What precisely do I mean then by *speaking to the body* in the analytic situation? A preliminary clinical vignette may elucidate this central question and prepare the ground for a discussion of theoretical concepts relevant to this inquiry.

Clinical vignette: leaning in

Clara, a highly sensitive and intelligent grad school student in four-times-weekly analysis, arrives for her session looking fearful and physically tense. She glances furtively at the couch and chooses to sit in a chair facing me without removing her winter coat. I take Clara's positioning herself at the greatest possible distance from me as an indication she feels vulnerable and unsure whether I am a safe person. Our verbal exchange is formal and remains superficial for the first part of the hour.

Eventually Clara sheds her coat and moves cautiously to the couch which puts her physically closer to me. However, she remains seated rather than lying down which I silently interpret as expressing her desire to reconnect with me as some-one she trusts while still feeling suspicious and needing to keep an eye on me. The conversation eventually turns to Clara's upset with me for being "cold" and "unfeeling," all the while keeping her eyes averted.

Clara thinks she should "just get up and walk out." Maybe then I would finally miss her (as much as she misses me) when we're apart, even though she's certain I don't miss her and never will. The whole situation is hopeless and she feels stupid for having let her guard down in yesterday's session leaving her too upset afterward to work on an important paper for one of her classes due at the end of the week. "I've put your ability to work in jeopardy," I say, "at school and here." No response.

At this point it seems I'm becoming increasingly menacing to Clara; I am someone who does not want to help her or, worse yet, someone triumphantly taking pleasure in her emotional unraveling. Anything I try to say to describe what I think is Clara's experience of me seems only to make matters worse. I feel increasingly tense in my own body and badly want to rub my eyes that are aching and dry from not blinking. Yet, if I move a muscle, I fear Clara will take it as further proof of my desire to get away from her.

Finally, in desperation I say something (I don't recall exactly what) about Clara trying to get away from her own feelings and therefore assuming I'm doing the same thing—that is, cruelly turning my back on her. With this, for the first time in the hour, she turns to face me directly and shrieks in a voice thick with rage, "You blame me for *everything*! Nothing is ever your fault. You hate me and I know it. Well, *I hate you too*. I *hate* you!"

As Clara begins shouting, without thinking, I lean my head and torso forward in my chair, bringing myself nearer to where she's perched on the edge of the analytic couch a few feet away. I see her eyes reflexively dilate as I tilt my body toward her, startled it seems by my unexpectedly moving closer. Then Clara's eyes soften and her shoulders slacken as fury gives way to heart-wrenching sobs. I feel my own eyes fill up with tears and make a concerted effort to keep breathing as deeply as I can. Neither of us speaks for a time. I can see that Clara notices the moistness in my eyes which seems to break the spell of her feeling entrenched with a feared and reviled maternal presence. She sees me differently from who she assumed I was moments before and is no longer terrified or hateful.

In the remaining time of the session we were able to talk together about what Clara had felt the previous day during our time together that left her feeling exposed and humiliated by the unbearable intensity of longing to be comforted by me, physically and emotionally. In the physical separation after the session ended she had lost her nascent ability to remember me as someone responsive to her distress and dread. And while all this made sense to Clara once she felt reconnected to me and could (literally) see my caring, what was most meaningful to her in the moment of greatest emotional turbulence, she told me later, was that I had leaned in and gotten physically closer. The "cold" and "unfeeling" person she was convinced I was at the beginning of the session would never have done that. Clara didn't have to take my word for it that I was a welcoming presence. She could feel it with her body, see it with her own eyes.[2]

My spontaneous movement *spoke* directly to Clara's body and affected her emotionally in a way that, I believe, words alone in that moment could not. Put another way, something sensorial was communicated between us, the result of which was an emotional transformation in the analytic field. Only then could we meaningfully talk about what Clara had experienced that has over time acquired symbolic significance and contributed to her greater trust in bodily experience as a basis for self and relating to subjective and external objects. More will be said later in the chapter about this crucial exchange and the nature of what was communicated via the subtle choreography of unconscious movements between us that in a healthy container/contained relationship words may (at least partly) come to represent.

To my mind, this vignette and others like it raise a number of questions including how to understand the state of bodymind from which intuitive actions like 'leaning in' may arise. What exactly is communicated that the body seems instinctively to understand prior to mentalization of experience? How does one account for the transformative nature of moments when physical or spatial contiguity between analyst and analysand suddenly shifts? These moments are similar to what the Process of Change Study Group (Stern et al., 1998) define as 'moments of meeting' but differ in how we theorize what is occurring.

How does *speaking to* the body differ from *talking about* the emotional significance of the analysand's psychosensory experience? Assuming both forms of communication are important at different moments in analysis, when should the analyst rely on verbal interpretation of bodily phenomena and when do somatopsychic interventions, including moments of silence, speak more powerfully than words?

In the following pages I address these questions and show how Winnicott's concept of 'direct communication' and Bion's concept of 'at-one-ment' provide theoretical support for the technical approaches taken in speaking to the body illustrated in four clinical vignettes. I conclude there are times when it is useful, even crucial, to offer verbal interpretations that explicate the body's role in expressing what is occurring in the analytic field, as well as times when talking is either unnecessary or may disrupt beneficial "shared psychosensory experience" (Goldberg, 2019) between analyst and analysand.

Winnicott's concept of 'direct communication': a pearl within

In seeking an approach that balances speaking to body and mind, Winnicott's (1962, 1963) concept of 'direct communication' provides clues as to how the analyst may usefully orient to the nonverbal aspects of analytic process and theoretical context for understanding body-to-body communication between analyst and analysand, as illustrated in my first vignette. However, I want to be clear that I differ from Winnicott's theorizing that views an individual's core state of being as one of isolation or "not communicating" (1962, 1963) with external objects, which I submit reflects his adherence to the concept of primary narcissism (Freud, 1914). Alternatively, I suggest direct communication is *bidirectional at a psychosensory level from birth* and becomes increasingly imbued with psychical qualities for the infant as a result of the mother's primary maternal preoccupation (Winnicott, 1956) and capacity for reverie (Bion, 2014 [1962]). Before discussing the clinical utility of direct communication, as I define it, it is important to recap Winnicott's remarkable contribution.

For Winnicott the infant communicates not by conscious effort to signal his needs to someone perceived as separate, but rather via the omnipotent illusion of being at one with his environment such that bodily and emotional needs are felt to be satisfied spontaneously. This illusion on the infant's part is made possible by the mother's primary maternal preoccupation through which she becomes "*biologically* and psychologically conditioned for special orientation to the needs of her child" [emphasis mine] (CW, Vol. 5, 1955–1959, Oxford University Press, 2016). I underscore the word *biologically* to show how Winnicott sees the mother's capacity for identification with her infant stemming from bodily attunement as well as emotional attentiveness.

Winnicott's (1962) view of direct communication is paradoxically founded on the infant's illusion of "not communicating" with an external object not yet perceived as separate from himself. In actuality, the infant's needs are facilitated by the mother's heightened sensitivity—listening with every fiber of her being—and responsiveness. In his view, direct communication allows the mother to be experienced initially by the infant as a subjective object in his internal world. Understood this way, direct communication preserves a degree of healthy omnipotence that results in the infant feeling 'real' to himself; 'real' because the infant's vulnerability is cushioned by the mother's provision of care in a way that Winnicott (ibid., p. 8) says allows for full establishment of the pleasure principle connected with satisfaction of bodily and emotional needs *before* being balanced with the reality principle.

Winnicott takes another step in his theorizing—and this is where I see things differently—asserting the individual's authentic sense of self "is essentially isolated" (1962, p. 15) such that feeling 'real' to one's self is based on "not communicating" except with subjective objects (ibid., p. 16). The implication of this way of thinking is that direct communication is *unidirectional*; that is, dependent on the mother's capacity for intuiting her infant's bodily and emotional needs and on the infant's illusion of "not communicating" (i.e. not needing to communicate) with external objects for this to occur.

By extension to the clinical situation, Winnicott believes it is incumbent on the analyst to intuit the analysand's direct communication and respond, at times, *without resorting to verbal interpretation*. Verbal interpretation at certain points in the analysis is to be avoided to allow for experiencing the analyst as a subjective object in the analytic field prior to the introduction of separateness in manageable doses. For example, Winnicott reports wanting to change an analysand's hour, so that he could work on a paper he was writing. However, he felt—that is, received the direct communication from his analysand—that it would be devastating if he prioritized his own needs by rescheduling the analysand's hour. Winnicott adds,

> Now *he will never know* that I refrained from altering his time... For him, he had communicated with me as powerfully as if he had shouted: 'for God's sake don't do anything tomorrow that will make me feel you hate me!' And I heard the silent communication that was never communicated [verbally], and in this way the trauma of a renewed insult was not inflicted.
>
> (Winnicott, 1962, pp. 11–12) [emphasis mine]

It is clear from this vignette that Winnicott views direct communication as occurring unidirectionally (from analysand to analyst) rather than bidirectionally (between analysand and analyst in both directions). No doubt Winnicott's ability to refrain from rescheduling was related to identification with his analysand's vulnerability prior to a long break. And although I agree with Winnicott that it would have been wounding to reveal his restraint, I remain unconvinced the analysand "will never know" at some level that he was kept in mind in this way. I have only to think of the not insignificant number of times analysands have dreamt of being in the exact geographical location where I have been during a scheduled break (that I have not revealed) to recognize to what degree the analyst's state of bodymind may be intuited, often quite accurately, by the analysand. Although I have no idea what Winnicott's analysand may have perceived, it seems at least possible that he unconsciously registered the impact of his analyst's discipline and compassion in maintaining the analytic frame.

Valuable as Winnicott's contribution is regarding the role of direct communication in nurturing an individual's sense of authenticity, I question his assumption that the foundation of one's core sense of self is based on "not communicating" or being insulated from unconscious communion with external objects. Rather, I believe as does Goldberg (2019) that the infant's experience of relatedness with subjective and external objects is entirely dependent upon a facilitating environment or, in Bionian terms, a container/contained relationship operating at a body-to-body level. That is, body-to-body relatedness inherently involves an external object, even before the infant is capable of consciously perceiving it as such.

This somatopsychic reverberation with internal and external objects is why, for example, infants and young children, and indeed many adults, find it easier to fall asleep with the murmur of human voices in the background than in the absence of these sounds. Conversely, why one of the cruelest, most dehumanizing forms of punishment is solitary confinement where one is isolated and deprived of psychosensory contiguity with fellow humans.

Remarkably, if we closely examine Winnicott's clinical work with parents and young children it is possible to see that he implicitly understood direct communication as occurring bidirectionally between analyst and analysand. What I am suggesting is that Winnicott's theorizing, based on his view of infants as initially incapable of self/other differentiation (primary narcissism), prevented him from grasping the full theoretical significance and technical value of his own, I think brilliant, conceptualization. If direct communication is understood as operating bidirectionally and continuously, as I believe it does, there is a 'pearl' inside Winnicott's metapsychology that provides a platform for integrating analytic theory and technique with respect to bodily phenomena. If seen as bidirectional and ongoing, direct communication becomes a primary building block in conceptualizing what it means to speak to the body in the clinical situation as illustrated in all the vignettes of this chapter including one from Winnicott's practice described in the next section.

Clinical vignette: the 'river' of direct communication

In keeping with the theme of this chapter, a clinical vignette described in a paper titled "On the Basis for Self in Body" written in 1970, a year before Winnicott's death, provides a clear and touching example of bidirectional direct communication between analyst and child patient. Therein he describes a psychiatric consultation in a hospital setting with a nine-year-old boy being treated for syndactyly or webbed fingers and toes. Treatment had already involved multiple surgeries and the boy's medical team was concerned because in many respects he seemed almost too cooperative. Interestingly, as it relates to the topic of this chapter, the boy spoke no English compelling Winnicott to rely largely on nonverbal communication with some assistance from an interpreter.

Winnicott engages the boy in an interchange of sketches (Squiggle Game), which reveals his great love of ducks which, like him, have webbed feet. The representational content of the drawings (i.e. ducks) which Winnicott astutely understood as linked to the boy's body image is important but not the element I wish to highlight. Rather, it is the relationship between drawing and visual imagery—tactile, fluid, and closer to the body and emotional experience than lexical communication—that deserves our attention in this situation. It is through the tactile and visual conversation (drawing together) that Winnicott comes to the privately held understanding that the boy can accept the need for multiple surgeries to correct his condition if he is "certain that first of all he was loved as he was when he was born..." (2016 [1970], p. 2). However, the analyst also believes a child such as this needs eventually to come to terms with the reality of his body being distorted after first being accepted in the "somatic shape and function" (ibid., p. 2) he was born with. How then does Winnicott convey this complex understanding and speak to the body in terms the body can understand?

Although Winnicott does not describe in any detail how he communicated with his child patient other than through mutual drawing, it is clear he believes an emotional transformation occurred as a result of their interaction. The boy was able, Winnicott thinks *for the first time*, to recognize the "fact of [his] deformity" even though this was not interpreted verbally (2016 [1970], p. 2). In other words, something was communicated by the analyst nonverbally that directly impacted the boy's experience of his body such that he was able to realize and begin to mourn his disfigurement without feeling narcissistically wounded or unloved.

Though speculative, I can imagine that Winnicott's awareness of his own bodily fragility and imperfection (he had suffered numerous heart attacks by this time in his life requiring medical intervention) contributed to his ability to tenderly accept the boy's ducklike body as well as identifying with its deformity. Winnicott's capacity to experience contradictory thoughts and feelings—the body accepted 'as is' and the body seen as misshapen—demonstrates alpha function as well as maternal and paternal function working in harmony. This understanding of the boy's needs might have been interpreted verbally by a different analyst or by Winnicott himself at a different moment in time. However, on this occasion the analyst's receptivity and intuitive grasp of a complex somatopsychic reality was *spoken* without words allowing us to see the powerful, sometimes transformative effect of bidirectional direct communication. At one level, Winnicott was able to communicate to the boy's mind something important *about* his body using nonverbal symbols (drawing). At the same time, their shared psychosensory experience of physical vulnerability did not rely on representational capacities or symbolization, and it is this level of communication upon which symbolic discourse depends.

Similarly, in the vignette with Clara described at the beginning of the chapter, my surrender as analyst to being experienced as a mother who fears, and therefore hates, her child's dependency as well as simultaneously trusting my body's impulse to 'lean in' seems to have contributed to a transformation in her and between us. If I had only attended to Clara's words expressing hatred at the moment of greatest emotional turbulence, I might have missed my body's impulse to move physically closer to her by leaning forward in my chair. As it was, the tension in her body *spoke* to my body, about her need for me to come closer even as her words were pushing me away. Additionally, seeing Clara's eyes dilate in response to my moving closer—a visual startle response—showed me how unexpected my action was because (as I came to later understand) it contradicted an unconscious phantasy of an analyst/mother coldly refusing to respond to her child's emotional needs. And whereas it did later in the session become possible to verbally interpret the emotional significance of Clara's experience and what had occurred between us, it was in the first place something that emerged within the context of an unconsciously driven body-to-body conversation.

Thinking about it later, it occurred to me that my pre-reflective movement when I leaned in and got closer to Clara may have been informed by my history working with horses in my youth; an unconscious procedural memory of how to contain fury when it is fueled by fear. When a horse startles and rears up or defensively strikes out with its powerful hind legs, the place of greatest safety is often to get close to its massive body as quickly as possible. Safe because it is harder for a horse to bite or kick when physically restrained and, more importantly, moving closer contains the animal's terror and fight/flight response in the face of perceived danger. Whether this history informed my response to Clara is unclear but it is interesting to consider from the perspective of the myriad and subtle ways mammalian bodies *speak* to one another continuously; although obfuscated much of the time by our attention to verbal speech and the symbolic meaning of words.

Reflecting on these vignettes and similar clinical experiences, I began to wonder if Winnicott's concept of direct communication, if seen as bidirectional, might bear some relationship to an intersubjective experience Bion (1965) describes as 'at-one-ment.' Even as these concepts derive from different models of the mind (or bodymind), both describe a process of unconscious communication that I suggest prominently involves the body. If direct communication is understood as an omnipresent feature of mental life, as I believe it is, might at-one-ment be considered a heightened manifestation of direct communication wherein two-person subjectivity momentarily recedes into the background and psychosensory union becomes briefly foreground?

In the next section, I examine Bion's concept of at-one-ment and show how it enhances Winnicott's concept of direct communication and facilitates understanding of the state of bodymind from which somatic interventions like 'leaning in' may arise. Additional vignettes illustrate how the analyst's evenly hovering attention to sensory experience can facilitate entrance into a state of at-one-ment rather than obfuscating it as Bion cautions. I suggest this more balanced view of bodily phenomena allows the analyst to make fuller use of somatic countertransference and reverie as technical tools and decreases the chance of erroneously attributing certain corporeal phenomena as outside the realm of analytically relevant communication at the body-to-body level.

From river to rapids: at-one-ment with the analysand's psychosensory reality

The ordinary meaning of the word 'atonement' is an act of reparation for sin or wrongdoing the purpose of which is to become reunited with the divinity or God. Bion (1965) takes this word and breaks it apart to create 'at-one-ment' by which he intends to convey an experience of being at one with ultimate reality as well as the process by which this occurs. López-Corvo (2003) notes at-one-ment is similar to empathy but more complex in that it requires a level of emotional 'nakedness' on the part of the analyst that can only exist in a state of mind [or bodymind] in which there is no striving for understanding. A paradox.

At-one-ment is an extremely complex concept to define much less to operationalize in analytic practice. Nevertheless, Bion came to believe late in his career that the analyst's at-one-ment with the analysand's psychic reality is of utmost importance to the psychoanalytic endeavor. Additionally, he believed any intervention or interpretation not made from this state is a distraction or a deviation from the fundamental aim of analysis. In Chapter 3 of *Attention and Interpretation*, "Reality Sensuous and Psychic," Bion writes

> The analyst must focus his attention on O, the unknown and unknowable. The success of psycho-analysis depends on the maintenance of a psycho-analytic point of view; the point of view is the psycho-analytic vertex; the psycho-analytic vertex is O. With this the analyst cannot be identified [known]: he must *be* it.
>
> (1970, in CW, 2014, p. 243)

Further on in the same chapter Bion (ibid., p. 248) links the analyst's task—to be at one with O—to the analysand's task saying, "It is difficult to conceive of an analysis having a satisfactory outcome without the analysand's becoming reconciled to, or *at one with, himself* [emphasis mine]." In other words, the analyst must become O of the session as it is evolving in order to nurture the analysand's capacity to embody their own essential being. To my ears, Bion's comment echoes Winnicott's emphasis on analysis nurturing the capacity for progressively being in contact with one's 'true self.' Yet, by claiming it is possible for the analyst to achieve moments of at-one-ment with the analysand's psychic reality, Bion sharply diverges—as do I—from Winnicott who insists on the impossibility of being at one with anything other than one's subjective objects.

Bion stresses repeatedly in Catastrophic Change (1966), Notes on Memory and Desire (1967), Attention and Interpretation (1970), and seminars given worldwide during the later years of his life how sensuous experience can interfere with at-one-ment or the state of mind most accessible to apprehending mental phenomena in the consulting room. Some have concluded from this, I think incorrectly, that Bion considered at-one-ment an intersubjective experience unrelated to bodily phenomena. As a counter point, it can be observed that Bion (1963) places beta elements or raw sense impressions before they acquire (full) psychical significance in Row A of his grid or map of psychological functions and designates this positioning as closest to O or ultimate reality. Then, a few years later in *Transformations* (1965, p. 272), Bion describes at-one-ment as T ß O (transformation in beta leading to O). Interestingly, by designating sense impressions 'beta' Bion implies there is some infinitesimal amount of alpha function or the potential for meaning making present in all bodily phenomena. In my view, Bion's nomenclature suggests that sense impressions are the building blocks of consciousness, indivisible (except conceptually) from mental life.

So, how does all this help us better conceptualize and speak to bodily phenomena in the clinical situation? If, as previously described, we consider Winnicott's concept of direct communication and think of it as operating bidirectionally at all times, what Bion's concept of at-one-ment adds is a more nuanced understanding of the intersubjective process by which analytic communication occurs as well as what is required of the analyst in opening to this level of experience. If direct communication is a river of ongoing body-to-body communication that carries analytic process, then moments of at-one-ment are the rapids or places in the watercourse where turbulence intensifies signifying heightened risk as well as the possibility of radical emotional transformation and psychic growth.

Having described how direct communication and at-one-ment provide theoretical footing for understanding the body's role in nonlexical communication between analyst and analysand as illustrated in the first two vignettes, I would like to show how the analyst's words may also directly impact (*speak* to) the analysand's body. In the next vignette taken from a paper by Henry Markman (2017) titled "Presence, Mourning, and Beauty: Elements of Analytic Process" an unanticipated comment by the analyst illustrates how heightened sensory experience may serve as a portal to at-one-ment leading to emotional transformation.

Clinical vignette: listening to the rain

Markman (2017, p. 981) describes the lead-up to an experience of at-one-ment with a man described as "schizoid," saying the session began with the analysand relating stories that, although not uninteresting, seemed to him a distraction from something else happening at a nonlexical register. It was a stormy day outside and toward the end of the hour the analyst found himself relaxing contentedly during a moment of silence, listening to the pouring rain beating rhythmically against a nearby windowpane. Then, quite unexpectedly, the analyst found himself saying, "Listen to that rain."

After some minutes of silence, as the downpour continued, the analysand spoke:

> In ninth grade I built a sailboat, ... and I was so proud of that boat. I raced it at the lake. It really planed and I was so excited. It had red sails and a spinnaker too ... I loved that ... I felt so free. It took most of a summer to build it and some kids I know at the lake started coming around to watch me work or to help. I was no longer an outcast. Up to that point in my life every activity

I did was solitary: my reading, my science projects, my drawing. And I never talked about what I did. This time I had help and companions.

(ibid., p. 981)

The analyst tells us the analysand's response was "entirely unexpected" and resulted in a sudden shift in the "texture" of his speech and "atmosphere in the room" in this and in subsequent sessions (Markman, 2017, p. 981). It strikes me that Markman wasn't simply sharing an observation with his analysand. Rather, he was inviting his analysand to join him in an intimate, psychosensory experience—listening to the rain. Markman spoke to his analysand's bodily consciousness from a state of at-one-ment or union with his psychosensory reality.

The analytic atmosphere thus created, for me, evokes the sense of security a child might feel being allowed to crawl into the lap of a loved and loving parent and together listen to the rain outside while feeling warm and safe inside. If we listen to the analysand's words as a transference communication, he's saying "up to [this] point" in the analysis "every activity I did was solitary." The analysand's isolated aloneness is transformed through a shared psychosensory experience, a moment of at-one-ment with the analyst, such that he can say from an authentic place in himself, "This time I [have] help and companions." This impression is confirmed by the analyst's report of the analysand commenting a few days later that the couch felt "like a boat," then adding, "We're sailing together" (ibid., p. 981).

It is important to bear in mind that moments of at-one-ment or union with the analysand's psychosensory reality, although sometimes pleasurable, may also be unnerving, even frightening for the analyst. For example, Markman (2017) acknowledges that what he unpreparedly said to his analysand about the rain made him anxious and contributed to his surprise in how it facilitated his analysand's emergence from a chrysalis state into a shared psychosensory experience. In the fourth and final vignette, I describe a moment in the analysis of a young man wherein verbal interpretation of bodily phenomena very nearly capsized the treatment before its metaphorical meaning could be fully appreciated.

Clinical vignette: erection

Harry began a second session of the week, on the couch, saying he felt fearful after yesterday's session in which he indicated his readiness to increase our agreed-upon fee.[3] He felt vulnerable acknowledging his desire to contribute more as it revealed deepening commitment to analysis and increasing financial sturdiness resulting from our work together. As he spoke, I noted a bulge in his trousers that suggested an erect penis. This observation was jarring, in part, because his words and tone of voice expressing vulnerability did not seem erotically charged. Something didn't add up. I felt puzzled by the seeming discontinuity between Harry's words and bodily expression and wondered if he would acknowledge his erection or avoid it out of embarrassment, hoping I hadn't noticed?

Harry continued talking about his hope that paying closer to my full fee would allow him to feel deserving of more from colleagues at work and from his analysis.

I could not for the life of me reconcile the disparity between his words expressing cautious optimism and his body communicating desire. Desire toward whom? I felt cornered; unable to dismiss the compelling nature of what I was seeing and powerless to think what, if anything, I might say to address what was happening between us. What was happening between us?

As I remained uneasily positioned behind the couch wondering if my analysand would say anything about the 'elephant in the room' a reverie materialized. In my waking dream, I saw an infant lying supine on a changing table; excitedly moving his arms and legs with penis at attention as his diaper is being changed by a mother who, although physically attentive, is deeply uncomfortable with her baby's, and her own, erotic aliveness. This internal vision gave me to wonder if my analysand's inability to acknowledge his erection might reflect an unconscious identification with a maternal object dissociated from her own body and the mutual pleasure associated in health with breastfeeding, bathing, diaper changing, and other aspects of caring for her infant.

I wanted to respect my analysand's privacy and give him room to speak to his own bodily experience. At the same time, as Harry continued talking about other things, I grew increasingly uncomfortable avoiding what was now occupying center stage in my mind. Was I being unconsciously recruited to play the part of an analyst/mother who denies what is right in front of her eyes, thereby disavowing responsibility for her role as signifier of her analysand's/child's bodily experience and erotic desire? Receiving this direct communication without speaking (in this case, verbally) to what my analysand's body was expressing felt like sidestepping my responsibility as analyst. At the same time, I feared that voicing my perception and its possible meaning could eroticize the transference or be experienced as intrusive.

With trepidation, I finally said, "I hear that you're feeling anxious about the change in our fee agreement. I wonder though if you might also feel excited about being able to do more as indicated by what appears to be your body's erection?"

It was as if a bomb had gone off in the room. Harry looked abruptly downward, put his hand on his crotch and quickly flattened the bulge in his trousers. He then proceeded to read me the riot act. Harry informed me that he most certainly did *not* have an erection, nor had he ever felt any degree of sexual arousal in my presence. Not now, not ever! What's more, he stated quite emphatically that it is not my place as his analyst to ever say anything about his body, particularly his genitals, unless he brings the topic into our conversation. My comment violated a boundary, confirming his fear that I want him to feel vulnerable and dependent because it is sexually exciting for me. He reminded me this sort of thing has happened before when he's trusted people in positions of authority. My "fantasy" about his having an erection proves to him that I'm as untrustworthy as they were.

Hearing this and realizing that I had in fact misperceived Harry's bodily state, I felt distraught and wondered if a scenario was being enacted in which a prurient parental object takes advantage of their child's vulnerability and trust, just as he claimed. At the same time, as the situation unfolded Harry remained on the couch and we continued working despite the emotional turbulence between us.[4] Moreover, I continued to feel that although my perception was inaccurate at one level (he did not have an erection), my interpretation about embodied aliveness and something opening up in our work together was not totally off the mark. Still, when the session ended I felt deeply shaken and wondered if this rupture could be worked through or if, as he feared, it repeated one more person in a position of authority failing him.

The next day when Harry returned he began the session on the couch saying, "I'm still upset about what happened yesterday but I think I may have overreacted. I've had a lot of thoughts about it." I listened intently as he described how what happened in yesterday's session echoed a number of painful experiences in his prepubescent youth including when his primary care doctor, who was also a member of his fundamentalist religious community, inquired if he masturbated. Harry responded that he did not. In truth, sensing his doctor's disapproval, Harry was afraid to admit he wasn't entirely sure what was meant by the term. Harry recalls his doctor telling him it was a good thing he didn't masturbate because if he did "it might break"—in other words, he'd be responsible for castrating himself by indulging his sexual desire. Sadly, this confusing and frightening prohibition from a trusted family friend and medical authority left him afraid to touch his own genitals for sexual pleasure until after he'd left home for college.

What followed from this turbulent episode in Harry's analysis has been a significant shift in the emotional atmosphere of our sessions. He seems to feel freer to talk about his bodily experience, including sexual feelings and fantasies, as well as when he feels I've misunderstood what he's telling me. I notice we both seem to feel free referring to this pivotal experience and how paradoxically a misunderstanding opened the door for his distrust of authority to come more fully into the open as well as his desire to be recognized and accepted as a sexual being. I no longer fear commenting on my perceptions of his bodily experience, nor does he. In hindsight, it seems my use of the word 'erection' put me in the direct line of fire from an internal object opposed to sexuality and, more generally, to carnal existence. In withstanding the attack usually aimed at himself, I demonstrated it is possible to survive the destructive force of a moralistic superego object without retaliating or collapsing. Not surprisingly, these developments give Harry to feel less afraid of his body and more trusting of his emotional experience including tender loving feelings beginning to emerge in the transference and in other relationships.

Discussion

This chapter's clinical vignettes barely scratch the surface of how the analyst may apprehend and speak to bodily phenomena in analytic practice. Nevertheless, what I have presented suggests how we may integrate conceptual understanding of bodily phenomena with how we *speak*, in both senses of the term, to analysands.

The first two vignettes ('leaning in' and Winnicott, 1970) illustrate how the analyst's interventions speak to the body without recourse to (or prior to) verbal interpretation. The third (Markman, 2017) and fourth ('erection') vignettes show how the analyst's verbal interpretations may operate synergistically with ongoing direct communication and moments of at-one-ment. Examining the similarities and differences in how the analyst speaks to the body in these vignettes in this final section of the chapter further elaborates how *speaking to* the body differs from *talking about* the meaning of the analysand's psychosensory experience, both of which are important at different moments.

As stated earlier, there are times when it is vital to offer verbal interpretations in an effort to clarify the body's role in expressing what is not-yet-represented in verbal thought or speech. At the same time, lexical communication can obstruct emerging psychosensory experience that needs to take up residence, so to speak, in the analyst's body before it can become part of the analysand's embodied sense of self. In these instances, speaking to the body is more likely to occur through nonlexical channels before acquiring lexical significance. The first vignette with Clara is a good example.

When Clara entered the consulting room, she appeared wary and this was underscored by her refusing the couch and keeping her winter coat buttoned up tight. Her emotional state was conveyed without words exemplifying the omni-present nature of direct communication. Clara and I were in the 'river' of direct communication and the water was icy cold. Both of us registered the tension at a conscious level and this was reflected in the stilted nature of our initial verbal exchange. Verbal interpretation of the transference at this point would have ob-structed or distracted from an important body-to-body conversation that needed time to evolve. Absorbing the strain of our interaction allowed me to identify physically and emotionally with Clara's fright and pent up rage. Becoming at-one with her simultaneous fears of attacking me and of losing me, permitted my body to unconsciously comprehend—awkward as it may sound to put it this way—that I needed to 'lean in' when her fury did emerge. In the metaphor of the river, when we reached the Class 5 rapids, the only sensible path was to go with the strength of the current to carry us through a turbulent emotional experience and hope we'd both survive.

There is a line from an NPR interview of Larch Hanson (2019) who's been hand harvesting seaweed from Gouldsboro Bay for many years where he says of the ocean, "the water remembers us." This comes to mind in thinking about the difference between speaking nonlexically to the body, as happened with Clara when I 'leaned in,' and reflecting on the significance of this moment as hap-pened later in the session. In the first case, the container for the analytic dyad is the river that 'remembers us'; another way of describing at-one-ment or becom-ing O of the session. Similarly, after I leaned in and Clara burst into tears and my own eyes became moist, the water was remembering us. Later, in reflecting on this crucial moment in the session, the quality of the experience was one of 'remembering going through the rapids' rather than being still in them. This, I believe, is the difference Bion had in mind in distinguishing O of the session from K or knowledge about an experience that, by definition, takes us out of the flow of the river.

José Bleger (2013, p. 240) writes that for the analysand, "the setting is his most primitive fusion with depressive position the mother's body and that the psychoanalyst's setting must serve to reestablish the original symbiosis" in order to repair bodymind disunity. The clear implication is that the analyst's body is part of the analytic setting; as much as the analytic couch (often associated with the analyst's body) or any other object that may obtain corporeal significance for the analysand.

If the original mother/infant symbiosis is disturbed, either because of a lack of reverie capacity on the mother's part or because of the infant's limits in utilizing maternal provision, this disturbance will be reflected in the analytic situation. For example, in the situation with Clara, this rupture was evident in her experience of my disappearance as a trustworthy object during times of physical separation between sessions. This breach in the original healthy symbiosis must be felt by the analyst in her body and responded to at a nonverbal level before verbal interpretation can hope to augment repair of bodymind disunity. Moments of shared psychosensory experience—such as when I leaned in and Clara experienced me as a maternal object wanting to be close and hold her—can serve a reparative function by disrupting the unconscious phantasy of an unbridgeable divide between mother and infant based on early life experience. Moreover, when I leaned in, although startled, Clara did not pull away. Thus, it may be that she unconsciously experienced the shift in spatial contiguity between us at a sensory level as if she too were leaning in.[5] If so, Clara's experience of getting closer also served a reparative function by restoring faith *in her own capacity* for healthy mother/infant symbiotic relatedness in an otherwise traumatized infant body.

Although it is not possible for me to address the analyst's inner experience in the vignette featuring Winnicott's work, I can comment on what I speculate played an important part in the direct communication with his child patient. As previously mentioned, Winnicott engaged the boy in the Squiggle Game or mutual drawing. Through this activity Winnicott intuited that his patient could accept multiple surgeries to correct his physical defect if he was first accepted as loveable in the body he was born with. Moreover, through nonlexical shared experience the boy was able for the first time to realize his body's deformity and begin to mourn its impact.

In the December 30, 2019 issue of *The New Yorker* in an article titled "Lost Art," author John Updike reveals that years before becoming a successful writer he had aspired to be a cartoonist. Ultimately, he relinquished this early career ambition but retained an understanding of how drawing engages and expresses the body in ways that words never do. "A drawing," Updike says,

> can feel perfect, in a way that prose never does, and a poem rarely. Language is intrinsically approximate, since words mean different things to different people, and there is not material retaining ground for the imagery that words conjure in one brain or another.
>
> (ibid., p. 16)

There is something conveyed, he goes on to say, "down to the tremor of excitement my hand may have communicated to the pen" that is lost in what can be represented lexically. Updike says he tried to bring the same sense of immediacy from his days as a cartoonist for *The Harvard Lampoon* to his writing, but it was "futile, and a disfigurement, really" (ibid., p. 16). When I read that line it allowed me to see Winnicott's work with his child patient in a new light.

The disfigurement that words represent from what the body conveys through ongoing direct communication, and more rarely, in moments of at-one-ment, is a necessary loss that if mourned (as Updike was able to do) allows for a more balanced appreciation of how the body speaks as distinct from lexical modes of communication. Winnicott, like Updike, seems to have achieved this balance, allowing him to appreciate what is conveyed by the body through drawing separate from what is communicated lexically. At the same time, as Winnicott and Updike were prolific writers, they both understood the power of words to give form and permanence to an infinite variety of human experience that transcends the temporality and transience of bodily existence.

In the third and final vignettes we see, in quite different ways, how the analyst's words can, if derived from an experience of at-one-ment, powerfully transform the analysand's bodily awareness and relationship with the analyst.

A great deal is made nowadays of Bion's wariness of sense impressions as an obstacle to intuition of non-sensory mental phenomena. Historically, this caution is rooted in Bion's adherence to Freud's "Two Principles of Mental Functioning" (1911) where Freud views the body as seeking pleasure or avoiding pain and fundamentally averse to reality. And yet, Parthenope Bion Talamo (1997, p. 51) makes it clear that "a very important leitmotiv in [her father's] work is the fundamental unity of soma and psyche and his clear positing of the biological, material, and corporeal basis of mental phenomena." Sensory experience may indeed obscure intuition of psychical qualities. At the same time, heightened sensory experience can, when it is not serving a defensive function, act as a portal to at-one-ment with the analysand's somatopsychic reality as beautifully illustrated in Markman's involvement with his analysand ('listening to the rain').

What stands out to me in Markman's response to his analysand is the degree to which he trusted his intuition emanating from sensory experience evidenced by unpremeditatedly saying, "Listen to that rain." The analyst admits he felt anxious as he spoke (as much to himself as to his analysand), revealing his somatic reverie and inviting a moment of uncommon intimacy. Markman doesn't say this, but I wonder if his *emotional nakedness* and courage in speaking without fully knowing what he was about to say—a quality López-Corvo (2003) notes is required for accessing at-one-ment or becoming O of the session—was unconsciously perceived by the analysand and contributed to what happened next. That is, the analyst's vulnerability and presence communicated through his tone of voice and (I'm imagining) slight hesitation before speaking may have induced a similarly *naked* response in his analysand.

Civitarese (2019) notes how the capacity to perceive time in Bion's metapsychology is embodied through the experience of satisfaction (the prototype of which is mouth/breast) followed by having to wait for the object's reappearance. He adds that for Bion it is the mother "who constantly 'hooks' herself onto the infant in moments of at-one-ment," establishing this rhythm of satisfaction/waiting/satisfaction culminating in the infant's first thought (ibid., p. 199). This thought, according to Civitarese, will have a sensory quality for the infant, but also a cognitive quality as seen from the mother's perspective. I agree but would add that thoughts contain a sensory quality for mother as well. Moreover, this dual sensory/cognitive dimension of thinking, in health, is present throughout life. If not, there would be no corporeal basis for a mother's hooking herself onto her infant's experience in moments of at-one-ment.

Applying these thoughts to the analytic situation gives me to wonder if the pleasure Markman felt listening to the rain and the satisfaction his analysand felt being invited to join him in this experience evoked a primordial rhythm—in this case, acoustic—of the object's appearance, disappearance, and reappearance. If so, the analyst's words ("Listen to that rain") were a lexical communication that simultaneously spoke to the body and served a symbolic function. The sensory quality is evident in the words 'listen' and 'rain' both of which touch on the aesthetic aspect of bodily experience. The symbolic register is evident, for example, in Markman's analysand saying some days after the session previously described that the couch "felt like a boat" that they were "sailing together." Although this sort of highly poetic verbal interpretation stemming from at-one-ment with the analysand's somatopsychic reality may be rare, it serves as an example of how words can directly impact the body and convey symbolic meaning.

In the fourth and final vignette ('erection'), words have a similarly powerful impact on the analysand's body consciousness, but do not initially function at the level of symbolization or metaphor. On the contrary, my attempt to language bodily phenomena evoked a catastrophic change in the analytic relationship.

In reflecting on the state of bodymind that gave rise to my interpretation linking (what I perceived to be) Harry's erection and his excitement about the changing nature of his relationship with himself and with me, I find meaning in Bion's (1970) concept of transformations in hallucinosis. According to Bion, hallucinosis is an omnipresent background state wherein sensuous impressions concretely perceived as 'the way things are' predominate over rational thinking. As such, it is the state of bodymind least tolerant of ambiguity or difference (Civitarese, 2015). At the same time—and this is surprising—Bion views it as an ideal state in which the analyst may attain at-one-ment with hallucinatory aspects of the analysand's psychic (or somatopsychic) reality. This poses certain risks for the analyst in that hallucinosis is based on unconscious denial of reality and absolute certainty that what is perceived is 'real' even as it later turns out to be false. Yet, this abandonment of reality is precisely what the analyst needs to be able to do; that is, to slip into a micro-delusion and then awake from it. Only then is it possible to utilize a transformation in hallucinosis as an analytic tool in the service of helping the analysand regain genuine contact with emotional reality.

What is most striking in hindsight about my (mis)perception of Harry's erection is how it was materially false and yet, at another level, precisely what he needed me to 'see' as a maternal object in the analytic field. This understanding of my hallucinosis is augmented by the reverie that visited me before I spoke in which an infant on a changing table (a metaphor for the analytic process) is being cared for by a mother dissociated from her own sexuality and uncomfortable with her infant's erotic aliveness. Interestingly, it never occurred to me until Harry reacted with indignation and moral outrage at what he perceived to be the inappropriateness of my interpretation that what I had perceived was not 'real.' I did not realize my micro-delusion or what it reflected about Harry's dissociated erotic aliveness that fortunately came to life in the session as a result of my 'error.' His anger and outrage were part of what enabled me to 'wake up,' completing the transformation in hallucinosis and rendering it useful as an analytic tool.

Speaking to the erotic body broke a taboo that had long been in place and reinforced by Harry's fundamentalist family and religious upbringing. Explicitly acknowledging the 'forbidden fruit' of bodily aliveness and desire allowed Harry to react to me—unconsciously identified with his disavowed sexuality—as if I had committed a cardinal sin. Violating this unconscious prohibition, fueled by at-one-ment with hallucinated somatopsychic reality and reverie opened the floodgates for Harry's moralistic superego, fueling his fear of sexuality, to explode with a force that, I believe, astonished both of us. If I had kept my (mis)perception of his erection to myself, which I might have done had it not seemed so 'real,' the portal to erotic aliveness might have remained closed, or closed until some other crisis unlocked it.

As it was, the fact that I spoke to Harry's erotic aliveness—even as it was founded on hallucinosis—served an invaluable function. He was able to react with vehemence against what he perceived to be my salacious interest in his body and taking advantage of his vulnerability and dependency. Although this was experienced as a dangerous 'rapids' in our work together, the value of speaking to the body in the way that I did was validated by Harry's ability to reflect on what had occurred between us *after* the session as well as by his curiosity and emotional openness the following day. That he could say, "I think I may have overreacted" and realize how his harshly censuring reaction to me the day before mirrored how he felt mistreated by his medical doctor and other authority figures indicated resurrection of normal projective-identification transformations and faith in the analytic process to tack toward truth.

Conclusion

Although the body has long been recognized as ground zero of human consciousness, it is only recently that psychoanalysts have realized the extent to which the body registers and catalogs phenomena that, although sensed or felt, are not represented in words or even thoughts. Even so, the emphasis in the consulting room has continued to be on translating unrepressed unconscious experience into what can be symbolized. Psychoanalysis has continued to be a talking cure with the addition of greater attention to bodily phenomena. Comparatively less attention has been paid to the process by which the analyst may achieve at-one-ment with the analysand's somatopsychic reality as part of speaking to the body in terms the body can understand.

Speaking, in this context, requires receptivity to direct communication of somatopsychic experience prior to what can be symbolized and expressed in thoughts or words. Clinical vignettes were provided to illustrate the ongoing nature of bidirectional direct communication between analyst and analysand and how this manner of *speaking* to the body facilitates emotional transformation whether or not it is rendered into verbal speech. Communication at this level is the basis of symbolic communication, not its opposite.

Winnicott's concept of direct communication and Bion's concept of at-one-ment were employed to suggest context for understanding the body's role in analytic discourse. If direct communication with internal and external objects is seen as an ongoing feature of intersubjective relatedness then at-one-ment signifies moments of intensified engagement ushering to the possibility of emotional transformation. If direct communication is a river of ongoing unconscious body-to-body communication that contains analytic process, then at-one-ment is the rapids where emotional turbulence increases signaling risk as well as the possibility of radical emotional transformation of the analytic field.

Whereas there are times when it is crucial to avoid making verbal interpretations to allow for moments of communion with subjective objects and shared psychosensory experience between analyst and analysand as exemplified in the first and second vignettes, there are other times when remaining silent represents an abdication of the analyst's responsibility to verbally narrate the body's contribution to analytic discourse. As seen in the third and fourth vignettes, the analyst's effort to language what the body is calling attention to, when emanating from a state of at-one-ment with the analysand's somatopsychic reality, is also transformative. Discerning the difference in how the analyst speaks to bodily phenomena is part of the art of psychoanalysis that, as Ogden (2009) reminds us, must be discovered anew by every analytic dyad.

Notes

1 I use the term 'bodymind' to connote the unity of body and mind, which is only divisible conceptually, not actually.
2 Civitarese (2019, p. 2) notes the close connection between bodily experience, visual imagery and thoughts. "Images," he says, "convey the knowledge of the body that is organized by rhythms and spacings that cannot be translated into words but which are no less important than words." For Clara, seeing me 'lean in' evoked bodily sensations and a series of visual images that eventuated in a narrative whereby I was restored as a trustworthy person in her eyes. According to Grotstein (2007) 'mentalization' occurs when sensations are converted to visual images, which becomes fodder for thinking under the influence of alpha function.
3 Harry's analysis began with his requesting and my granting a reduced fee based on a careful assessment of his financial circumstances. Our agreement included his letting me know when he could pay more, until reaching my full fee.
4 This moment with Harry exemplifies what it is like when analyst and analysand are catapulted from the smooth flow of the analytic 'river' into the 'rapids.' In the best of

circumstances, these experiences are transformative in the positive sense when analyst and analysand are able to go with the physical and emotional force of current and allow themselves to be carried through to quieter waters. On the other hand, if the analyst strives for understanding—to get control of the raft, so to speak—the possibility of growth will be jeopardized.

5 I am grateful to my colleague, Oscar Romero, for pointing out that the experience of space in the unconscious is infinite. Thus, if one celestial body comes closer to another the distance changes, but it is impossible to say which one moved without some other point of reference.

References

Abel-Hirsch, N. (2019). Alpha-function and the body: Interpretation breast. Not complete unpublished manuscript.

Bion, W.R. (2014 [1962]). Learning from experience. In C. Mawson (Ed.), *The complete works of W. R. Bion* (Vol. 4, pp. 303, 305). Karnac Books.

Bion, W.R. (2014 [1963]). Taming wild thoughts: The grid. In C. Mawson (Ed.), *The complete works of W. R. Bion* (Vol. 5, pp. 87–114). Karnac Books.

Bion, W.R. (2014 [1965]). Transformations. In C. Mawson (Ed.), *The complete works of W. R. Bion* (Vol. 4, pp. 115–280). Karnac Books.

Bion, W.R. (2014 [1966]). Catastrophic change. In C. Mawson (Ed.), *The complete works of W. R. Bion* (Vol. 6, pp. 19–43). Karnac Books.

Bion, W.R. (2014 [1967]). Notes on memory and desire. In C. Mawson (Ed.), *The complete works of W. R. Bion* (Vol. 6, pp. 203–210). Karnac Books.

Bion, W.R. (2014 [1970]). Attention and interpretation: A scientific approach to insight in psycho-analysis and groups. In C. Mawson (Ed.), *The complete works of W. R. Bion* (Vol. 6, pp. 211–330). Karnac Books.

Bion Talamo, P. (1997). Bion: A Freudian innovator. *British Journal of Psychotherapy*, *14*(1):47–59.

Blechner, M. (2011). Listening to the body and feeling the mind. *Contemporary Psychoanalysis*, *47*(1):25–34.

Bleger, J. (2013 [1967]). *Simbiosis y Ambiguedad: Estudio Psicoanalitico*. Buenos Aires: Paidos Argentina. *Symbiosis and Ambiguity: A Psychoanalytic Study*. Routledge.

Bronstein, C. (2014). 'I am not crying. I am rubbing my eyes': Annie and the hollow object. *Journal of Child Psychotherapy*, *40*(2):135–149.

Busch, F. & Sandberg, L. (2014). Unmentalized aspects of panic and anxiety disorders. *Psychodynamic Psychiatry*, *42*(2):175–195.

Civitarese, G. (2015). Transformations in hallucinosis and the receptivity of the analyst. *The International Journal of Psychoanalysis*, *96*(4):1091–1116.

Civitarese, G. (2019). The concept of time in Bion's "A theory of thinking". *The International Journal of Psychoanalysis*, *100*(2):182–205.

Connolly, A. (2013). Out of the body: Embodiment and its vicissitudes. *Journal of Analytical Psychology*, *58*:636–656.

De Toffoli, C. (2011). The living body in the psychoanalytic experience. *The Psychoanalytic Quarterly*, *80*(3):595–618.

Freud, S. (1911). Formulations on the two principles of mental functioning. In J. Strachey (Ed. and Trans.), *The standard edition of the complete psychological works of Sigmund Freud* (Vol. 12, pp. 215–226). Hogarth Press.

Freud, S. (1914). On narcissism: An introduction. In J. Strachey (Ed. and Trans.), *The standard edition of the complete psychological works of Sigmund Freud* (Vol. 14, pp. 67–102). Hogarth Press.

Godsil, G. (2018). Residues in the analyst of the patient's symbiotic connection at a somatic level: Unrepresented states in the patient and analyst. *Journal of Analytical Psychology, 63*(1), 6–25.

Goldberg, P. (2019). Winnicott's remarkable presentation on communication. Not complete unpublished manuscript.

Grotstein, J. (2007). *A beam of intense darkness: Wilfred Bion's legacy to psychoanalysis*. Karnac Books.

Grubb, K. (2014). Craving interpretation: A case of somatic countertransference. *British Journal of Psychotherapy, 30*(1):51–67.

Hanson, L. (2019). Lulu Garcia-Navarro, October 6, 7:59 AM ET, 'What it's like to harvest seaweed,' Weekend Edition Sunday, National Public Radio.

Küchenhoff, J. (2019). Intercorporeity and body language: The semiotics of mental suffering expressed through the body. *The International Journal of Psychoanalysis, 100*(4):769–791.

Levine, H.B. (2018). Body-mind dissociation in psychoanalysis: Development after Bion. *The Psychoanalytic Quarterly, 87*(2):360–368.

Lombardi, R. (2011). The body, feelings, and the unheard music of the senses. *Contemporary Psychoanalysis, 47*(1):3–24.

López-Corvo, R. (2003). *The dictionary of the work of W. R. Bion*. Karnac Books.

Markman, H. (2017). Presence, mourning, and beauty: Elements of analytic process. *Journal of the American Psychoanalytic Association, 65*(6):979–1009.

Martini, S. (2016). Embodying analysis: The body and the therapeutic process. *The Journal of Analytical Psychology, 61*(1):5–23.

Miller, P. (2014). *Driving soma: A transformational process in the analytic encounter*. Karnac Books.

Ogden, T.H. (2009). *Rediscovering psychoanalysis: Thinking and dreaming, learning and forgetting*. Routledge.

Sletvold, J. (2013). The ego and the id revisited Freud and Damasio on the body ego/self. *The International Journal of Psychoanalysis, 94*(5):1019–1032.

The Process of Change Study Group, Stern, D.N., Sander, L.W., Nahum, J.P., Harrison, A.M., Lyons- Ruth, K., Morgan, A.C., Bruschweiler-Stern, N. and Tronick, E.Z. (1998). Non-interpretive mechanisms in psychoanalytic therapy. *The International Journal of Psychoanalysis, 79*:903–921.

Tsolas, V. & Anzieu-Premmereur, C. (2018). *A psychoanalytic exploration of the body in today's world: On the body*. Routledge.

Updike, J. (2019, December). Lost art: A writer who wanted to draw. *The New Yorker*, December 30, pp. 14–16.

Willemsen, H. (2014). Early trauma and affect: The importance of the body for the development of the capacity to symbolize. *Journal of Analytical Psychology, 59*(5):695–712.

Winnicott, D.W. (2016 [1956]). Primary maternal preoccupation. In L. Caldwell & H. Taylor Robinson (Eds.) Collected Papers. *The collected works of D.W. Winnicott: Volume 5, 1955–1959*. Oxford University Press.

Winnicott, D.W. (1962). Communication between individuals examined with reference to the development of a capacity for communication in the individual infant. A not final not complete unpublished manuscript presented to the San Francisco Psychoanalytic Society and Institute on October 8, 1962.

Winnicott, D.W. (2016 [1963]). Communicating and not communicating, leading to the studies of certain opposites - BPAS (not final version), 15 May 1963. In R. Adès (Ed.) *The collected works of D. W. Winnicott: Volume 12, appendices and bibliographies.* Oxford University Press.

Winnicott, D.W. (2016 [1970]). Basis for self in body. In L. Caldwell, L. & Taylor Robinson, H. (Eds.), *The collected works of D.W. Winnicott: Volume 9, 1969–1971.* Oxford University Press.

Part V

Body in breakdown

14 Introduction

Caron Harrang, Drew Tillotson, and Nancy C. Winters

In each chapter of this part, analyst and analysand are confronted with body in breakdown. Comparing the similarities and differences in how these analytic authors understand and address the intersecting significance of physical and emotional illness provides a rich opportunity for enhancing appreciation of the mind–body relationship in psychoanalytic work with all patients.

The search for understanding the mechanisms involved in psychosomatic illness has been a longstanding challenge for psychoanalysts. Oscar Romero takes a novel approach in "The self as a refugee in the psychosomatic condition." Departing from the association of psychosomatic primarily with illness he says, "We are all psychosomatic living organisms." Interestingly, this suggests 'psychosomatic' expresses the mind–body relationship that is balanced in health and only problematic under certain circumstances. When things go awry psychosomatic illness can develop. This is an important distinction because it draws attention to the ongoing importance of the mind–body relationship in health as well as in disease.

With this evolutionary lens Romero sets out his hypothesis. A key clinical feature in psychosomatic conditions is their persistent, enduring, and recalcitrant character. By 'psychosomatic condition' Romero means "any physical illness or organic dysfunction (conversion disorders excluded) in which psychological factors play a significant dynamic role in the origin of the illness or in the aggravation of latent organic disease in a constitutionally vulnerable person." He also includes transient "somatizations" that emerge during psychoanalytic treatment.

How is healthy psychosomatic balance disrupted? In an effort to unlock this puzzle, Romero takes as his starting point the notion that the body is experienced unconsciously as if it were an external object and the psychosomatic symptom experienced as a 'bad object.' For example, in comments such as, "My back is *killing* me!" Where then, in the internal object world the author wonders are these bad objects located? Drawing on concepts from British object relations, Romero suggests they are located in the interior of the body-object, thus becoming 'psychosomatic objects' that wreaks havoc on healthy aspects of the self. In developmental terms, a psychosomatic disorder may arise in the face of trauma coming from the environment or the internal world, both of which may overwhelm the self, thwarting access to good internal or external objects.

DOI: 10.4324/9781003195559-14

Applying his theoretical understanding, Romero details the course of analysis with a young man suffering from chronic esophagitis as they journey through the often confusing, sometimes maddening underworld of psychosomatic illness in search of refuge for the beleaguered self. Remarkably, in light of the patient's presenting problem ("my ulcer"), he fails to adhere to comprehensive medical treatment and shows no curiosity or concern for this incongruence. For a time, the analyst too loses his capacity for reverie and becomes consumed with fantasies of, for example, resolving the patient's difficulties by helping him to end a frustrating external relationship. Awakening from this "psychosomatic folie à deux" ushers in a phase of analysis wherein the analyst feels "immersed in the irrational inner world of the patient" including muscle aches, diffuse abdominal pain, and sensations of sliding or falling. Then, in a fascinating turn of psychosomatic events, the patient suddenly develops "severe torticollis" simultaneous with his gastric symptoms completely abating. Without spoiling the ending, this transient psychosomatic symptom proves rich in meaning when the patient reveals a surprising fantasy to the analyst. This transformation of bodily symptom into a waking dream signals liberation, for both members of the analytic group, from psychosomatic illness and a return to normal psychosomatic living.

In Drew Tillotson's "Body as enemy: the risk of coming alive" we are allowed intimate access to the analyst's experience working with a young man suffering from debilitating self-doubt and a chronic bodily illness for which there is no current cure. Through a series of detailed clinical vignettes, the reader is invited into the unsettling process of discovery as Tillotson struggles to form a durable therapeutic bond with Kage.

Their union, as it evolves, is challenging because it conscripts both analyst and patient into a battle being waged in the body between powerful unconscious forces for and against aliveness. For the analyst this requires palpably feeling the shadow of death (Kage means 'shadow' in Japanese) while trusting in his own aliveness to contain their ongoing uncertain analytic journey. For example, when they first meet the analyst is jolted by his patient's frozen expression suddenly shifting to a socially rehearsed smile. "It did not seem genuine," Tillotson says, "and struck me as slightly dangerous." Then, toward the end of the initial consultation after a silence, Tillotson finds himself saying "you are…so *very* sad." Kage bursts into tears, overcome with emotion. This jarring oscillation between false-self relatedness and bursts of genuine emotion followed by a return to melancholia is one of the powerful leitmotifs of the analysis.

Over time, Tillotson learns of two intersecting losses in Kage's life that gives him to experience his body as enemy and early death as inevitable. First, in his childhood, Kage's father dies after a protracted illness; a loss he's not been able to grieve. Then, in college, Kage develops wrenching gut pain, eventually diagnosed as Crohn's disease. These losses, the analyst tells us, intertwine resulting in Kage's unconscious identification with an idealized dead father that pits him against his own bodily aliveness when his gut becomes inflamed. Both losses are, literally and figuratively, undigestible. Thus, mourning and recovery are compromised. Tillotson's primary source understanding of his patient is linked to theoretical constructs including melancholia (Freud, 1917), inability to mourn (Steiner, 1990), being and aliveness (Winnicott, 1970), and catastrophic change (Bion, 1966).

In one of the more fascinating sections of the chapter, Tillotson describes a speech pattern he calls 'looping' wherein Kage tells a story about something, then minutes later, repeats it almost word for word. The analyst sees this as Kage's getting stuck in an endless loop, unable to face the pain of loss or perceive that anyone exists outside of himself who can help him. In his reverie, Tillotson "dreaded [these] sessions, getting caught in his loops with no way of reaching him." Although not mentioned in the chapter, Tillotson's description of 'looping' brings Meltzer's concept of the claustrum to mind; both analyst and patient stuck inside a diseased intestinal chamber with no way out. Yet, Tillotson does not try to escape what is agonizing to experience with Kage. Rather, he trusts if he accompanies Kage into the depths of despair this will allow mourning to resume and new life in its wake. For example, Kage says, "I feel hopeless and depressed at times…" Tillotson comments, "You're fighting for your life, inside." Kage replies, "Yes, growing into feeling more alive…it's terrifying."

Tillotson notes at the beginning of his chapter that coming alive is experienced "for some patients" as dangerous, risky, and destabilizing. However, in light of what the COVID-19 pandemic has revealed of our need for and fear of physical contiguity, it seems the themes explored in this chapter apply, in some measure, to everybody. This is because no matter how energetic and healthy one is at any stage of life; the inevitability of decline and physical death is a reality none of us can escape.

Nancy Winters' chapter "Autoimmune Autoimmunity as a response to analytic change," is an ambitious undertaking and a highly gratifying journey for the reader. Drawing on Freud, Winnicott, Bion, Anzieu, Rosenfeld, Britton, Green, LaPlanche, Catalina Bronstein, and the French psychosomaticists among others, Winters employs the case of her analysand Ariel, who surprisingly develops an autoimmune disorder at a critical juncture in her analysis when her bad maternal objects have been relinquished, thereby freeing libidinal forces to emerge perhaps for the first time in a meaningful way. This emergence, while longed and hoped for by both patient and analyst, catalyzes a catastrophic change (Bion, 1970) in the form of somatic dysregulation. In the analytic process of her reintegrating split-off aspects, Ariel's body attacks itself: she manifests an autoimmune disorder. Advantageously, illness interrupts Ariel's heretofore defensive and distracting "hyperactivity" by restricting her movements: her body must slowdown in order to keep pain at a minimum. This slowdown also provides Ariel some stillness to become more reflective, allowing tender feelings toward her analyst to be present and acknowledged.

This remarkable turn of events (from bodily betrayal and pain to unfamiliar contact with her analyst) understandably piques Winters' curiosity enough to posit a bravely innovative hypothesis: she sees autoimmunity both as a metaphor and a parallel process, in which body and mind are essentially indivisible ... but are apprehended from different vertices. I propose the very psychic change we aspire to in analysis may engender a shift in the equilibrium of the body's immune system that can pose a threat to physical health.

Winters offers a startling, compelling paradox: the *destructive* processes of illness may lead to *productive* reflective capacities that become significantly mutative.

In assiduously reviewing different theorists' ideas of 'psyche/soma' and 'mind/body,' comparing and contrasting conflict and deficit models, examining metaphors of psychic autoimmunity, revisiting Freud's death instinct, then turning to contemporary biological theories of autoimmunity, Winters develops a novel theory of how psychic change may induce a state of unregulated chaos, unleashing self-destructive capacities and engendering a "revolt of the body against itself, essentially a war within the psychesoma." Winters makes a significant contribution by following "Freud's use of biological models to establish guiding principles" in exploring recent developments in immunology to discover parallels in psychic life. She contemplates metaphorical and biological dynamics of an autoimmune process to reconsider the applicability of the death instinct in somatic illness. Running adroitly throughout the chapter, Winters' overarching theme is her position in the ongoing psychoanalytic debate regarding the "cesura of body and mind," which she notes was also a major concern for Freud: "the puzzling leap from a mental process to a somatic innervation" (1909, p. 157).

Winters' scholarship and clinical acumen are manifest and meritorious: she never loses the thread of questioning the relationship between body and mind, how unmentalized phenomena manifest bodily for some patients, and how that may or may not cross the crevasse to be "decoded" within the mind. The case of Ariel is a moving, profound example of how powerful emotional life and unconscious dynamics may be so threatening that they surface somatically, demonstrating—as Winters indicates—Bion's "unbridgeable gulf between mind and body in which meaning cannot get through." Winters' inspirational work with Ariel is a testament to her claim that "an important aim of analysis is to bridge that gulf."

References

Bion, W.R. (1970) *Attention and interpretation: A scientific approach to insight in psycho-analysis and groups*. Tavistock Publications.

Bion, W.R. (2014 [1966]). Catastrophic change. In C. Mawson (Ed.), *The complete works of W. R. Bion* (Vol. 6, pp. 19–43). Karnac Books.

Freud, S. (1909). Notes upon a case of obsessional neurosis. In J. Strachey (Ed. and Trans.), *The standard edition of the complete psychological works of Sigmund Freud: Two case histories ('Little Hans' and the 'Rat Man')* (Vol. 10, pp. 151–318). Hogarth Press.

Freud, S. (1917). Mourning and melancholia. In J. Strachey (Ed. and Trans.), *The standard edition of the complete psychological works of Sigmund Freud: On the history of the psycho-analytic movement, papers on metapsychology and other works* (Vol. 10, pp. 237–258). Hogarth Press.

Steiner, J. (1990). Pathological organizations as obstacles to mourning: The role of unbearable guilt. *The International Journal of Psychoanalysis, 71*:87–94.

Winnicott, D.W. (1970 [1986]). Living creatively. In: *Home is where we start from* (pp. 39–54). W.W. Norton & Company Ltd.

15 The self as a refugee in the psychosomatic condition

Oscar H. Romero

We all are psychosomatic living organisms. Similar to the early mother–baby relationship that constitutes a unit, the mind and the body are also an inseparable unit. However, when things go wrong, we can develop a psychosomatic illness. I am limiting the use of the term psychosomatic condition to any physical illness or organic dysfunction (conversion disorders excluded)[1] in which psychological factors play a significant dynamic role in the origin of the illness or in the aggravation of latent organic disease in a constitutionally vulnerable person. I also include the term in reference to transient somatization that can emerge during any psychoanalytic treatment.

The search for an understanding of the mechanisms involved in the development of psychosomatic illnesses has been a historical challenge in medicine. Object relations theory provides a useful means toward the understanding and psychoanalytic treatment of such conditions. The approach presented in this chapter is founded in the vicissitudes of the world of internalized object relations and its overlap with external reality.

Fairbairn called our attention to Freud's description of the superego as an internal object and implied that "object-relationships exist within the personality itself as well as between the personality and external objects" (Fairbairn, 1994, vol. I, p. 106). Melanie Klein described a multiplicity of internalized objects in addition to the superego. She stated, "There are in fact very few people in the young infant's life, but he feels them to be a multitude of objects because they appear to him in different aspects." Both Klein (1952, p. 54) and Fairbairn viewed the world of internal object relations as separate from and overlapping with external reality.

We are, then, surrounded by a human and a non-human environment with which we establish vital relationships. We also live in our internal world, where representations of ourselves (self-representations) and representations of others (object-representations) are in a constant complex interaction, rich in dynamic meanings. In early development, and based in the necessary human inconsistency of the mother's ministrations, the baby experiences her as a loving mother separated from an unloving mother (a good and a bad external object). These and other external objects are internalized throughout development forming the world of internal object relations.

DOI: 10.4324/9781003195559-15

I accept that, in psychoanalytic terms, the body is experienced as if it were an external object. There is an intrapsychic representation of the body and this representation is an internal object. It is the body as an internal object, which I refer to as the 'body-object,' and it is in a dynamic relationship with a multiplicity of internal self-representations.

We are all familiar with colloquial expressions that refer to physical pain or discomfort as if the affected part of the body were an external object. This experience is expressed in statements such as, "My back is bothering me again," "My migraine kept me from going to the party," or "My shoulder won't let me work." The internal representation of the affected part of the body is experienced unconsciously as a bad object. A central question emerges that I explore in this chapter: where in the internal world is this bad object located? I suggest it is located in the interior of the internal body-object, and refer to this internal bad object that modifies the body-object as the 'psychosomatic object.'

A British object relations view of psychosomatic conditions

A clinical challenge of psychosomatic conditions is the persistent, enduring, and recalcitrant character of their presence in the suffering patient. This implies these conditions have their origin in early childhood experiences. In my view, the libidinal tie to a seductive and rejecting internal objects explains the strong addiction patients have to the psychosomatic condition, often to the point of unconsciously sabotaging medical care and psychoanalytic treatment to the dismay of health-care providers and the psychoanalyst.

Referring to the early anxieties experienced by the infant, Melanie Klein (1957/1975, p. 229) states, "I have previously suggested that greed, hate, and persecutory anxieties in relation to the primal object, the mother's breast, have an innate basis." She sees envy as being constitutional adding,

> Another factor that influences development from the beginning is the variety of external experiences through which the infant goes … My accumulated observations, however, have convinced me that the impact of these external experiences is in proportion to the constitutional strength of the innate destructive impulses and the ensuing paranoid anxieties.
>
> (ibid., p. 229)

The central self is forced to take protective measures when under siege in the face of innate and preexisting internal persecutory objects energized by a person's recent external traumatic experiences. In these circumstances, when the self's capacity for symbolization and sublimation is limited, due to regression or developmental deficits, the body may be recruited as a defensive instrument. This defense is necessary to prevent the vulnerable central self from being overwhelmed by persecutory internal objects. I suggest a psychosomatic condition may emerge when a significant external trauma or an accumulation of micro-traumatic experiences (Crastnopol, 2015) upsets the homeostatic equilibrium we are naturally inclined to maintain. In what follows, I demonstrate how such events may result in the development of psychosomatic disorders.

I propose a person can develop a psychosomatic disorder when his security is affected or his survival is threatened by traumatizing external object(s) that attack the self through physical or emotional abuse, neglect, or a combination of the two. The attack may also be the result of an internal persecutory object projected into an external object that cannot contain it and therefore responds aggressively. Using displacement as a defense mechanism the individual tries to protect the relationship with the object by partially displacing the source of the aggression into a vulnerable body organ that then becomes a psychosomatic object. However, the external traumatizing object relationship remains activated. An example is the case of a child who experiences a strong aggressive response toward an abusive parent. To protect the parent, the child displaces the painful experience from the relationship with the parent to the relationship with a vulnerable body organ. The organ becomes the perceived attacker, over which the child omnipotently feels he has control.

In an effort to gain control and reduce the fear and pain brought about by contact with an external object into which the self has projected a persecuting object, the self internalizes it along with the traumatizing impact of the object's hostility and lack of containment. The newly internalized persecutory psychosomatic object is added to preexisting internal persecutory objects which together activate additional persecutory objects acquired through earlier primitive experiences.

I find Ogden's (2012) restatement of Fairbairn's theory of object relations compatible with my understanding of the genesis of psychosomatic conditions. I agree with him when he says that in trying to gain control over the internalized relationship with an unloving mother, the infant "… divides the unloving (internal object) mother into two parts; the tantalizing mother and the rejecting mother" (p. 61). A part of the infant's self-representation feels "powerfully [and] uncontrollably attached to the alluring aspect of the internal object mother, while another aspect of the infant's personality [self-representation] feels hopelessly attached to the rejecting aspect of the internal object mother" (p. 61). Both attachments are split off from the healthy body ego or central self. For Fairbairn, there is a libidinal link between the tantalized or seduced self and the tantalizing or seductive object, as well as a libidinal link between the rejected self and the rejecting object.

As stated above, the physical body is psychically experienced as an external object, which becomes the internal body-object. The body-object may include a persecutory symptomatic part of the body internalized as a bad object. This internal bad object is what becomes the psychosomatic object that then modifies the body-object.

Ogden (2012) believes, as do I, that the libidinal tie to the rejecting object represents an attempt by the rejected self to transform the rejecting object into a loving and accepting one. The rejected self feels it must coerce the rejecting object into recognizing the incalculable pain it has caused. At the same time, the seduced self is tied by addictive love to the seducing object. I agree with Ogden when he concludes that the infant's "efforts to transform unsatisfactory objects into satisfactory objects, is the single most important motivation sustaining the structure of the internal object world" (ibid., p. 63).

Looking at the early development of the psychosomatic condition, we can say that the infant internalizes the unloving mother together with a vulnerable malfunctioning organ (perhaps genetically determined) that becomes the psychosomatic object. Once internalized, the infant splits them into tantalizing and rejecting objects. The psychosomatic object that has entered and modified the body-object then attacks the central self. Besieged by this internal persecution, the infant splits off two parts of his central self in an attempt to protect himself from further fragmentation.

I suggest these two split-off parts of the self then attempt to neutralize the seductive and rejecting parts of the psychosomatic object. The relationship between these parts is very powerful due to their being libidinally tied (Ogden, 2012). As a result of these defensive mechanisms, the central self is impoverished and its operations become concrete due to the loss of symbolic functions.[2] We can deduce that when the central self splits off parts of itself, it undergoes regression to the paranoid-schizoid position where there is poor cohesiveness of the self and weak self-object boundaries and differentiation. This is the price the self pays in order to protect its integrity when powerful persecutory internal objects, coupled with the relative weakness of loving, welcoming internal objects, unite.

I agree with Meltzer in *Dream Life: A Re-Examination of Psychoanalytic Theory and Technique* (1984) that negative emotional experiences evoke or mobilize persecutory internal objects which need to be transformed into symbolic representations. In psychosomatic conditions the internalized psychosomatic object energizes the persecutory internal objects Bion (1967, pp. 38–40) describes as "bizarre objects" that imprison the self. As a result of external trauma, negative experiences that cannot be symbolized energize internal bizarre objects which then attack the self. The vulnerable and disturbing part of the body internalized as a psychosomatic object enters and dominates the body-object. This psychosomatic object undergoes splitting into a seductive (or tantalizing) object and a persecutory object. Under the threat of disintegration by bizarre objects, the self splits off parts of itself and these parts take refuge in and adhere to the psychosomatic object. Although weakened by the split, part of the central self remains protected preventing a more devastating psychotic disintegration. That is, split-off parts of the central self find refuge in attaching to a psychosomatic object. The weakening of the central self is unconsciously perceived as better than dangerous exposure to bizarre objects.

When psychoanalytic treatment is successful, the patient can gradually internalize the alpha function provided by the analyst's 'good enough' responses, consistent analytic attitude, and availability as a new good object. These internalizations tilt the balance toward greater reliance on internal good objects. The central self is fortified and recovers its symbolic function. With the use of symbols, the central self can respond to the internal trauma and persecutory objects by exercising control over them through a process similar to dream work. I would say that the patient can now dream the embattled internal object world and communicate it to the analyst and receptive others. Once this level of symbolization is achieved, the interpretation of meaning at the level of content is made possible. At this point, the use of the psychosomatic object is not necessary and split-off parts of the self are recoverable. The psychosomatic object can be abandoned and the body-object is freed from it.

In the next section of the chapter I describe my analytic work with a young man who at the beginning of treatment offered strong unconscious resistances proportional to the libidinal character of his attachment to a psychosomatic condition. His physical disorder had failed to improve with medical treatment. Later, transference and countertransference experiences reached catastrophic proportions that required painstaking analysis. The eventual development of a good internal object, which could compete with the psychosomatic object, led to a successful outcome.

Clinical vignette: a refugee hiding in the body

Paul was 27 years old when he came to the first appointment, referred to me by his primary care physician. Contrasting with his very formal presentation, he surprised me by asking to be called by his first name, even as he preferred to address me as "doctor." Paul told me he was seeking psychoanalysis because he feared marrying his girlfriend of five years whom, he said, often reproached him for being overly "demanding and controlling." He complained that she had "mood swings" giving him to experience her as critical, inconsistently passionate, and unpredictable. His anxiety was constant and severe and he had developed gastric symptoms diagnosed by his internist as chronic esophagitis. He called it "my ulcer" and said he would not marry until it was cured. Despite his very well regimented home life and work in the technology industry, he failed to adhere to his comprehensive medical treatment. He showed no concern about this particular incongruence, explaining that he had a very busy life.

Describing further his relationship with his girlfriend, he told me she was very caring and soothing when he was more ill with his "ulcer," but became distant and avoided him when he did not improve. He said she seemed "very frustrated after a while."

Paul is the youngest of three children, his brothers being 10 and 12 years older than he. He grew up in a wealthy family who lived in a cosmopolitan city outside of the United States. As his parents were very busy, active professionals, and frequent travelers, he had been since infancy mostly under the inconsistent care of multiple loving family members. "Nothing to complain about," he commented. However, he remembers missing his parents and playing alone with toys "for hours." He said his parents never played with him but when they came back from their trips, they brought him new attractive toys.

Paul is a very pleasant and polite young man; always formally dressed and arrived to sessions on time. Initially, he seemed to idealize me. He told me that contrary to "the failure" of other clinicians, he was sure I was going to cure his illness.

During the first months of analysis (four times a week on the couch) I developed a countertransference response to Paul's unquestionable trust and confidence in my capacities. I listened for associations that could indicate the possible dynamics of his somatic problem. Like his girlfriend, I too felt frustrated with him. It took me a while to realize that I was overly involved in the intellectual task of thinking about the conceptual meaning of his symptoms as a defense against the frustrating character of Paul's recalcitrant somatic condition. I was missing the fuller picture through my unconsciously motivated grandiose effort to live up to his idealization. He reported no dreams, and in the sessions his narrative was very detailed and concrete about his day-to-day life, work activities, and often angry interactions with his emotionally inconsistent girlfriend. Frequently, he interrupted his own narrative by stating that he was having too much pain in his epigastric area to continue speaking.

As treatment continued, I realized I felt angry because he was limiting my analytic abilities by not bringing material that could be analyzed. Feeling narcissistically injured, I withdrew into an intellectual pseudo-analysis. Similar to his concreteness, my approach became for a time similarly constricted. Gradually, however, I became curious about my countertransference response and realized there was a parallel between Paul's defensive concreteness and my own. This realization opened the way to renewed interest in establishing better contact with my patient and my more imaginative self. I had become relatively detached and distant, often thinking about medical ways to study and treat his gastric symptoms. I was afraid his medical condition had not been adequately evaluated, diagnosed, or treated. I had doubts about the quality of the medical care he was receiving. At the same time, I realized more and more how powerful was his psychosomatic condition and what a hold it had on us both!

Paul did not seem to miss me or his analysis during our breaks, after which he would resume reporting life events and his medical condition, focusing on his "ulcer" described as "acting out." As analysis continued, I regressed to hoping for a more productive analytic process. I recall switching my attention away from the possible correlation of the somatic problem with any internal dynamics and instead explored his anxieties regarding the threatening nature of getting married. I expected this shift would open new avenues of exploration and understanding in our work together. However, these expectations were not realized and I felt increasingly frustrated. Retrospectively, I realize I was being unconsciously pulled ever increasingly into Paul's world of concreteness. Inattention to my own internal world and Paul's inattention to his were practically indistinguishable. Looking back, I see we were engaged at this point in a psychosomatic folie à deux.

As the patient's physical condition continued unchanged, I began to wonder if perhaps Paul was not analyzable, or if he was not analyzable working with me. I arrived to the point where I began to 'like' his somatic illness, rationalizing that he could 'live with it.' After all, I mused to myself, it wasn't going to kill him. Alternately, I noted my private fantasy that he would get better if only he terminated his relationship with his girlfriend. Moreover, that I could help him to end the relationship. Reflecting privately on these fantasies gradually allowed me to notice the striking contrast between my growing frustration, despair, and anger at the lack of progress in Paul's analysis and his apparent impassivity.

After ten months of analysis with sessions that for the most part seemed repetitive and boring to me, Paul inexplicably began to appear calmer and reported feeling more secure and productive at work. I experienced myself as present but fluctuating between feeling close to him at times and emotionally distant at others. In an effort to understand this unexpected shift in Paul's experience, I turned my attention to analyzing my lived experience in the analysis. In so doing, I seemed to be in a position of experiencing Paul's early life internal representations projected into my body–mind. I now palpably felt the distant and distancing presence of his parents, at times, and the crowding of my physical space at other times. I felt the inconsistent closeness of his other family members eroding the continuity of my internal sense of security. I felt bored because at a deeper level I was feeling lonely and angry. The transference meaning of my countertransference responses had previously been unclear to me because my analytic activity had been hampered by the concreteness Paul and I were sharing. However, the analytic frame and, at another level, my curiosity and openness (beyond the countertransference) continued to be a consistent and predictable part of the analytic frame.

Gradually, Paul seemed to become aware of his feelings about moments of my emotional distance and became openly angry with me. He began to openly criticize me and the analysis and threatened to leave. Something was changing in him and between us. I sensed that a critical time in the treatment was approaching and I needed to be able to weather the storm. In a sense, his storm was now joining the storm in me and they had almost become one. I remember in one session angrily thinking to myself, "This is becoming a perfect storm." In more lucid moments outside of sessions, I reflected on the meaning of the term "perfect" and the meaning of the negative power generated by the two of us during this phase of the analysis.

During some sessions in this period of the analysis, I felt temporarily immersed in the irrational inner world of the patient. Paul was visibly agitated when expressing his anger. He spoke in a raised voice, in short, incomplete sentences. This was a big contrast with his habitual composure and politeness! I had difficulty at these times formulating a possible interpretation of the situation because confusing, competitive ideas kept crossing my mind. I felt very tense, had muscle aches in my upper and lower back, and a diffuse abdominal discomfort. I found comfort recalling Meltzer's comments on the importance of entering into a state of reverie, as suggested by Bion, to be able to immerse one's self in the patient's chaos, which meant being in touch with a psychotic part of my own personality triggered by my own psychosomatic feelings and symptoms. Meltzer (1984, p. 43) states, "[Bion's] conception of the development of the baby's capacity to think implied that it is not only dependent on the mother's reverie to put order into the chaotic experience, but on her availability as an object for internalization."

This part of the analysis, although painful, was no longer predictable or boring. Sometimes I practiced brief meditation to recover after sessions. During sessions, as I listened to Paul, I tried as best I could to enter into a state of reverie
as I sometimes do when reading poetry. My reveries during these sessions were
accompanied, at times, by a whirlpool of fragmented, occasionally disturbing images impossible to describe verbally. During one disturbing reverie, I visualized
the patient's esophagus as a tube of passage; like the dark tunnel of a cave with
salient slippery rocks with bats flying around as I desperately looked for a light to
show me the way out.

On another occasion, I had in my abdomen a sensation I recall having as a
child when I was going down a slide. Then, a thought came to my mind. The
slide was analogous to a tortuous passage from the schizoid-paranoid to the depressive position. I told Paul that I thought we were going through a difficult time
in the analysis and that he was afraid we were not going to succeed. Up until that
moment I had been dreaming the patient's turbulent internal world, but had not
yet been able to awaken from the nightmare. Paul did not immediately respond
verbally but in subsequent sessions reported a worsening of his esophagitis. At the
same time, I noticed that his rage had diminished.

Paul continued to attend sessions punctually but with increasing interest. This
observation was comforting in some respects, yet I worried about the worsening of his psychosomatic symptom (esophagitis). I limited my comments to brief
descriptions of what was happening in the sessions. He listened quietly and appeared less tense. I believe he felt respected and contained by my presence. At
the same time, periods of calm like these were typically followed by periods of
upheaval, although of lesser intensity.

When we had advanced beyond this stormy period, Paul suddenly developed
a severe torticollis requiring x-rays, an MRI of his neck, and symptomatic treatment provided by his primary care physician and a consulting neurologist. Simultaneously, his gastric symptoms completely abated. This new symptom felt more
open to exploration in that Paul was curious about how one illness had seemingly
"cured" another. Moreover, he was now seriously contemplating marriage.

Eventually, Paul reported a dream in which he saw himself as a pilot flying a
small test airplane. He was alone, sitting next to an empty copilot seat. He was
afraid of being helpless and had lost control of the airplane. After reporting the
dream, Paul told me he remembered reading "The Little Prince" during one of
those long days waiting for his parents to come home and hoping "this time they
will stay." He later learned that the author of the book had been a pilot. He told
me he was interested in understanding the meaning of dreams and was reading
about them. I suggested his thoughts in the dream were a reference to our work
together. After a pause, Paul said he trusted me but during the last few sessions
had felt a strong urge to turn his head and look behind him so that he could see
me in an effort to dissipate a disturbing fantasy. The fantasy involved his fear
that I might be distractedly using a mobile phone he had seen on my desk rather
than listening to him. He said this fantasy was accompanied by strong feelings of
abandonment and he'd felt like crying. I realized Paul was no longer splitting me

into a loving object and an uncaring object, but experiencing ambivalence when establishing closer contact with me. He both wanted to, and did not want to, look at me. Having reached a symbolic mode of communication, we understood how the antagonist muscles in his neck were in conflict and had become painful. He listened to my interpretation and smilingly commented, "You are right, this analysis has become a pain in my neck." Subsequently, the muscle tension and pain in his neck resolved.

The remainder of the analysis with Paul continued with transference manifestations that had symbolic characteristics and word representations that allowed for relatively easy interpretative work as the psychosomatic condition subsided. There were brief regressive episodes with transient somatic symptoms that seemed to momentarily block or slow the progress of the analysis. It was possible to overcome these obstacles by reducing or suspending my interpretative interventions, by patiently listening to the Paul's efforts to communicate his affective states and, most importantly, by joining him in these efforts. I noticed with relief that I too was now free of somatic symptoms during his (or our) regressive states.

Discussion: integrating theory and technique

Paul had experienced significant trauma as a result of the parental neglect he suffered very early in life. In response to severe frustration and anxiety he developed defensive mechanisms that later in life were triggered by new external trauma. His defenses included regressive splitting of the external object into a loving object and an unloving persecutory object.

To further understand the complexities brought about by the development of his psychosomatic condition, I propose we apply some of the aforementioned insights described by Fairbairn.

When Paul came to analysis, he had a steady job, a highly controlled predictable lifestyle, and relationships with friends that were emotionally distant, intellectualized, and organized around his only hobby: video games. Looking for emotional connection, he engaged in a relationship with his girlfriend that he experienced as complex and challenging. The perspective of making the relationship more stable and lasting through marriage, as his girlfriend desired, produced intense anxiety, and a psychosomatic symptom developed. Paul did not want to lose her but the prospect of marrying her terrified him.

Paul's girlfriend, as described by him, seemed to have personality features that limited her capacity to tolerate frustration and impairment in the modulation of her own emotional responses. These limitations, by themselves, would not constitute a serious handicap in her relationship with Paul if it wasn't for his projecting into her an internal persecutory object split into a tantalizing, seductive object and a rejecting object. A massive projective identification phenomenon ensued. She alternated in her identification with the tantalizing object and the rejecting object, and due to her own psychological difficulties, she was unable to extricate herself from these projections. Acting on them confirmed Paul's perception of his girlfriend as lacking constancy in her care for him including his medical condition. He couldn't trust her care.

Based on the theoretical formulations presented in the first section of the chapter, I suggest that Paul tried to protect his relationship with his girlfriend by unconsciously displacing his emotional investment from her into his own body; that is, into his affected physical object. He projected the split tantalizing and rejecting internal objects into his vulnerable somatic object that then became symptomatic. This dynamic understanding helps to clarify Paul's suffering from the symptom *and his attachment to it.*

Trying to control his somatic external object, Paul internalized it and this became his internal psychosomatic object, split into tantalizing and rejecting part objects. The psychosomatic object with its two components became attached to and modified an existing internal body-object. At this point, with the addition of the persecutory somatic object to other preexisting persecutory objects, the central self had to defend itself from being overwhelmed and fragmented. Defensively, the central self split-off part of itself into a rejected self and a seduced self that joined the psychosomatic object to neutralize it. The integrity of the central self was protected but lost its capacity to symbolize due to excessive splitting and projection. Paul's concreteness during this phase of the analysis is understandable.

The aforementioned describes the state of affairs when Paul arrived to treatment. During the initial phase of analysis, he idealized me, thus keeping me at a distance. He projected into me the seductive, tantalizing object and I unconsciously identified with it. I was the 'great analyst' who was going to cure him. At the same time, his esophagitis persisted and the analytic treatment stalled. I despaired and distanced myself from him. However, despite my frustration, I maintained an analytic frame and, as a result, Paul sensed I had not given up.

In the next phase of analysis, Paul became aware of my emotional distance which activated the other component of the internal split psychosomatic object. He projected into me the split rejecting object, and became angry with me. He felt abandoned and I temporarily identified with the projection but, in realizing this, did not reject him. An internal detachment of the psychosomatic object from the body-object took place and, as a result, Paul's central self became unprotected and fragmented. He went into a psychotic state that was massively projected into me. In response, I too regressed and experienced a psychotic state of body–mind within the analytic frame. This was a very difficult phase of treatment. Containing Paul's fragmented psychotic elements and my own became critical. My capacity for reverie and the unconscious communication with my patient allowed Paul to internalize a cohesive sense of himself. Eventually, the internalization of my analytic functioning created a new good internal object that overpowered the persecutory objects including the psychosomatic split object. Paul's central self over time recovered and the defensively created psychosomatic object ceased to exist.

Not surprisingly, transient regressions to the states described above continued to occur in the remaining phases of analysis but they were easily analyzed as he gained better insight and quickly recovered his capacity to symbolize.

Eventually, neurotic conflicts were more easily analyzed with transference interpretations. For example, he was able to recognize as a fantasy his thought that I had "abandoned" him in the session involving imagined attention to my mobile phone rather than to him. Moreover, Paul joined me in the interpretation of my imagined action (looking at my phone) linked to his experience of busy, absent parents. His doubts about whether I was listening to him, expressed through the onset of his neck tension, could now be understood as symbolizing his ambivalence.

In sum, I believe Paul's internalization of my analytic attitude, emotional presence, and predictable holding environment of the sessions contributed to the development of a more solid structure of reliable, good internal objects and to his movement into the depressive position. The predominance of new welcoming objects allowed split-off parts of the self to leave the place of refuge and reintegrate into the central self. The strengthening of the central self accompanied the dissolution of the no longer needed psychosomatic object. Paul recovered his capacity for symbolic thinking, brought dreams and metaphors that could be interpreted, and developed a transient hysterical symptom easily amenable to transference interpretations. Further psychosomatic manifestations that emerged, as they can in any analysis, no longer overwhelmed Paul's capacity for depending on his good internal or external objects.

Concluding thoughts

The analyst's engagement with the psychosomatic condition

I concur with Meltzer (1984, p. 37) that we must discover the emotional experience the patient is unable to dream, through dreaming with and for him. As presented in my clinical vignette, the psychic survival of my analytic function throughout the treatment with Paul was a critical factor in the outcome of an analysis involving numerous enactments and subsequent interpretations of the transference and countertransference.

In my work with Paul, when projective processes dominated during regressive periods of the analysis, excessive projective identification obliterated differentiation between self and object resulting in a confusion between reality and fantasy and regression to concrete thinking (Rosenfeld, 1990). At these times, I needed to contain my patient's projections, some of which were somatic, and dream both with and for him. In analyzing patients with psychosomatic conditions, I have come to believe the analyst needs to enter into an unusual depth of reverie and be able to tolerate immersion in the psychotic field including contact with the psychotic part of our own personality. We need to survive the onslaught of excessive projective identification and maintain curiosity. This does not always happen.

My work with Paul required frequent reestablishment of my internal relationship with what Eaton (2011) calls "projective identification welcoming objects" and an openness to overcoming personal obstacles. By personal obstacles I am referring to a process that involves examining moments when the analyst can become transiently fused with the patient's psychosomatic object or concrete ways of thinking or frustration to the point of turning to medical solutions in lieu of remaining curious about what is as yet unknown. I agree with Eaton (ibid., p. 29) when he suggests that psychoanalytic work, and I would say especially when working with psychosomatic disorders, involves turning toward our internal welcoming objects "rather than giving in to the temptation to slam the door on the potential of living through and transforming both the analyst's and the patient's distress."

We know that psychoanalytic treatment demands significant effort and takes time. This is particularly so in the analysis of patients with psychosomatic conditions. In my view, it is possible for the analyst and patient to emerge from a primitive world without symbols into the symbolic order where poetry can emerge after a prolonged period in which the analyst is immersed in the psychosomatic world of bodily illness concretely expressed. As this progression occurs, the analyst becomes for the psychosomatic patient the internal projective identification welcoming object that provides the alpha function necessary to transform unrepresented experience into lived experience symbolized and shared through language.

Object relations theory in combination with the analyst's capacity for personal reflection on deeply disturbing psychosomatic countertransference experiences offers us a powerful means of increasing psychoanalytic understanding of psychosomatic conditions. As previously stated, when the patient is severely threatened by primitive persecutory objects and has a very limited capacity to symbolize, he may seek protection by using, as a place of refuge, an internalized psychosomatic object that attaches in the internal body-object to split-off parts of the central self. The internal dynamics of these processes can be examined and understood by the analyst in a way that facilitates the capacity to endure the demands placed on us by the lengthy and cautious treatment of patients with psychosomatic conditions.

From my analytic work with Paul I learned how extreme and entrenched a psychosomatic condition can be and how arduous is the road toward a positive outcome. However, treatment of psychosomatic conditions is *not* always successful. This leads me to appreciate Paul's ability to find refuge in my presence as a welcoming object and ultimately rescue from imprisonment within a psychosomatic object. Still, I wonder what it is that may impair internalization of a new object and suggest that further research is needed to more fully address these questions.

The psychosomatic in everyday life

As this exploration ends, I find myself wondering if psychosomatic phenomena, outside of pathological conditions, may be present in the day-to-day experiences of most individuals? That is, are we often, momentarily, 'somatizing,' or displacing and internalizing stressful everyday life experiences in an affected organ and freeing it again when our central self recovers through internalization of positive experiences? I'm also left wondering whether the statistical increase of somatic pathology in communities where material and emotional resources for coping with social stress are limited can be fully accounted for on the basis of the individual dynamics explored in this chapter? Or are there other ways of thinking about the etiology of psychosomatic conditions that involve socioeconomic and political hardship and the impact of these factors on unconscious group dynamics? I believe the doors remain open to further psychoanalytic research of these and other questions related to psychosomatic conditions.

Notes

1 Conversion disorders in classical Freudian theory are conditions in which somatic symptoms develop unconsciously as a symbolic expression of intrapsychic conflict. In these conditions, the patient's capacity for symbolization is maintained although they lack the conscious awareness of the conflict and thus cannot verbalize it. They are operating in the realm of the depressive position. Antonino Ferro (2019, p. 57) uses the term 'conversion' to denote the discharge of "balpha elements" and their correlatives in the form of fragments of derived narratives. By contrast, he uses the term 'somatization' to indicate evacuation of beta elements that have not been mentalized or metabolized.
2 Meltzer (2018 [1986]) refers to an aspect of Bion's theory of thinking; that if an emotional experience is not processed into a symbolic representation, like dreams or thoughts, the accretions of stimuli are evacuated in some way by hallucinations, psychosomatic disorders, and [regressive] group behavior. The failure of the alpha-function leads to an increase of beta-elements that must be evacuated by regressive group mentality or somatic innervation, as the symbol is lost (p. 23). And, Searles (1962) suggests that concrete thought disorders result from diffuse ego boundaries, and symbolic thinking develops when the boundaries are gradually firmly established in treatment (pp. 22–49).

References

Bion, W.R. (1967). *Second thoughts: Selected papers on psycho-analysis.* Jason Aronson.
Crastnopol, M. (2015). *Micro-trauma: A psychoanalytic understanding of cumulative psychic injury.* Routledge.
Eaton, J. (2011). *A fruitful harvest: Essays after Bion.* The Alliance Press.
Fairbairn, W.R.D. (1994). *From instinct to self: Selected papers of W. R. D. Fairbairn (Vol.1).* (D. E. Scharff & E. Fairbairn Birtles, Eds.). Jason Aronson.
Ferro, A. (2019). *Psychoanalysis and dreams: Bion, the field and the viscera of the mind.* Routledge.
Klein, M. (1975 [1952]). The origins of transference. In *Envy and gratitude and other works 1946–1963* (pp. 48–56). Free Press.
Klein, M. (1975 [1957]). Envy and gratitude. In *Envy and gratitude and other works 1946–1963* (pp. 176–235). Free Press.
Meltzer, D. (2018 [1984]). *Dream life: A re-examination of psychoanalytic theory and technique.* Karnac Books.
Meltzer, D. (2018 [1986]). *Studies in extended metapsychology.* Karnac Books.
Ogden, T.H. (2012). *Creative readings: Essays on seminal analytic works.* Routledge.
Rosenfeld, H. (1990 [1987]). *Impasse and interpretation.* Routledge.
Searles, H. (1962). The differentiation between concrete and metaphorical thinking in the recovering schizophrenic patient. *Journal of the American Psychoanalytic Association,* *10*(1): 22–49.

16 Body as enemy

The risk of coming alive

Drew Tillotson

Being and staying alive in clinical work is not always a welcomed experience. Counterintuitively, at times the analyst's aliveness collides with patients' anxieties, their psychic walls, or dead spaces. This is the dilemma of two minds coming together: temporary but growthful disturbance. Hopefully these encounters penetrate barriers, awaken nascent or truncated psychic development. At times we help enliven psychic deadness or awaken paralysis. For some patients this is experienced as dangerous, risky, destabilizing. For a multiplicity of reasons enumerated in this chapter, such is the case with my patient, Kage.

In the first section of the chapter, using clinical material from analysis with Kage, I illustrate the impact of a chronic bodily illness on his object world and its interdigitation with his struggles to come alive—both psychically and bodily—and to *stay* alive. I explore how, for this patient, illness sealed an early object identification with a dead parent. This particular psychic knot caused the patient to experience a deadness inside, an "essential depression" (Marty, 1968) that preserves an un-mournable object tie that blocks experiences of aliveness, and bodily vitality.

I describe how Kage's analysis attempts to liberate the hold of powerful object ties that deaden his body and mind by helping him to mourn. Yet, liberation from painful objects produces its own terrors. Coming alive engenders significant risks; the benefits of change, while poignantly sought, are also unconsciously dreaded due to an inability to mourn an object tie that has shaped Kage's internal life. The experience of being with a helping other is foreign and confusing, accepted at times, rejected at others, even in the midst of relief from psychic isolation, and bursts of aliveness and pleasure. Kage's growth and transformation will be enumerated in the chapter.

In the second section of the chapter, I theorize how for Kage coming alive adds an additional layer of complexity to mourning in a body formerly experienced as vital and strong. Management of chronic illness requires *acceptance* of illness and discovering the psychological meaning of it. Something is locked in Kage's soma forming a massive resistance to recognition of the life-long nature of a disease with no current cure. Management of his illness requires use of immunosuppressant medication leaving Kage open to opportunistic infections and a chronic feeling of malaise. This paradoxical situation puts him in an intolerable bind:

DOI: 10.4324/9781003195559-16

treat his chronic illness and experience forms of illness as a side effect or forgo medication and suffer continuing bouts of inflammation and the subsequent sequelae of such.

I contend this paradox enhances the move toward a compromise of psychic deadness: sadness, disillusionment, resignation, and lack of hope prevents longed-for change. Change involves coming alive, in mind and body, all of which evoke catastrophic repercussions (Bion, 1970). Kage lives in an isolated mind, with limited enlivening, reciprocal psychic contact with others. How the risk of coming alive in a body seen as the enemy was navigated in my work with Kage is the analytic journey I describe in what follows.

Section I: Clinical considerations

First encounter

The following vignette describes what it was like to first meet Kage, my initial impressions and the experience of being with him before knowing of his chronic illness, and ongoing physical and psychic vulnerability. The vignette shows both the conscious and unconscious dynamics that later led me to understand more about his terror of coming alive, and how powerful the deadness in him obstructed his capacity for aliveness. We see a response in me that foreshadows anxieties about letting him into my mind.

Kage, a tall, good looking young man sat stiffly in my reception area awaiting his first session with me. As I greeted him, out of what seemed a frozen expression suddenly came a broad smile, a socially rehearsed expression one sees at parties sometimes when guests are introduced. It did not seem genuine, and struck me as slightly dangerous, although it was not a fully formed thought, but rather a quick intuitive jolt.

Kage sat down across from me in a formal manner, hands folded, legs together, very still. He was cautious and reticent with me, stiff and intellectualized. He explained in a soft voice I could barely hear, and in interrupted half sentences, that he was finally seeking help because he had the distinct impression life was passing him by. He felt like a "spectator," but had no idea why this detached feeling was so pervasive throughout all aspects of his life. He questioned his current relationship with Alea, his girlfriend of several years, because she had languished after graduate school, working part-time odd jobs here and there. Kage had grown increasingly uncomfortable with her lack of ambition. He felt he should accept her choices but could not escape privately feeling profoundly disappointed in her once "great potential," given her superlative education and initial professional ambitions. He talked about how over time he had become her "caretaker," how she cycled through bouts of deep depression and sporadic jobs and had come to depend on him financially and emotionally.

I wondered what Kage was bringing to me, what help he hoped for, who I might become in the transference, indeed, what I was already unconsciously becoming for him in this first hour. Would he become disappointed in me, like Alea, and would I not live up to his expectations? Would he become my caretaker? Would he try to rely on me only to have the roles reversed where I depended on him for something, and was this part of an unconscious phantasy about his objects?

Kage went on describing how he and Alea gradually settled into a "roommate-like" relationship with little to no sexual intimacy. He mentioned not enjoying sex much at all, felt little libido, and when he did have sex it was to "get it over with." His work life, while intermittently enjoyable, had become a deadened routine and he questioned how becoming a geology research assistant, something that appealed to the "scientist" in him, nevertheless left him unfulfilled.

He spoke of how, outside of work, he had become very involved in sculpture and pottery work and had become quite skilled in it, but this had become frustrating over time given he had some difficulties getting his work shown, or accepted into large and widely known arts and crafts festivals. After submitting photos of his work, he sometimes never heard back from them or was rejected by them. However, he continued to work long disciplined hours trying to perfect his technique. He said he was "obsessed and overly focused" with long hours of molding and sculpting clay, sometimes unable to stop even though many hours had passed, as it could absorb an entire weekend. He had difficulty falling asleep unless he felt he had "produced enough" for the day. When he was able to quiet his mind somewhat, he would lie awake, afraid of the dark, and worry some danger would apprehend him. He sometimes worried he was being observed from outside his apartment because he was a "white dude in an almost all minority neighborhood."

After telling me all this, Kage and I sat silently for a long time, while he looked off into the distance. Then, without much forethought I found myself saying "you are … so *very* sad." Suddenly, he started to weep. Intermittently, he tried to speak through tears, but the impact of his sudden emotional response overwhelmed him. Actually, it startled us both. He had not described feeling sad thus far in the hour. In fact, I had noted how cut off from his emotions he seemed and was relieved and moved when something deeply hidden surfaced.

Then, I noticed a distinct shift inside me: I felt some hope of Kage being reachable after questioning for most of the hour whether to take him as a patient at all since he seemed so deeply encased and rigidly defended. Heretofore, his profoundly encased presence left me a bit hopeless for him, and I suspect, caused me anxiety about being with him in intimate psychic contact. And I had felt that whiff of dangerousness when I greeted him in the waiting room.

The hour came to an end and I asked if he wanted to make another appointment. He accepted and we scheduled for later in the week. As he left, he extended his hand. We shook hands and with tears still in his eyes he peered tenderly into *my* eyes. This intimate moment no longer felt dangerous to me. He seemed deeply grateful for our conversation.

I did not understand my apprehension at that time. Looking back, I may have been consciously and unconsciously anxious about the degree of suffering in Kage, even though the encased-ness I encountered, the deadness, and flatness in the telling of his troubles did not overtly suggest a deep well of pain inside him. Perhaps I was unsure of being able to stay alive in the presence of these elements in him or what I would be undertaking by letting him into my mind. Maybe this accounted for the dangerous element I sensed in the waiting room when we first met. At times in other first encounters in my waiting room I have had similar chills of danger with certain patients, usually attributable to fear of the unknown or paranoia projected into me due to anxiety regarding their first hour with me. However, with Kage it did not strike me this way; it was juxtaposed against his shy demeanor and socially rehearsed smile.

I was immediately curious about the dramatic shift in my willingness to let him in once he opened emotionally, a mixture of surprise and relief which enabled me to access empathy for him. It was a powerful moment. I was struck by how trapped and sad Kage was for a man his age, but not clear what it was that evoked this feeling. Was I unconsciously anxious about something I sensed and dreaded? Perhaps I was caught in the poignancy of the level of suffering in a man ostensibly heading into the prime of his life, yet caught in a matrix of confusing sadness and isolation. The simultaneity of my desire to help him and the dread of the potential cost of doing so was elusive in this initial session, but I was curious. I was able to let him in, and he took me in enough for me to have some hope of helping him. Kage likely felt some hope that day as well which I imagined he hadn't felt in a very long time, if ever. Yet, some significant risk lurked in the corners of both our minds: my hesitancy to take him as a patient, his hesitancy to experience his deep sadness.

Illness revealed

In the first two weeks of sessions, Kage and I talked more about his suffering and he decided to embark on an analytic treatment. I noticed in these earliest sessions a deep sadness emerged in him when I grew curious about his father. Eventually, he told me when he was still a child, his father had died after a protracted period of frequent hospitalizations and in-home hospice care. He talked about cycles of false hopes for successful treatment followed by inevitable bad news for over a year. In speaking about it, Kage was tearful, admitting he'd not been able to fully mourn this loss and could not imagine doing so.

Kage was bringing his feeling of the futility of mourning to my attention: hope for help from me, yet resignation that no hope was possible. What kept coming to mind was how the stakes seemed so incredibly high and acutely profound for this kind of resignation in a man so young. More than once he talked about the lack of hope for a better life.

This was compelling for me because of something I felt in the first session: his words and stories had a somewhat numbing impact on me, it was difficult to think, then suddenly his tears and pain would bring me back to feeling emotionally engaged with him. This pattern repeated in the first several sessions: I would feel disconnected and bored by his numbing reports replete with copious details, only to respond emotionally to his dropping into something painful.

One day near the end of the third week into analysis, Kage revealed a complex, crucial element of his suffering which gave a larger context to what I likely encountered unconsciously in the initial hour. He walked in, laid on the couch and remained quiet for a lengthy period. Eventually, he spoke about a powerful fear of dying young, a sense of being resigned to a life cut short. When I queried about the intensity of this fantasy, he revealed when he was in his third year of college, he started having bouts of wrenching gut pain, blood in his stool, and diarrhea. Lab tests revealed he'd developed Crohn's disease, a serious but medically manageable inflammatory bowel condition. However, the severity of symptoms required surgery, then an extended leave from college. Kage said ever since his diagnosis and surgery, he felt his body was damaged and an early death was inevitable. Simultaneously, he felt an increasingly urgent need to accomplish something significant before being betrayed by his own body.

Looping

Early in my work with Kage, I observed a pattern that was challenging to be with: he could become at times so robotic, dry, and ruminative, that it was difficult to sit with. I thought about this in a variety of ways including, a schizoid retreat, a defense against anxiety, and a fear of contact with me. I concluded after some time he was not really alive in his mind and thought it likely related to his compromised bodily aliveness.

I noticed in several sessions Kage would tell me what I thought of as a *theory* about himself; obsessive intellectualizing, a kind of masochistic *looping*. For example, he noticed feeling highly anxious in social situations, usually at a party, and worried about not being interesting to others. He presumed he was not interesting because he had nothing noteworthy to add to conversations. He imagined people were bored by him if conversations lagged or there was a silence: he concluded the silence was because he was boring and people likely wanted to get away from him, but felt awkward stepping away. To mitigate anxiety *he* would step away and then felt isolated. Kage's solution then was to use cocaine or ecstasy to make himself disinhibited, more "interesting." He knew he used recreational drugs because he was anxious. Then, in slightly different words, he would go back and tell me the exact same sequence, with no apparent awareness he had just told me this. This looping could happen three to four times in a session.

His repetitive narratives grew increasingly irritating in ways that registered bodily. I struggled to not fidget in my chair and became aware I would cross and uncross my legs repeatedly. I tried to contain my impulse to sigh. I felt warded off, not seen by him, likely the way he felt in the social situations he described. However, knowing he was showing me what it was like to be him did not help with my irritation.

I noticed in Kage's ruminative narratives an *absence* of anxiety or distress. He would tell me a story about being anxious, yet his affect was blank, robotic. I came to understand he was trapped inside himself and could not escape or be reached. He needed to tell me his stories, but could not imagine I was there as any kind of help. It was as if he just needed to 'play' an endless vocal loop, hoping it would rid himself of something painful, and then he could leave. If I interrupted one of these loops, he would look at me, listen, then when I finished speaking, he would say "yeah," pause briefly, look puzzled and then return to looping.

I concluded over time this sequence expressed Kage's way of being in the world: a mind-numbing deadness. He used intellect to narrate experience, but without emotion or real psychic contact with himself or with me. He needed to list his experiences, some of which baffled him, with an air that all was *a fete accompli*. Things were what they were and nothing more.

The challenge of being with him in this intensified. I sometimes dreaded his sessions, getting caught in his loops with no way of reaching him. I felt consigned to be a witness, not to be able to contact him in any meaningful way. The agitating aspect of this was knowing he was communicating something he wanted help with but could not imagine there was help outside these stories of resignation and despair. Yet, he showed no evidence of despair or discomfort in the telling. It was a motoric recitation; Kage standing outside himself, outside of us, reporting.

I began to wonder how these bodily experiences relatively early in Kage's life had factored into his hopelessness of having a meaningful, pleasurable, and fulfilling life. Both his father's illness and death and his own chronic disease involved profound loss of bodily robustness and vitality. Mortality—his late father's and fears of his own—intruded into his conscious daily awareness, resulting in a defensive detachment from his bodily experience and paralyzing anxieties about his inability to feel meaningfully connected to others.

Signs of aliveness

Alongside these challenging, deadening hours there were occasionally times when Kage spoke sincerely about what I thought of as signs of life: pleasure and enjoyment, awakenings of newer ways of being and thinking. These arose more predominantly during a period when, after about nine months of our work together, he decided to end his frustrating relationship with Alea and moved into his own apartment. I saw his ending this relationship as a sign of healthy growth, a product of our work together taking hold, as he had been increasingly frustrated in a relationship he no longer found satisfying. He felt he was more a "parent" to Alea than a romantic partner and the two ended their seven-year relationship amicably.

Moving into his own apartment, entering a new chapter, created an opening for more liveliness in Kage's inner world. Soon after moving, he became romantically involved with Clara, whom he had been close friends with for a few years. He described a deep, growing attachment to her, something he said he had never felt with any other romantic partner.

Kage started mentioning how on certain weekends when attending arts and crafts festivals with other artists, he felt engaged, present, not anxious in his interactions with others. He described in great detail the power and intensity of beautiful art, sculpture, and pottery, how it moved him deeply, "penetrated his soul." He found participating in the group experience of artists appreciating each other's work to be immensely satisfying, and helpful in creating his own art. In sessions he became embodied and enlivened when describing how meaningful it was to feel part of a community of fellow artists. He took pleasure in feeling connected and relaxed with people, versus feeling boring or awkward. In contrast to the robotic reporting, he seemed alive, with access to a more fluid emotional life. Over time, I came to learn he was highly intelligent and deeply thoughtful when not caught in the grips of looping despair or meaninglessness. It was like two different Kages: I never knew who I would see from one session to the next.

This seemingly paradoxical presentation was puzzling until I began to notice a pattern emerging: after a particularly enlivening experience of attending an arts festival, a day or two after he would retreat into a state of bitter depression and hopelessness. Another way this pattern became evident was after spending a weekend with Clara and feeling close with her, deepening their sexual and emotional connection. When she left his apartment on Sunday evenings to go back to her place, he would say goodbye at the door, then soon thereafter feel overcome with sadness and dread. He was puzzled by his response because the weekend would be so good, only to be followed by emptiness and a fear he would inevitably lose Clara.

This pattern of aliveness followed by dread and a return to robotic relating was evident in our work together as well. I knew Kage warded off real contact through obsessive, intellectual defenses. I understood when contact was made between us, he could be quite impacted by our work, moved to tears at times, but psychic contact also increased his anxiety. He could feel lively, more connected, then confused and unsure how to be in this new psychic space. I surmised a retreat to intellectualizing and obsessing was part of maintaining psychic equilibrium (Joseph, 1989) at the cost of aliveness.

Clinical material

Over time I started speaking to Kage about this pattern of aliveness followed by a strong experience of despair, in hopes of engaging his curiosity. The following material includes excerpts from sessions on two successive days illustrating Kage's sense of coming alive in his mind and his body, and the inherent anxieties and conflicts accompanying it, along with the pleasure:

TUESDAY
KAGE: I've had terrible sleep the last two nights, hard to even get to sleep…then lying awake most of the night.

[Silent a bit, then]
   I feel hopeless and depressed at times because I don't feel I can defend myself. [Pauses] If I exist, it has to be defended.

DREW: You're fighting for your life, inside.
KAGE: Yes, growing into feeling more alive…it's terrifying

[Silent]

Trying to understand where this inherent sense of defensiveness—at what point did I feel I had to shoot down my own ideas? [pauses] I've felt *rude* at times for having my opinions and thoughts—insensitive to others—like I'm being mean or aggressive for having my own thoughts. I'm realizing I'm having negative feelings about anything that comes from myself.

DREW: Yes.

KAGE: [Pauses] I guess I'm starting to feel like there's a lot of joy on the other side of this—learning to *believe* what I'm feeling and experiencing. [Pauses] I'm worried I'll become too self-absorbed, which stops me…maybe I'll be less rigorous in trying to understand my thoughts. Even the most simple things require rigor. Like there's no amount of rigorousness to create a sense of validity of it—caught in a place of hope that something like that exists—that some authority will tell me it exists. Like things I talk about in here—my internal response to things—like nobody can look inside me to tell me it's real—there's nothing to make it valid to me.

DREW: Nothing on the outside …

KAGE: Exactly…I think I'm realizing that. Ohhhh, my mind feels like it's been racing forty-eight hours straight. [Pause] I've been trying to meditate because it's been so hard to focus on anything. I can't even sit still. [Pause] Maybe it's a positive thing that I suddenly have a lot to say [laughs].

Here, I was particularly struck that Kage could articulate how feeling more alive evoked terror. Yet, amidst terror he was beginning to wonder about "a lot of joy on the other side of this." Hope was emerging in a different way, an excitement that elicited laughter. He was registering some of this bodily:

DREW: I wonder if you're actually excited by all this.

KAGE: I feel it's hard to distinguish between exciting or torment—but it's like an adrenaline rush—like a rush of riding my bicycle. Maybe it's more exciting than terrifying.

DREW: And you feel it acutely in your body.

KAGE: Yes, more than anything, I feel it in my body, energetic in a way I don't usually feel. All this energy feels confusing [inhales deeply several times] I feel it mostly at night, when I go home from work, up to trying to go to sleep.

DREW: You're more with yourself and your thoughts at home alone.

KAGE: Yeah, in a way, it's exciting to have my own thoughts…but also challenging.

DREW: New.

KAGE: Yes…the challenging part is feeling this need to defend them as soon as I have them. It's exciting to start actually believing my own ideas… [pauses, breathing deeply, something he's not done in sessions before]. I want to feel I'm finding my voice. It's been hard to feel I don't have one. At other times I think I have much more of a voice than I've been able to believe. I've spent so much time reading or thinking alone.

Here he is able to describe having his own thoughts, finding his "voice," which I believe is fostered by my presence; a sense of being alive in the presence of an Other. I comment on this, and he takes it up:

DREW: You've been doing that more here with me—not being alone.

KAGE: I think, even in this environment, I still find myself being very… selective with what I say. Not because I'm afraid of what you will think … but more a habit that I don't question. I stop myself without even thinking about it.

DREW: I think you're starting to realize that I'm here to talk to, discovering I'm really *here*—another mind to take in your thoughts. That's been daunting, or unknown, with me, and in the world with others.

KAGE: I think it's been challenging because when I'm here, you're listening, *that's* a new experience for me. What's been challenging here is someone is actually listening. Almost a sense of not wanting to be wasting your time. Not to just say what first comes to my mind. To move the opposite way—to present something to you that's clear, more understandable. It feels new that someone's really listening to me. At times I don't know what to make of it.

Later in this hour, we see how enlivenment becomes a dangerous element to contend with: a fear of narcissistic destructiveness if he experiences pleasure in speaking his mind. His conscious fantasy is others will attack or reject him for it:

KAGE: [takes a deep breath and exhales slowly]. I think I worry I'm going to start talking too much. That I'll stop listening to people—become too concerned with my own worries and thoughts.

DREW: Forget the other…

KAGE: Yeah. These extremes that I've talked about. If I don't do one thing, I'll drift to the opposite extreme. If I warm to feeling comfortable with speaking my mind, I'll stop listening to others.

DREW: Take too much space.

KAGE: Yeah, exactly. I remember in school among friends, I talked too much, being too opinionated, saying things I regretted. But eight or nine years ago, it drifted to the total opposite direction. So difficult to participate in conversation. [Pauses] I went to a show this weekend with some friends. Afterwards, Clara got into this intense conversation with this guy about their childhoods. At one point she asked me if I had any thoughts. I wasn't sure I had anything to say. Wondering if I had anything interesting to add. I was enjoying just listening to them … it didn't feel necessary to add anything—it was different from being too afraid or locked up or frozen to contribute.

[silence]

I think something comes up when I think about it more deeply—a real fear of being rejected by people. Their response to what I would say would be harsh and critical. People may respond with anger that's hard for me to understand. People would be really cruel, if I allow people some info about me, they'll use it against me, I'll be ridiculed or bullied for thinking or feeling something. When I say something, I lose control of it. I think that's what makes me so self-conscious, if I don't say exactly what I mean.

DREW: You'll be attacked unless you curate it.

KAGE: Yes, it has to be a *strong* idea—like in my arts and crafts community, something I'll say will be miscommunicated. I'd be ostracized. I see that happen a lot in the world I'm in, the social setting. I really love this community and would hate to feel I said something to hurt them, then lose my ability to be friends with them.

Here, there is danger I could attack Kage for having pleasure or use his vulnerability to betray him. Also, a fear I will abandon or reject him. The next day, he expresses how bodily aliveness generates hope and excitement regarding new ventures:

WEDNESDAY

KAGE: Had a lot of trouble sleeping again last night ... was so energetic. I feel terrible when I don't get enough sleep [pauses]. I feel like I'm still in this place of being unable to relax my thoughts. Last night I was looking at PhD programs. Like, if I should get a PhD in what I'm doing now ... feeling like what I'm doing with my life is missing something for me, something more connected with people. My work is so cut off from people. I'm wondering if I might do something more helpful for people, the world. To do some version of what I'm doing for the rest of my life? It feels too far removed from people. It's so physical, mathematical.

Later, Kage speaks of a research director at work. A man he'd worked closely with relocated to another country leaving him feeling more unmoored and alone, at work, more open and curious about making a change professionally, dreaming of possibilities. Yet again, fear of making "bad decisions" threatens to curtail his aliveness:

KAGE: I'd really relied on him, to talk about things that were interesting ... so, before he left the company, it would be motivating to read about and learn new stuff about my industry. This experience now of me actually looking at what I really want to do is exciting.

DREW: Opening your head up to this possibility of changing ... it's keeping you up at night.

KAGE: Yeah, trying to figure out what's right for me and what's missing from my current work. [Pauses] I'm scared I'm trying to make a decision at a time I feel less sure of myself. Hard to know what I'm feeling and where the feelings are coming from. Worried about making a bad decision.

[He pauses. Silence for a bit]

KAGE: Maybe what's been difficult lately is nobody has been asking me what I think ... most of my work the last month or so is simple, not challenging. Yesterday I actually got to talk some with the research team.

DREW: That was stimulating.

KAGE: Yes, I felt really better at my job yesterday, talking to the team, it gave me things to research and to be excited about what I *could* research.

DREW: You felt more alive with them.

KAGE: Yeah, more excited, connected to them and to the job. [Pauses] It's hard to understand what's going on. I've felt the desire to leave the company for a while but recently it's been more intense, finding work I really want to do. Also thinking about going back to school, what that's going to look like. I've always been interested in teaching. Maybe teaching is actually something I'd enjoy... I used to teach tennis. I was a tennis instructor to kids when I was in high school and college. But I'm worried I may be too socially awkward being in front of people, and it's hard for me to communicate with people sometimes. I don't feel that great at it. I have such a hard time sharing my thoughts with people.

[silent]

I've been reading a lot lately ... Foucault's *History of Sexuality*, and *Eroticism: Death and Sensuality*, by Georges Bataille.

DREW: Sexuality and eroticism are compelling?

KAGE: [laughs lightly] Yeah. I'm surprised I've been drawn to it. Reading is only one part of it, but it's designed for discussion with others. Reading alone has made me miss school. The books about sexuality have been really compelling.

DREW: Looking for yourself in them.

KAGE: Yeah, it was a part of why I came to you in the first place, my inability to enjoy sex.

In these excerpts, we see Kage opening his mind, becoming hopeful, excited. He even brings in sexuality, a renewed interest in eroticism albeit an intellectual exploration. I see this as a procreative process emerging in his mind born of our work together, a burgeoning capacity to play with ideas although worried what I will think of his generativity. Will he bore me? Will he talk too much in sessions? Will I attack him for enjoying an enlivened and productive interplay between us? He dreams of movement, of change and relating more with people, spending less solitary time encased in deadening work that becomes laden with meaningless abstraction. Lying in wait, however, is the danger of being humiliated, betrayed, or abandoned if he hopes for or attempts to find enlivened fulfillment in mind and body. In all of this, the object tie to his abandoning father emerges in the transference alluded to in his feelings toward the departing research director he'd come to rely on.

The following material is from a week later. It shows Kage in what I call 'looping,' described earlier in the chapter as a retreat from the risk of coming alive. He starts by mentioning a pleasurable weekend experience, then moves quickly to a mode of complaining in a way that indicates irritation, yet is lacking in affect; how things are not right in his world, how life is lacking and monotonous. He struggles to hold on to what was good and pleasurable just a few days before:

KAGE: I went down south to the mountains for the weekend …went to this sculpture workshop. Had a really enjoyable time. Met new people. I was less anxious about it. I was wondering what it would be to live down there. [Pauses] Then, going back into work yesterday, I was realizing I'm not happy in my work. I'm not engaged. Part of me is feeling I should be looking for a new job. I'm so disconnected from my work. I've invested so much time and skill, but the work is so exhausting, uninteresting.

DREW: This, on the heels of feeling more alive over the weekend …the artistry, the pleasure of being with others.

KAGE: Yes, going from something I love, back to something I hate. My friends down there spend a lot of time with each other there. Here, everybody is so busy. I wish the way they spend time together down there, I could have *here*. I used to have that, but everybody is off living their lives now. [Pauses] It's weird how I don't like what my work is now.

DREW: Not meaningful.

KAGE: It *used* to be meaningful. [Pauses] Honestly, I don't feel appreciated at work anymore. I've been a part of every project, so it doesn't feel good that the amount of time and work isn't seen or rewarded at all, even though the work is more challenging now.

DREW: You're not being cared for.

KAGE: [he says something about his fantasy that when he eventually does get a raise, it won't be available for seven months] … like a nightmare. So, moving on instead of sticking around and fighting them seems it won't amount to anything. It's hard to feel the energy of what it would take to get new work. Part of me wants to step away and figure out if this is what I want now. I don't understand now why I do this work. It doesn't excite me anymore, which is confusing because for a long time my work was a kind of stability in my life.

This material feels distinctly different from just a week before. It is deadening for me, I have to struggle to keep my mind. He has an almost monotone voice, punctuated occasionally by anxious laughs. I don't feel we are connecting and keep trying to engage:

KAGE: At work, I'm doing a lot more research, which is what I enjoy, but lately it's so difficult. There's nobody that's senior anymore to talk to.

DREW: A mentor recently left.

KAGE: Yes, he knew a lot, he was a great resource, and could help me. But without that, I'm on my own. All these expectations and deadlines, it's so challenging. So, without him, I'm taking twice the time to try to figure things out.

Here, we can hear in the transference, unlike last week, I am now the mentor who has left Kage on his own, unable to think, use his mind. The object has abandoned him, and while I try to make psychic contact, it is as if I am not really there to be made use of:

KAGE: ... like you said, it's been hard to feel alive and connected to the world then to come back and feel I'm not connected... to be with people where it was meaningful, to coming back here then feeling I don't know where I am in my life. [Pauses] I'm worried no matter what I do, I'll lose interest and be frustrated.

[Silence. Then, he lets out a big sigh]

I'm searching for some meaning in what I'm doing with my life. Even with making sculpture, pots, understanding if I'm connected to it. I also feel burned out on it. This past weekend, I didn't feel any pressure when sculpting. I felt like even if no one likes it, it would have been special. I don't feel the need so much to be *seen* as an artist. The studio, sculpting, and pottery is not really that exciting. But if I'm just working the clay for *me*, it's not meaningful. Whereas if people are moved by it or impressed, it's more meaningful.

Again, after pleasurable experiences, both aesthetic and psychic, Kage complains bitterly, but without emotion. He returns to *looping* in an internal world where meaninglessness predominates, and hopelessness consumes even his artistic endeavors where normally he feels most alive. In the material, we see his despair and frustration. Yet in the room, I am with a child in the corner caught in himself, ruminating and cataloguing his pain without realizing I am truly there with him. He needs to pour out his internal deadness and resignation and have a witness present, a "live third" (Gerson, 2009) who doesn't intrude, but also one who can't comfort or offer aliveness through ideas, empathy, or being in our bodies together. At times like these, Kage feels beyond my reach.

Staying alive: a body's impossible paradox

After two years into treatment, I discovered a critically impactful truth which added a new layer of complexity to my thinking about Kage's internal world. He came for his first session following a break where I had been away for a week. I noticed immediately he seemed a bit fragile, a delicate quality, yet a significant presentness. He began telling me about his body: he'd had a flu a few weeks ago and since then his chest felt tight, breathing was difficult, and he had sporadic gut pain. During our break, he'd gone to see his medical doctor concerned about how badly he felt. His doctor noted he'd not had a blood panel for a few years or regular check-ups for his Crohn's disease. Lab tests revealed significant elevations signaling inflammation. A CAT scan of his gut revealed inflammation at the site of prior surgery. Kage said he'd quit smoking during the flu after his doctor reminded him smoking was one of the worst things for his disease because it contributed to gut inflammation.

This led to a larger conversation between us where he confessed he'd stopped taking medication for his disease two years ago. I said this was not what he told me then, when he indicated his disease was managed by medication and regular medical monitoring. In fact, recently when I inquired how he was handling his illness, he'd told me he was taking medication and his disease was "managed."

I realized, given the timeline, Kage had stopped his medication *before* beginning treatment with me. He rationalized he'd stopped medication because "it kills white blood cells" to prevent inflammation. This immunosuppressive effect left him vulnerable to colds and flu and "feeling ill all the time." Without medication he felt "more normal at least" even as his disease went untreated. But this was a despairing trade-off for Kage: the sacrifice for *staying* alive was a susceptibility to lesser kinds of illnesses, a constant malaise reminding him of the larger enemy within his body.

I was taken aback by the profundity and paradox of the choice he'd made. He could see my reaction, and to my surprise it led to a deeper admission from him about his relationship to his illness and, more importantly, to his body. He revealed he often tried to ignore bodily sensations because he experienced bodily aches and pains as something possibly fatal, like lung disease or worse, which terrified him. He talked openly about his recreational drug use and smoking as a denial of disease and the despair he felt about it being with him for the rest of his life. He'd been trying to escape these feelings, and in so doing had ignored his health.

These revelations, unexpected as they were, created an opening in our work together. Kage spoke at a level of truth and intimacy not previously shared between us. More details kept pouring out. We entered the deep, coarsely graveled floor of his experience in a way we hadn't before. The poignancy of this *staying-alive-by-weakening* paradox moved me, and opened a new space between us; a shared psychic mobius strip experience wherein any way we twisted and turned, there was no separation between life and death.

In revealing this new information, an important mind–body dynamic emerged. Prior to the first appearance of symptoms, Kage had been a tennis instructor and avid cyclist during high school. In sports, Kage had been near the top of his class in physical strength and capabilities. His first bout of illness caused massive weight loss due to deteriorating muscle mass and a level of bodily weakness he'd never felt before. It terrified him.

After taking leave from college and lengthy recovery from surgery, each time he went back to the gym to rebuild his strength, because of the immunosuppressant medication, he would inevitably get a bad cold or flu, be in bed for several days, lose weight and motivation to return to the gym, "what was the point of trying?" This conundrum coalesced into a much deeper conflict than I had realized:

his body had become an enemy, seemingly betraying him at every attempt to regain health and resiliency.

As a young adult, Kage started smoking cigarettes and using drugs in nightclubs where he socialized with friends who used stimulants and hypnotics to stay up late at night and dance, and hear music in the clubs. Drugs reduced his social anxieties and offered the illusion of feeling temporarily "normal." Yet recently, visiting his doctor and seeing the lab results forced him to rethink his self-destructive behavior. He had been pretending his disease wasn't real, hadn't come to terms with the permanence of his illness. When he let himself think about it, he became deeply depressed about how taking medication to suppress his immune system was so difficult to reconcile, "It's a kind of despair." I commented on the irony of taking something to help his disease, which ended up making his body feel worse and vulnerable to infections.

This was the most Kage had ever revealed about living with his disease, of being in his body. He not only faced the risk of *coming* alive, he'd been coping with the trade-off of feeling worse and more vulnerable all in the service of *staying* alive. The compromise had been to use drugs to enliven, because disease would always win out in the end; he'd been warding off mourning his once healthy, vital, strong body.

This new information opened the door to understanding Kage's frequent oscillation between aliveness and deadness in our work, enlivening contact followed by retreating to despair. At last, the psychic knot I had detected when I first met Kage—the feeling of disease as yet unnamed—was beginning to make sense. The compromise formation (Freud, 1923, p. 242)—aliveness perceived as intolerably painful and life-threatening—would not be solved without untangling this complicated knot.

For Kage, catalyzing hope and aliveness signals catastrophic change (Bion, 1966), a loss of an old object tie, but also the recognition and acceptance of a chronic disease with no current cure. Going off "toxic" medication and instead taking stimulants and hypnotics denies a diseased body: a manic defense preventing him from feeling the loss of his prior healthy body. It fills him with false enlivenment and wards off grief. Yet using substances inevitably leads to increased complications from his autoimmune disease. Moments of sober clarity allow Kage to recognize he's been avoiding mourning the vital body of his past, and in so doing shutting himself out of the aliveness he might otherwise experience in his present life.

Coming alive psychically in analysis carries *multiple* risks for Kage including facing life in a compromised body capable of illness. Pleasure is fleeting because it means aliveness in a body he has tried to fool himself into believing is *not ill*. Denial of his disease, to be like everybody else, is a falsehood. How can Kage feel alive when it means acknowledging the limits to aliveness and requires mourning? He can realistically expect only so much pleasure with the specter of illness looming in the background; a cruel irony sometimes felt as aliveness is exclusively for those who are not living with a chronic disease.

Section II: Theoretical discussion

Thus far, using detailed clinical material, I have described Kage's dilemma as one of coming alive and staying alive against the challenges of living in a body with chronic illness. I have illustrated challenging aspects of his psyche that resist aliveness and a sense of bodily vitality: depressive withdrawal, a sense of resignation, meaninglessness, self-reproach, and crippling anxieties about relating to others.

I turn now to theoretical considerations to conceptualize Kage's dilemmas and our analytic journey together thus far. First, I explore the impact of his father's untimely death coupled with the later impact of developing a chronic disease. Both events required mourning that he was incapable of prior to seeking treatment with me. I contend he suffers from melancholia (Freud, 1917, p. 243) and an inability to mourn (Steiner, 2005, p. 97) the double loss of a father and a healthy enlivened body. I then turn to Winnicott's (1970) ideas about aliveness, transitional phenomena and potential space (1971) to understand Kage's early life and adolescence before the discovery of his Crohn's disease and subsequent surgery. Finally, I consider Bion's (1966) concept of catastrophic change as a way to understand how Kage's analysis catalyzed the struggle between aliveness and a resignation to a deadened existence with limited capacities for pleasure and hope.

Melancholia: impediments to mourning

Freud (1917) famously drew a distinction between the process of mourning and that which produced a more pathological response to loss, or "melancholia" (p. 244). For Freud, mourning is a normal reaction to the loss of a loved one, a reaction that follows a course of time, then gradually abates as loss is integrated allowing one to move forward and love again rather than becoming encapsulated in a prolonged state of grief.

Kage came to treatment feeling cut off from the world. He had very little libido and described life passing him by, as if he were in a bubble. Freud would likely have found Kage to be melancholic, noting there is a predominant feature in melancholia not found in mourning:

> an extraordinary diminution in his self-regard … In mourning it is the world which has become poor and empty; in melancholia it is the ego itself. The patient represents his ego to us as worthless, incapable of any achievement and morally despicable; he reproaches himself, vilifies himself and expects to be cast out and punished.
>
> (p. 246)

The self is turned inward, and harsh; life becomes devoid of meaning:

> The distinguishing mental features of melancholia are a profoundly painful dejection, cessation of interest in the outside world, loss of the capacity to

love, inhibition of all activity, and a lowering of the self-regarding feelings to a degree that finds utterance in self-reproaches and self-revilings, and culminates in a delusional expectation of punishment.

(p. 244)

all of which are descriptive of Kage's psychic life.

As described earlier, Kage said he could not imagine being able to fully mourn the loss of his father. In one session, he described feeling he was supposed to follow in his father's footsteps, a highly regarded and well-respected man in their community. Yet, he could not articulate how he came to believe this. In one sense, he had overidentified with a dying, dead father, and because of this had been living in what Reis (2019) calls a "zombie state... [in which] they are living a deadness that they have come to inhabit as if it were a full experience of aliveness" (p. 34). Winnicott (1986, p. 50) describes it thus: "The symptom of uncreative living is the feeling that nothing means anything, of futility, I couldn't care less."

Steiner's (2005) ideas augment Freud's on the conflict between mourning and melancholia, and further elaborate the difficulty Kage has had in what I am calling a double or *fused mourning* of his identification with his lost father and a lost bodily robustness he once enjoyed. Of particular interest to me in Steiner's work is his conceptualization of failed mourning relevant to what I believe led Kage to finally seek treatment. He intuitively realized he had no idea how to relinquish a powerful identification with a larger than life father who died (a bodily illness as powerful signifier of death). Nor did he know how to come alive in psyche and soma (Winnicott, 1949, p. 243) while living with a chronic illness whose management requires a compromised immune system. Steiner precisely captures this fused mourning of paternal object and *body-as-object* I hypothesize is a source of profound and painful conflict within Kage:

> ... the patient attempts to deny the loss by trying to possess and preserve the object, and one of the ways he does this is by identification with it ... Because of the identification with the object, *the mourner believes that if the object dies, then he must die with it, and, conversely, if the mourner is to survive, then the reality of loss of the object has to be denied* (my emphasis). It is often at this first stage that mourning becomes stalled, as the defenses leading to melancholia are deployed ... melancholia can be thought of as a failed mourning.

(p. 97)

I contend this "stalled" mourning led Kage to realize he did not want a life without hope, a meaningless existence with some sporadic bright moments, without a sustained sense of purpose, creativity, or libidinal pleasure. Yet he was caught in a compromise formation (Freud, 1923, p. 242), a conflict between an unconscious identification with a dead father object and a conscious loss of bodily integrity, preventing him from mourning either loss. He could feel inner pain and consciously observe his lack of liveliness and pleasure, his fear of engaging with others, while yearning to break out of this encasing bubble:

> The conflict becomes more conscious as the patient's reality sense persuades him that the loss can be faced, while the patient's preferences, in contrast, create the illusion that the object remains alive. The compromise provided by the melancholic solution that up to now has sustained an equilibrium no longer satisfies the patient, as he begins to become aware of the wish to once more engage in life and to allow development to proceed.
>
> (Steiner, 2005, p. 98)

I believe it was the pressure of his "wish to once more engage in life" that ultimately led him to believe there might be help from someone other than himself, that seeking help was and is one of his key strengths. Kage's awareness of this painful conflict led him to consider his losses could potentially be "faced," and he somehow knew he could not face them alone.

Coming and staying alive as catastrophe

Winnicott's (1970) ideas are pertinent to formulating Kage's dilemma in coming alive, particularly his struggle with holding on to moments of pleasure or times of enlivenment through aesthetic experiences:

> To be creative a person must *exist and have a feeling of existing* (emphasis mine), not in conscious awareness, but as a basic place to operate from. Creativity is then the doing that arises out of being. It indicates that he who is, is alive … unless at rest, the person is reaching out in some way so that if an object is in the way there can be a relationship … *Be* before *Do*. *Be* has to develop behind *Do* (emphasis mine) … The origin … is the individual's genetically determined tendency to be alive and to stay alive and to relate to objects that get in the way when the moment comes for reaching out, even for the moon.
>
> (pp. 41–42)

Goldberg (this publication) elaborates this idea further: "Winnicott insists that only through the experience of living in the psyche-soma can a person feel alive and real … the ongoing well-being of self depends upon the psyche's embeddedness in a living body." Kage was capable of reaching out and relating to objects "in the way," yet he had an inconsistent sense of personal existence: the creative act of being alive by having an embodied place to operate from. Winnicott's (1971) ideas regarding the transitional object and transitional phenomena (pp. 1–34), as well as his concept of potential space (pp. 144–148) illustrated in *Playing and Reality* are relevant here. Indeed, it is this very reaching out *for* and *to* objects, this "tendency to be alive and to stay alive" (Winnicott, 1986, p. 42), that ironically destabilizes Kage's sense of hope, creativity, or enlivening contact between us.

In seeking to understand Kage's moves toward coming alive followed soon-after by regression to a melancholic stasis, as well as obstructions in mourning his dead father and his vital body prior to illness, Bion's (1965, p. 4) concept of catastrophic change most closely illustrates Kage's terror of mourning and relinquishment of old object ties. Bion suggests psychoanalysis may be viewed as a group of transformations and utilizes the visual arts to create an analogy between a painter and a psychoanalyst:

> The original experience, the realization, in the instance of the painter the subject that he paints, and in the instance of the psychoanalyst the experi-ence of analyzing his patient, are *transformed* (emphasis Bion's) by painting in the one, and analysis in the other into a painting and a psycho-analytic description respectively. The psycho-analytic interpretation ... can be seen to belong to this same group of transformations. An interpretation is a trans-formation; to display the invariants, an experience, felt and described in one way, is described in another.
>
> (p. 4)

Transformations in the analytic setting occur in a more or less controlled envi-ronment, in the sense that the analyst provides a frame aimed at containing the disturbing impact of psychoanalytic work. The setting then is apt to evoke intense or sudden bodily and emotional phenomena in patients, but at what cost? How are we to know when we begin work with a patient what is their psychic struc-ture or capacity for tolerating regressive experiences? In Kage's case, I had hints in the beginning of his profound sadness alongside his intellectualized defenses. However, it wasn't until I was able to observe dramatic oscillations between en-livenment and melancholia that I could ascertain the depth of what might be threatening to erupt.

Bion (1965, p. 8) describes the power of catastrophic change:

> It is catastrophic in the restricted sense of an event producing a subversion of the order or system of things; it is catastrophic in the sense that it is accompa-nied by feelings of disaster in the participants; it is catastrophic in the sense that it is sudden and violent in an almost physical way.
>
> (Levine, 2009, p. 77)

raises an important question pertinent to my work with Kage (whom I consider having a neurotic structure) when he notes Bion's description of catastrophic change is accompanied by a clinical vignette from the treatment of a border-line psychotic patient. Yet, according to Levine (2009, p. 77) Bion later avers in *Attention and Interpretation* that "all emotional growth and change is at some level experienced as catastrophic and threatening, even for the neurotic patient or the nonpsychotic portions of the patient's mind." In light of Levine's astute observa-tion, which I agree with, every analytic treatment eventually reaches a potential for catastrophic change.

Others have taken up Bion's catastrophic change (e.g. Gaddini, 1981; Lombardi, 2009, to name a few). Goldberg's (2008, p. 6) ideas resonate most in my work with Kage:

> Catastrophic Change ... is not only a necessary feature of psychical growth, but is its apotheosis. If we are to grow and develop, it is imperative that we become permeable to new experiences of psychical and external reality, even as this permeability disturbs our equilibrium ... But why should this openness to experiencing the reality of things ... cause such disruption to our consciousness, and bring such turbulent intimations of catastrophe? What is so disturbing about encountering reality?

Goldberg's question about encountering reality is crucial in understanding Kage's losses: loss of his actual father as well as diminished bodily vitality and integrity due to chronic illness. These are conscious experiences, yet their hold on him has significant implications for his unconscious life. How best then to help him mourn and integrate such losses, to be with his intellectual explanations without inadvertently shaming him (i.e. my bodily restlessness, my impulse to sigh) while encouraging reflection that will catalyze mourning? Kage's fused losses are extensive and psychically entangled. Grief opens a series of life losses, but can this catastrophe be facilitated in such a way to engender a life with bodily vitality? Can he mourn the father he lost by relinquishing melancholic ties to an idealized object? Can he hold a damaged body with tenderness *and* his fears of more illness as a result of attempts to save it? Can he come to accept his body on terms that mitigate fear of sickness and mortality?

Conclusion

The genesis of this chapter came through an experience of being captured by the profundity of Kage's suffering. Of particular curiosity was his relationship to a chronic disease with no cure, diagnosed in his young adulthood, which left him deeply depressed and resigned to a shortened existence and feeling of doom.

As Kage's analysis took hold, I grew perplexed about his internal life as more was revealed about his past and I lived with him in the transference and countertransference. Ultimately, discovering his not taking medication for his disease prior to beginning analysis along with manic flights into recreational drug use as disavowal of the seriousness of his disease led to a watershed moment in his analysis; a place where were able to begin again with truth laid out before us.

Yet, this new beginning also revealed a more complex dilemma, a *double mourning*. As stated throughout, Kage's psychic dilemma centered on his inability to mourn the loss of his father and subsequently the loss of his own robust, sturdy body. In order to successfully mourn and to come alive psychically, Kage needed to face anxieties linked to his own bodily pleasure and excitement of mind, as well as anxieties associated with encountering me as an enlivening object. The ensuing catastrophe involved letting go of idealized and deadening object ties. Coming to terms with illness required relinquishing manic flights into a fantasied disease-free body.

Questions remain relative to Kage's prognosis for a more contented, pleasurable life. Rather than an extensive review of psychosomatic literature related to inflammatory bowel diseases, I utilized detailed clinical material to bring alive for the reader Kage's movements forward followed by retreat and our efforts together to untangle this weighty psychic 'knot.'

I employed Freud's ideas on mourning and melancholia, Bion's concept of catastrophic change, and Winnicott's thoughts on creative living to explore various theoretical contributions applicable to understanding Kage's dilemma. I agree with Winnicott (1966, p. 511) when he asserts that

> ... any intellectualized attempt to make psycho-somatics easy keeps clear of the very clinical clutter-up which bogs us down in our actual [psychoanalytic] work. We find ourselves involved in attempts to build a theory where the word should be *theories*.
>
> [emphasis mine]

This chapter speaks to the need in contemporary psychoanalysis for increased understanding of psyche and soma relative to psychosomatic conditions generally and chronic autoimmune disorders in particular. At the time of this writing, a review of Psychoanalytic Electronic Publishing revealed a mere eight references to 'autoimmune disorders.' Charles Hogan's (1995) was the only book I found specifically addressing psychoanalysis and Crohn's disease. As other authors have noted (several in this book), psychoanalysis has only recently begun to show renewed interest in the unconscious meaning of bodily phenomena after being ignored or taken for granted for many years.

The question remains what Kage and I will be able to accomplish toward a successful mourning and integration of more enlivened aspects of his psyche. 'Aliveness' has once again been threatened by the specter of COVID-19—a highly destructive, contagious, potentially deadly disease that is—as of this writing—still spreading across the globe. This has required continuing analysis via remote technology; this too requires mourning. Eventually, resuming analysis in my office will be complicated; we must navigate our reunion and the impact of parallel embodiments.

Kage has taught me how crucial coming alive in mind and body is for all patients who struggle with mourning, psychic deadness, retreats into deeply encapsulated places, and dissociative spaces. I have come to appreciate through our work together how important it is in facilitating my patient's aliveness to be in touch with my own. Understanding how coming alive psychically is at times felt as catastrophic allows us to take account of the arduousness of this task for both analyst and patient. Appreciating the risk of coming alive helps us to be with and hold patients throughout an uncertain, yet potentially mutative process toward growth.

References

Bion, W.R. (2014 [1965]). Transformations. In C. Mawson (Ed.), *The complete works of W. R. Bion* (Vol 4, pp. 115–280). Karnac Books.

Bion, W.R. (2014 [1966]). Catastrophic change. In C. Mawson (Ed.), *The complete works of W. R. Bion* (Vol. 6, pp. 19–43). Karnac Books.

Bion, W.R. (2014 [1970]). Attention and interpretation: A scientific approach to insight in psycho-analysis and groups. In C. Mawson (Ed.), *The complete works of W. R. Bion* (Vol. 6, pp. 211–330). Karnac Books.

Freud, S. (1917). Mourning and melancholia. In J. Strachey (Ed. and Trans.), *The standard edition of the complete psychological works of Sigmund Freud: On the history of the psycho-analytic movement, papers on metapsychology and other works* (Vol. 10, pp. 237–258). Hogarth Press.

Freud, S. (1923). Two Encyclopaedia Articles. In J. Strachey (Ed. and Trans.), *The standard edition of the complete psychological works of Sigmund Freud: Beyond the pleasure principle, group psychology and other works* (Vol. 18, pp. 233–260). Hogarth Press.

Gaddini, R. (1981). Bion's 'catastrophic change' and Winnicott's 'breakdown.' *Rivista di Psicoanalisi.*, *27*(3–4):610–621.

Gerson, S. (2009). When the third Is dead: Memory, mourning, and witnessing in the aftermath of the Holocaust. *The International Journal of Psychoanalysis*, *90*(6):1341–1357.

Goldberg, P. (2008). Catastrophic change, communal dreaming, and the counter-catastrophic personality. Unpublished work.

Goldberg, P. (this publication). Embodiment, Dissociation, and the Rhythm of Life. In C. Harrang, D. Tillotson & N. Winters (Eds.), *Body as psychoanalytic object: Clinical applications from Winnicott to Bion and beyond*. Routledge.

Hogan, C. (1995). *Psychosomatics, psychoanalysis, and inflammatory disease of the colon*. International Universities Press.

Joseph, B. (1989). *Psychic equilibrium and psychic change: Selected papers of Betty Joseph* (M. Feldman & E. Spillius, Eds.). New Library of Psychoanalysis, *9*:1–222. Routledge.

Levine, H.B. (2009). Reflections on catastrophic change. *International Forum of Psychoanalysis, 18*(2):77–81.

Lombardi, R. (2009). Symmetric frenzy and catastrophic change: A consideration of primitive mental states in the wake of Bion and Matte Blanco. *The International Journal of Psychoanalysis*, *90*(3):529–549.

Marty, P. (1968). A major process of somatization: The progressive disorganization. *The International Journal of Psychoanalysis*, *49*:246–249.

Reis, B. (2019). Zombie States: Reconsidering the relationship between life and death Instincts. In *Creative repetition and intersubjectivity: Contemporary Freudian explorations of trauma, memory, and clinical process* (pp. 33–46). Routledge.

Steiner, J. (1990). Pathological organizations as obstacles to mourning: The role of unbearable guilt. The *International Journal of Psychoanalysis*, *71*:87–94.

Steiner, J. (2005). The conflict between mourning and melancholia. *The Psychoanalytic Quarterly*, *74*(1):83–104.

Winnicott, D.W. (1949 [1958]). Mind in its relation to the psyche-soma. In *Through pediatrics to psychoanalysis* (pp. 243–254). Basic Books.

Winnicott, D.W. (1966). Psycho-somatic illness in its positive and negative aspects. *The International Journal of Psychoanalysis*, *47*:510–516.

Winnicott, D.W. (1970). Living creatively. In *Home is where we start from* (pp. 39–54). W.W. Norton & Company.

Winnicott, D.W. (1971). *Playing and reality*. Tavistock Publications.

Winnicott, D.W. (1986). *Home is where we start from*. W.W. Norton & Company.

17 Autoimmunity as a response to analytic change

Nancy C. Winters

> The danger of death does not become acute until it is clear to every beholder that a resounding success is at hand.
>
> (Bion, 1991a, *Memoir of the Future*)

As Bion reminds us, change is experienced as a catastrophe when the container of the mind is strained by an explosion of the contents of the contained (1970). In his example of the man who stammered,

> the words that should have represented the meaning the man wanted to express were fragmented by the emotional forces to which he wished to give only verbal expression; the verbal formulation could not 'contain' his emotions, which broke through and dispersed it as enemy forces might break through the forces that strove to contain them.
>
> (ibid., p. 94)

The stammerer struggles not only with language but also with his body (his mouth) as he tries to produce speech. The body too is a container and subject to being overwhelmed by the forces within. In this chapter I explore the analysis of Ariel, whose body was unable to contain the catastrophic change resulting from productive analytic work, and responded with an eruption of autoimmune disease.

Ariel was an anxious young researcher who came for analysis after a boating accident left her with arm pain that persisted inexplicably even after the injury had healed. Not knowing when or if the pain would go away, her chronic anxiety went "off the charts." Ariel's physical pain resolved early in the analysis, uncovering the existential psychic pain of her life, a deep despair at feeling she had never been loved, even as an infant. Her current romantic relationship was convenient and stable, but platonic and lacking in desire. Ariel managed her anxiety with incessant activity, a dizzying schedule of work and social events. When she began to experience new and unfamiliar seedlings of desire and erotic feeling as an outgrowth of the analysis, her body called a halt to the change. A debilitating

DOI: 10.4324/9781003195559-17

somatic autoimmune condition that made movement painful interrupted her hyperactivity and made her question the safety of her emerging erotic feelings.

In my effort to understand the role of her mind in bringing about this bodily illness I investigate Ariel's autoimmunity both as a metaphor and as a parallel process, in which body and mind are essentially indivisible, that is, are one and the same, but are apprehended from different vertices. I propose the very psychic change we aspire to in analysis may engender a shift in the equilibrium of the body's immune systems that can pose a threat to physical health. Paradoxically, the underlying disequilibrium of this physical illness may offer an opportunity for progressive psychic reorganization and growth. It is critical to understand how the analyst can enable the potential for a higher level of organization rather than progressive disorganization (Marty, 1968) at these nodal points in an analysis.

I also argue that the biological processes of autoimmunity provide new evidence for the death instinct in that the body/mind has the capability and readiness to attack and destroy itself; this capability is held in abeyance by regulatory processes of the immune system that can be disrupted by 'rocking the boat' of a previously established psychic equilibrium (Joseph, 1989). How the 'catastrophe' of psychic change might cause such a profound disruption in the soma gets to the enigma of the mind–body relation in somatic illness, which psychoanalysts have grappled with since Freud's time.

The leap from mind to body

A major concern of Freud's was the puzzling "leap from a mental process to a somatic innervation" (1909, p. 157). Subsequently, psychoanalysts of varied theoretical orientations have found the relationship between mind and body to be a rich yet enigmatic area for exploration. This relationship becomes particularly salient in somatic illness, where the psychic meaning of physical symptoms presents itself as a critical question for psychoanalytic treatment. When Ariel was in a particularly productive phase of her analysis, and considerable working through had occurred, a painful autoimmune response was unleashed. While a greater ability to suffer emotional pain is part of the analytic process, this emergence of physical pain was perplexing.

Psychoanalysis offers a process aimed at increasing psychological resilience, but in the case of Ariel, new self-experience seemed to have engendered a revolt of the body against itself, essentially a war within the psychesoma.[1] I assumed that greater emotional freedom would enhance her overall health, yet her body reacted as if its integrity had been threatened. How was I to understand an eruption of somatic illness in the wake of positive psychological developments?

Ariel's autoimmune illness had its onset just as she was becoming less static and frozen emotionally. A new ability to experience her erotic life as exciting and pleasurable seemed to be emerging along with new feelings of tenderness toward me. Such feelings had previously been either inaccessible or resolutely off-limits. In considering this apparent paradox, I wondered whether a seemingly beneficial psychic change in the course of analysis can pose a danger to one's body, and, if so, how does this happen? This possibility represents a particularly puzzling leap from psyche to soma. We are familiar with the notion of negative therapeutic reaction (Freud, 1923), according to which analytic progress leads not to health but to psychological symptoms, which Freud postulated was a form of unconscious self-punishment related to the death instinct. But here what is striking is the development of a new symptom, a physical one. The body has taken center stage; is there a message from the body that needs to be decoded?

The psyche/soma link in health and illness has been written about extensively in the psychoanalytic literature. In reading various authors, including Freud, one detects various ways of construing the mind–body relationship in somatic illness that are relevant to this exploration, and may be briefly summarized thus: (1) mental contents may be *causative* factors in somatic illness; (2) mental contents and illness are *correlates*, without a clear causal relationship (Marty, 1952); (3) the mind and body are inseparable and are different representations of the *same processes*, although our minds may apprehend them differently (Grotstein, 1997); and (4) somatic symptoms and our names for them serve as *metaphors* that help us to understand how we experience our body. For example, heartburn as a metaphor for acid reflux speaks to a fire burning in the 'heart' of oneself.

There may be various relationships between these different assumptions (the causative, the correlative, the same processes, and the metaphorical). In my view, all of these assumptions have heuristic value and stand in dialectical relation to each other, a process, as described by Ogden (1988), "in which opposing elements each create, preserve and negate the other" (p. 517). In my exploration of Ariel's progression from analytic working through to somatic illness, I found all four assumptions relevant to my thinking, but most relevant were assumptions (3) and (4), and the dialectical relationship between them. These assumptions would imply both that autoimmunity can be seen as a single process in which mind and body are indivisible albeit apprehended differently (the *same process* assumption), and that autoimmunity can be explored as a metaphor to further understand the psychic situation suffered by Ariel when seemingly desirable change 'rocked the boat' of her psychic equilibrium (*metaphor* assumption).

In this chapter I touch briefly on some differing conceptualizations of 'psyche' / 'soma' and 'mind' / 'body,' which express fundamental assumptions about mind–body relationships. Relevant contributions of authors who have addressed the mind–body question in physical illness are reviewed, starting with the foundational contributions of the Paris psychosomatic school, as well as others who have somewhat differing viewpoints. Included are several authors who explicitly use the concept of autoimmunity as a psychical metaphor. Since metaphors inform how we experience the body, and therefore the meanings we assign to our bodily experience, I pose the question as to whether intuitive metaphors of autoimmunity are consistent with contemporary biology. For example, Ariel felt that her autoimmune condition meant that she was attacking herself, and she came to see her body as a battleground between forces for change and against change. Was this description touching on a deep insight of Ariel's, or missing something more profound?

If the metaphor we use to think about a somatic condition such as autoim-mune disease is sufficiently different from what is currently understood of the biology, might the psychical mechanisms also need to be reconsidered? Newer perspectives on biological autoimmunity might enlarge our analytic understand-ings of the process of change during an analysis as registered in the psychesoma. Following Freud's use of biological models to establish guiding principles, and relying on what he referred to as "biological parallels" (1930, p. 118), I refer to recent developments in immunology, not to provide the reader with a particular understanding of the biological process, but for the principles it teaches us that may find parallels in psychic life. Therefore, no attempt was made to provide a comprehensive review but rather to ascertain principles that might provide clues about autoimmunity as both a biological and a psychic phenomenon, or to use the *same processes* assumption, a phenomenon that is singular but can be under-stood from two different vertices of observation. Finally, I consider the metaphor of autoimmunity informed by contemporary biology invites us to re-examine the relevance of the death instinct in somatic illness.

Defining the psyche/soma relationship

A discussion of psychic and biological autoimmunity begins with the variety of meanings of the terms *psyche/soma* and *body/mind* in the psychoanalytic literature. For Winnicott, who took a particular interest in this area, the infant's attainment of a "unit self" begins with the "psyche indwelling in the soma" (1965); the mind develops as a special function of the psyche-soma. In 1949 he writes,

> The mind does not exist as an entity in the individual's scheme of things provided the individual psyche-soma or body scheme has come satisfacto-rily through the very early developmental stages; mind is then no more than a special case of the functioning of the psyche-soma... I suppose the word psyche means the *imaginative elaboration of somatic parts, feelings, and functions,* that is, of physical aliveness... Gradually, the psyche and soma aspects of the growing person become involved in a process of mutual interrelation.... At a later stage the live body, with its limits, and with an inside and an outside, is *felt by the individual* [emphasis Winnicott] to form the core for the imaginative self.
>
> (p. 244)

Winnicott focuses on the psyche in relation to the soma: psyche as an imagina-tive elaboration of the soma, mind as a "special case" of psyche-soma, and body experienced later when the self has an inside and outside. Green (1975, 1998) further distinguishes between soma as purely biological, and body as psychically charged soma. Bronstein (2011) adopts Green's (1998) distinction, noting that the *body* is the "libidinal body (erotic, aggressive, narcissistic)" whereas "the *soma* re-fers to the biological organization (p. 174)." Bronstein notes that some psycho-somatic schools of thought see the patient as "bringing their 'soma' and aim at helping the patient acquire a 'libidinal body' so that the physical symptom can acquire meaning" (Fine, 1998, cited by Bronstein, 2011). Perhaps the libidinal body of Green could also be seen as relating to Winnicott's notion of a "live body" which forms "the core for the imaginative self." From Green's perspective it is possible to think of Ariel's difficulty as one of transforming libidinal energy from soma to body.

Bion's formulation emphasizes the tension between mind and body where body is seeking its autonomy from the mind. A view of a body and mind inherently at war is depicted in Bion's (1991b) late work, *A Memoir of the Future* (pp. 433–434) also cited in this volume by Robert Oelsner.

MIND Hullo! Where have you sprung from?
BODY What—you again? I am Body; you can call me Soma if you like. Who are YOU?
MIND Call me Psyche—Psyche-Soma.
BODY Soma-Psyche.
MIND We must be related.
BODY Never—not if I can help it …
MIND Funny—the meaning does not get through whether it is from you to me, or from me to you.
BODY It is the meaning of pain that I am sending to you; the words get through—which I have not sent—but the meaning is lost.

(ibid., 433–434)[2]

In this provocative dialog, mind and body vie for dominance and are unable to cooperate. The meanings of each cannot get through to the other, despite body's sending pain to the mind. Bion's view of the body and mind unable to bridge the 'caesura' between them is consonant with many views of psychosomatic disease, including Winnicott's, as a dissociation of psyche and soma (1966).

For Ariel, the meaning of her pain is indecipherable, other than that it hurts her to move, and slows her down. Yet she is convinced that it has a meaning beyond the physical. It is interesting here to consider Bion's idea of incommunicability between mind and body as a failure of translation, both in the Freudian (1896) sense in which repression is understood as a failure of translation of psychic material from one epoch to the next and Laplanche's (1987) idea of the body ego formed through the infant's successive translations of enigmatic communications from its mother's unconscious. Could Ariel's physical symptom mean that a message is not getting through from mind to body or body to mind, in a failure of translation?

Deficit vs. conflict and the death drive

Within the psychosomatic literature, Bronstein (2011) has emphasized a central issue is whether the model is based on conflict or deficit. In the Paris School, psychosomatic symptoms are believed to relate to a lack of psychic structure, called 'pensée operatoire' or "operational thinking" (Marty and de M'uzan, 1978), associated with concrete thinking and an impoverished fantasy life. Accordingly, unrepresented or unmentalized anxiety is transformed into somatic illness. This theory relates to Freud's (1917) concept of "actual neurosis" in which libidinal energy goes into the body and remains psychically unrepresented. Winnicott's (1949) view of psychosomatic illness as a seduction of the psyche from the mind back to its "original intimate association with the soma" (p. 254) bears some resemblance to Freud's idea of libidinal energy regressing into the body through repression, implying a lower level of psychic organization (Loewald, 1973).

McDougall (1986) has a related but alternative view that links actual neurosis to primitive phantasies and the need to act rather than reflect, referred to as "archaic hysteria." Marty (1968) described the state of "progressive disorganization" which cancels all libidinal activities and can produce an "essential depression" which "is also pursued on the somatic level where it ... causes a real physiological anarchy" (p. 248). Marty saw this process as an assertion of a death instinct that can eventually lead to physical death.

In contrast to these views emphasizing a structural deficit in psychosomatic illness, the Kleinian school, as articulated by Bronstein (2011), would see it as impossible for there to be an early state prior to the existence of unconscious phantasy, and holds that anxiety is always "linked to some sort of mental representation, however concrete and primitive this might be" (p. 184). Thus, there may be different levels of symbolization rather than either presence or absence.

Where these different views of conflict vs. deficit get more interesting is around the role of the death instinct in psychosomatic illness. Marty's (ibid.) view is that the death instinct exerts a regressive, anti-libidinal pull that leads to progressive disorganization, including at the somatic level. While Klein doesn't address this issue, it may be suggested that the death drive may not only be associated with annihilation anxiety, but also be experienced as an attack on one's own body.

Particularly relevant to Ariel's case is Laplanche's (2004) reframing of the death drive as the "sexual death drive" (p. 86). In contrast to the bound, more adaptive libido of what he calls the "sexual life drive" (ibid.), the sexual death drive is unbound, aggressive, and chaotic. For Laplanche, both are essential aspects of sexuality; the unbinding serving the constructive aim of taking apart and reorganizing problematic organizations, what Laplanche refers to as forming new translations.[3] Applying Laplanche's distinction between the sexual death drive and the sexual life drive would seem to be helpful in understanding Ariel's response to the emergence of new libidinal energy, the chaos and destruction that her new erotic desires brought into what had previously been a secure yet limited life.

Consideration of the various theories of deficit and conflict in psychosomatic illness is relevant to my search for the metaphor that fits Ariel's somatopsychic situation. A deficit model implies deprivation and absence, a failure to develop psychic structure, whereas conflict implies intrapsychic prohibitions of desire and suggests the metaphor of an internal war or at least a repressive regime.

This distinction, or perhaps dialectical relationship, will help us as we now return to the process Ariel underwent in the course of her analysis.

In the early part of the analysis Ariel had little hope that her body would ever relinquish the pain from her accident; she became unbearably anxious, leading to suicidal depression. She sought analysis to understand her extreme response to this injury. Starting in a four times weekly process on the couch, she initially felt held and cared for by me, and her physical pain resolved quickly. She was then able to turn to her deeper psychic pain, her experience of feeling profoundly unloved by a self-absorbed mother. For Ariel, her mother's eyes were black holes that reflected nothing back, no love, and no self that could be mirrored through them (Winnicott, 1971). Her mother's apparent lack of primary maternal preoccupation had, in Winnicott's terms made it difficult for Ariel to *be* rather than *do* (1971); and as she was unable to *be*, embodied desire and erotic feeling was also unknown to her.

Ariel had been on a lifelong, unsuccessful search for a replacement for the absent maternal love she longed for. Each romantic partner ultimately failed her, and after an initial period of hopefulness that I would be such a replacement, she became convinced that another rejection by me would ensue. As the transference deepened under the shadow of her certainty of rejection, Ariel had dreams of destructive female characters, phantasies of sadistic maternal figures who, in her associations to the dreams she connected with me. In one dream there was a female pilot who threatened to attack a baby she was responsible for, and in another dream a nurse leaves her in a hospital room with her unsafe mother. At that time Ariel had little or no transitional space in the analysis. She could not feel me as protective or as an accompanying presence as she confronted her fear of the dangerous maternal introject. The dreams heightened her sense of being controlled by me, and Ariel resisted the control she perceived by planning trips, coming late to sessions, and engaging in whirlwinds of exhausting activity.

At this stage, I felt drawn to understanding Ariel's conflict along the Kleinian lines that Bronstein (ibid.) suggests, while at the same time there seemed to be an involvement of a kind of deficit along the lines that Marty (ibid.) was speaking about and which I found useful in the analytic work. These deficits presented as notable gaps in her self-knowledge and the presence of 'unthinkable' areas, especially in her erotic life. These gaps were often portrayed in her dreams as concrete signs that were visible but unreadable, or messages locked away in boxes. But more notably, the gaps limited Ariel's ability to see her behavior as connected or linked to what was going on in her mind, leaving her vulnerable to psyche/ soma dissociation as well as thoughtless, impulsive behavior. I should add that although Ariel's depriving early environment seemed to have produced what appeared to be a deficit (a kind of cognitive limitation of her capacity for insight) this state was also influenced by the complex dynamics of her hatred of the maternal object and fear of retribution for her murderous impulses.

After several years of actions to weaken my control and my interpretations of her anxiety and rage about feeling unloved and unlovable, something began to thaw in Ariel. She had glimmerings of my benevolence, even if I might not love her as she wished. She smiled at me at the beginning and ending of sessions, and tried to make me laugh with gently flirtatious comments ("You look cute today"). She brought her first erotic fantasies and dreams to the analysis. In one dream, she observed another couple touching each other tenderly and recognized her own longing for this experience. She imagined the possibility of a future with a truly compatible partner, one whom she might feel loved by. This aroused a fear of losing the stable albeit passionless life she had created. Her sense of security being paramount, Ariel felt she simply could not brook such a loss. It was out of the question. So, she got busy and planned another round of business travel. Shortly thereafter, she started complaining of severe joint pain that forced her to slow down. She sought medical advice and was diagnosed with an autoimmune condition that couldn't be specified. As her analyst, it was so disappointing to feel she was on the verge of new libidinal energy breaking through the repressive forces, and just then being stopped by somatic illness! I searched for a way to understand this paradox of becoming healthy and ill at the same time, starting with what became Ariel's own metaphor of an internal battle between the forces for and against change—a conflict between a known famine and an uncertain harvest.

The metaphor of psychic autoimmunity

Autoimmunity as a metaphor is explicitly discussed by Britton (2004), Anzieu (1989) and the postmodern philosopher Jacques Derrida. Britton (2004) describes a narcissistic group of patients in which "hyper-subjectivity" may predispose them to a "*failure of maternal containment.*" The patient experiences any difference from her own mind as a "malignant misunderstanding" such that there may be "an allergy to the products of other minds, analogous to the body's immune system—a kind of psychic atopia" (p. 60). Britton asks (ibid.), "Are there psychic allergies and is there sometimes a kind of autoimmunity as an 'allergic reaction' to the products of other minds?" Britton's ideas capture the excessive and self-damaging aspect of autoimmunity, but there seems to be a problem. A close reading of his idea reveals that the 'auto' part of autoimmunity is not actually addressed. He seems to be describing immune hypersensitivity, or allergy, which is a pronounced response to something from the 'outside' and thus a different process from an autoimmune disease. Britton's notion of allergy could be amended to emphasize the 'auto' aspect of autoimmunity by postulating an allergic reaction to the products of one's own mind, whereby previously projected, split-off aspects of self are attacked in the process of reintegration. Although these are not the products coming from another mind, they may be unconsciously experienced as such. In Ariel, her projected cruel maternal introject was being reintegrated as her own aggression against her analyst/mother, for which she could now experience some guilt.

In his book *The Skin Ego* (1989, translation, Turner) Didier Anzieu introduced the concept of the skin ego because of the need for a "narcissistic envelope for the well-being of the psychic apparatus" (Anzieu-Premmereur, 2015, p. 660). In his book he describes nine functions of the skin ego. The ninth function is a negative one, "an anti-function, so to speak, in the service of Thanatos, having as its goal the *self-destruction* of the skin and the Ego." Noting with interest the biologists' use of "self" and "non-self" he compares the rejection of organ transplants when the "biological personality" of the donor differs from the recipient, to the attack on "one of the body's own organs as if it were a foreign transplant." He further asserts,

> As an analyst, I am struck by the analogy between the auto-immune reaction on the one hand, and on the other the turning of drives against oneself, the negative therapeutic reaction, as well as attacks on linking in general and against psychical contents in particular.
>
> (Anzieu, 1989, p. 106)

Anzieu's notion of autoimmune attacks against one's psychical contents accounts for the presence of both conflict and deficit.

Like Britton and Anzieu, Solan (1998) and Bach (2011) liken narcissism to an immune system that attacks non-self. For Bach it is the experience of the analyst's interpretation, for Solan, previously dissociated aspects of self that go against the homeostasis of the "self-net-code" (p. 173).

Autoimmunity is used metaphorically at a socio-cultural level in the work of the postmodern philosopher Jacques Derrida. As quoted by Giovanni Borradori (2003, p. 108), Derrida described the attacks of September 11th as a "Cold War in the head," a global head cold that had now mutated in an "*autoimmunitary process…* that strange behavior where a living being, in quasi-suicidal fashion, 'itself' works to destroy its own protection, to immunize itself *against* its 'own' immunity."

As used by Britton, Anzieu and Derrida, autoimmunity is a psychic phenomenon in which the self is attacked. Their explanations for psychic autoimmunity include narcissistic hyper-subjectivity in Britton, attacks on one's "psychical contents" (p. 106) in Anzieu, and a virulent form of excessive self-protection that has become suicidal in Derrida and attacked the immune system itself. Metaphors of autoimmunity as a psychic phenomenon, as illustrated by these examples, generally assume that autoimmunity is a pathological state that occurs due to either: (1) a failure of self-recognition (i.e. self is felt to be alien) as in Anzieu, Solan and Bach, or (2) because of an over-reaction to non-self, as in Britton and Derrida.

Contemporary biological theories of autoimmunity

To better understand what was happening in Ariel psychically and in her bodily concomitants, it is important to go beyond the metaphorization of autoimmunity to explore the known mechanisms of physiological autoimmunity, and to determine whether prior conceptualizations of psychic autoimmunity are consistent with currently understood principles of biological autoimmunity. Taking a cue from Freud's interest in biological models as a way to inform and test the theoretical viability of his ideas, I review current knowledge of the biology of autoimmunity in health and pathology. My intuition had been there is a parallel between the somatic processes and the psychic representations of an attack on the self not recognized as self. What I discovered is far more complicated and closer to Ogden's (1988) description of a dialectical process in which disparate elements seem to "create, preserve and negate" each other (p. 517).

Autoimmunity is a particularly rich area in which to explore the link between mind and body. The immune system has been described as the closest analog to the nervous system (Nataf, 2017; Schwartz and Kipnis, 2011). Both systems are involved in the organism's adaptational interactions with the external environment, and both systems have the capacity for memory, which, interestingly, means they learn from experience (Bion, 1962). In the immune system, disease fighting cells 'remember' their exposure to pathogenic antigens (substances that engender an immune response); this is the basis of immunity in vaccines. It is interesting to think of the contemporary opposition to vaccines, which highlights how much the immune system is the subject of unconscious phantasy and expresses our narcissistic fear that the *other* is 'bad' and dangerous.

In contemporary immunology, autoimmunity is not thought of in terms of a de novo attack on the self, but rather a loss of normal *self-tolerance*. What is the distinction? In health, there are multiple immune cell types that are programed to react (defensively) against self-antigens (one's own antigens that have the capacity to generate an immune response). Self-tolerance exists because these self-reactive cells are thought to be either eliminated in a programmed way or are regulated by specialized cells not to react. Autoimmune disease has been thought to represent an unexplained loss of self-tolerance, postulated to be related to genetic factors or an environmental insult such as infection. Now the catastrophe of psychic change (Bion, 1970) can be added to the list of such insults.

While still holding the view of autoimmunity as a loss of self-tolerance, there has been a shift in the immunology literature toward a different view of autoimmunity. There is now believed to be a *natural autoimmunity* which involves an extensive spectrum of self-reactive cellular mechanisms. In health, these mechanisms enable the organism to perform appropriate programmed cell death, to repair injury such as in wound-healing and to recognize and defend the body from self-like cells that are being over-produced, such as in cancer. Of interest is that the same autoimmune mechanisms that can destroy cancer cells can also cause tissue damage; this is considered one of the paradoxical aspects of autoimmunity (Toomer and Chen, 2014).

To restate, *self-tolerance* means the body is prepared with specialized self-reactive cells to react defensively against itself. But this potentiality is kept in check either by groups of specialized regulatory cells, or elimination of self-reactive immune cells. So-called natural autoimmunity is a newer idea[4] recognizing that autoimmunity is involved in normal self-maintenance, which involves wound-healing, and minimizing tissue destruction in states of injury (Schwartz and Cohen, 2000). Thus, there seems to be a state of equilibrium in which healthy autoimmunity is maintained. In pathological conditions, the balance is shifted such that these specialized regulatory mechanisms are less effective and self-reactive immunity may act against the body, often damaging a specific organ such as the pancreas in diabetes. In such a case as animal models have shown, one regulatory cell type may fall short in numbers.

It is fascinating to contemplate that in a sense, we have a whole arsenal lined up to attack ourselves, and this arsenal is held back by highly specific regulatory mechanisms that can go awry under various conditions. One might therefore say the autoimmune disease represents a shift in homeostatic balance from a more regulated state to a less regulated state—in essence, to a lower level of organiza- tion. This might be seen as new evidence for Freud's notion of the death instinct, adding to earlier biological findings regarding single-celled organisms that Freud (1920) relied on in arguing that a drive toward death is an inherent tendency of all organisms, including humans.

The loss of regulatory control could also be seen as relating to Laplanche's (2004) construct of the unbound drive energy in the sexual death drive. In Ariel, the autoimmune process and its underlying dysregulation seemed to emerge with the freeing up of erotic libido and a new object cathexis of her analyst. As Freud (1914) stated in his paper on narcissism, "not until there is object cathexis is it possible to discriminate a sexual energy—the libido—from an energy of the ego-instincts" (p. 76). We might hypothesize such freeing up of sexual energy shifted Ariel's physiological equilibrium away from what we now understand is a finely tuned state of immunological self-tolerance, and toward a state of chaos that could either be destructive or creative.

Ariel and her autoimmune response to working through

It was most unexpected that Ariel would become physically ill just as she reached a watershed moment in her analysis and was able to experience me as a benevo- lent and whole object for whom she could have tender feelings. Yet we know that psychic change has many meanings to the analysand, which can be threatening, including the pain of mourning the eventual ending of the analysis and the loss of the analyst. Also, as described by Rosenfeld (1971), emergence of the libidinal parts of the self may be opposed by a destructive internal 'gang' fueled by the death instinct.

In exploring the biology of autoimmunity both as a metaphor and as a parallel process to a psychic situation, I was able to expand my thinking and capacity for reverie. I could imagine Ariel's *self-tolerance*—inhibition of defensive reactions against herself—involved a tenuous balance in which her maternal introject was split into a phantasied evil mother and an idealized adoring one. When these split-off parts were reintegrated following the weakening of the tie to the internal sadistic bad object, and new sexual libido emerged, it 'rocked the boat,' caus- ing waves of somatopsychic dysregulation. From the standpoint of Laplanche's (2004) unbound sexual death drive, new libido led to a loss of equilibrium. The autoimmune arsenal that was at the ready to defend against self-like invaders such as cancer was unleashed against her incrementally healing self.

Perhaps the 'penseé operatoire' aspect of Ariel's mind put her at greater risk for this eventuality (Marty and de M'uzan, 1978). Her incessant activity to block reflective thought, and the consequent gaps in her self-awareness prevented meaning from getting across the caesura between her mind and body. Laplanchean theory might allow us to speculate that the risk of this unbound energy was greater because of such a failure of transcription of meaning, of an underlying message, into a represented form. The meaning of destructive maternal sexuality used for control and not love had been violently intromitted (see Note 4), unable to be represented until made conscious in the analysis.

To understand what happened in the analysis, we return to Winnicott's notion of the mother as mirror discussed earlier, with Scarfone's (2018) discussion of the neuroscientist Ramachandran's treatment of phantom limb pain. The idea is essentially that the body as represented in the mind is 'stuck' at the moment of the loss of the limb and has not re-transcribed the new state, so the body itself is frozen in the traumatic loss. Ramachandran uses an actual mirror to 'fool' the mind into releasing the frozen position of the lost limb. Perhaps Ariel had been frozen in the trauma of loss that was her mother's "black-hole" eyes, and has needed me as a mirror to unfreeze herself from her frozen, locked emotional state of being the unloved child.

The next phase of the treatment

Although I will not recount all the developments of this analysis, which concluded several years later, the next phase of Ariel's treatment was quite interesting. The onset of an autoimmune condition served as a signal to Ariel that she needed to slow down; she felt that she had a war going on inside of her and that analysis was her only path to recovery. She recommitted herself to the work, with the intention that she would complete the analysis, whatever it took, and one day would be without me, the figure who inspired such intense feelings of both love and hatred. She had never been able to imagine life without me, but now accepted that there would be a mourning process. There was a different quality in her. The autoimmune illness made physical movement painful for her but it made stillness possible. With stillness, Ariel developed more of an 'as-if space' in which she could both experience and reflect upon her impulses to use chaos to create a breach between herself and me. She could now say that she missed me on the weekends or during my vacation and expressed some affectionate feelings. She didn't know what would come out of this phase of work but believed that she could survive making changes in the way she lived her life to correspond with inner changes in analysis.

Sometime later Ariel discussed a ring she had bought for herself, as she was unable to accept a ring from her current partner. Only she could give herself the impressive ring she wanted. As I watched her playing with the ring, I felt she was telling me that in her omnipotent phantasy, love from another was inferior to the 'jewels' she could provide for herself. She *must* be self-sufficient in order to survive. I thought about her wish to be loved by me, to be a special analysand;

and her difficulty accepting me as a benign object who wanted the best for her rather than a sadistic maternal figure who wanted to control her. I said, "There is also something from me you're struggling to accept." After a considerable silence, she said,

> I'm embarrassed to say this ... What you want to offer is your own brand of love for me and your own brand of caring and I can't accept it because I can't believe in it. But what if it were true?

Ariel was taking some steps in binding Eros and the destructive drive, taking a step across the caesura of body and mind. Freud (1937) emphasized the necessity of such binding: "Only by the concurrent or mutually opposing action of the two primal instincts—Eros and the death instinct—never by one or the other alone, can we explain the rich multiplicity of the phenomena of life."

I wonder if in my words to Ariel "... something from me ...," there was a direct, bodily communication of an offering (Harrang, Chapter 13) allowing her to take a step across the body–mind caesura.

Discussion

There seems to be something about the disruption and dysregulation of physical illness that brings about the possibility of a new organization at a different psychic level, perhaps allowing Ariel take steps toward relinquishing a bad object tie and to have the beginnings of a capacity for a pleasurable erotic life. How does a new understanding of autoimmunity as discussed above illuminate our understanding of the psychic processes involved in this disruption (and opportunity), and help us develop a more suitable metaphor? It doesn't really fit to say the forces of change are at war with the forces of stasis, or that the narcissistic envelope has been punctured (as in Anzieu, Solan and others). Understanding that the loss of self-tolerance represents removal of a regulatory function, a new metaphor might be the "unleashing" of the arsenal that is already aimed at the self. It's as if the immune system is saying, "I'm not going to stop you from attacking yourself, because this attack may be part of a process of repair. But it may not, so you'll have to figure it out." In essence, the immune system does not distinguish between processes leading toward death and those leading toward life. It is akin to the binding of life energy, which too, as Freud describes is a life-preserving process or one ultimately leading toward complete discharge, that is, death. Discernment between the two is required, and that is a significant part of what takes place in analysis.

A remaining and central question is why Ariel's response to stirrings of change during her analysis became a somatic, rather than purely psychic phenomenon. This has been a major concern of both the French psychosomatists and Bion in several ways. Bion's (1970) notion of catastrophic change suggests that powerful emotional contents may break through the container, which I posit may be the body. Also, as discussed previously, a reading of Bion's *Memoir of the Future* (1991b) suggests a barrier between body and mind where the symptoms are somatic, but no meaning gets through. What has prevented meaning from getting through? In Ariel's case it seems less like a deficit of structure and more akin to Freud's and Laplanche's theories of repression, understood as a failure of translation. Thus, perhaps today's increasingly common autoimmune illnesses may be like the hysterics of yesteryear.[5]

Perhaps we could say Ariel's experience of illness helped to create a mirror function in the analysis, allowing both of us to expand the bounds of our imaginations as to what was going on inside of Ariel. The mirror function for Ariel told her that she was doing something destructive to herself that was being expressed in her body. Ariel came to understand her disease as representing her untrammeled campaign to feel powerful and thus armored against rejection by her analyst through opposing the analytic process. As mentioned earlier, this destructive force could also be understood as the work of the death instinct. The shift to a less regulated state of her immune system that unleashed destructive self-reactivity could be seen in various ways: as Rosenfeld's (1971) gang opposing change; as Laplanche's unbound sexual death drive involving the mixture of aggression and pleasure; or as Freud (1940) explained:

> The aim of [*eros*] is to establish ever greater unities and to preserve them thus—in short, to bind together; the aim of the other [the *death instinct*], on the contrary, is to undo connections and so to destroy things.
>
> (p. 31)

This brings us to the paradoxical qualities of a destructive process. It may proceed relentlessly to Marty's (1968) "progressive disorganization" or even death. Or, as I propose happened to Ariel, it has the capacity to progress to something more constructive: a greater reflective capacity ushered in by the illness. Meaning was getting across the body–mind caesura that was no longer the unrepresented pain of the classic psychosomatic patient.

Conclusions

In this chapter I describe the analysis of Ariel, when her body's destructive reaction to psychic change spurred me to investigate both the metaphor and biological dynamics of an autoimmune process. What I found is instead of the more popular notions of an abnormal attack on self, in the current understanding of autoimmunity the *normal* capacity for self-attack is kept in check by regulatory mechanisms, and autoimmune disease represents a disruption of these restraining forces. It is profound to consider we are always prepared to kill ourselves from within. This opens avenues for consideration of how the life and death instincts exist in a state of ongoing tension throughout life, maintaining a kind of balance between them that can be disrupted even by change toward greater psychic freedom.

This understanding enriches my thinking about the process of psychic change in analysis. I see that it can put the patient on a potentially dangerous precipice:

on the one side is the possibility of reorganization, and on the other entry into a progressive state of disorganization. In Ariel, the preceding analytic work which allowed her to re-integrate split-off parts posed both a danger and an opportunity. These reintegrated parts (related to the sadistic maternal introject) were felt as foreign antigens, but my explorations into autoimmunity also suggest that Ariel's productive work in the transference released new libido which disrupted her immunologic equilibrium. The immune mechanisms regulating self-attack that had served as a container were weakened by the perceived danger of change. On that precipice, the opportunity for reorganization at a higher level is helped by a growing capacity for representation. Clinically, the mirror function of the analyst and the analysis works in some way analogous to Ramachandran's mirror to help the patient's mind free itself from a frozen state by expanding the capacity for mentalization. This increased capacity may make the difference between constructive disorganization as happened to Ariel, and a psychic dead-end.

The relationship between the mind and body—the "mind–body problem"—has concerned philosophers for many centuries (e.g., Aristotle, Descartes, Kant). It could be argued that psychoanalytic theory has not progressed far beyond Freud's description of the puzzling leap from mental states to somatic innervation. We still struggle with basic definitions, dualistic perspectives, and the absence of a comprehensive mind–body theory. Until recently psychoanalysis has tended to separate the mind from the body, emphasizing the role of the former at the expense of the latter. There has been limited interest in the body's internal operations such as its immune system, from both a metaphoric and an organismic perspective. Current scientific knowledge locates the mind throughout the body in the sense that the nervous system is widely distributed, yet the mind is often equated only with the brain. However, we should take note that even when the mind and body are regarded philosophically and scientifically as inherently tied, they are still separate in some ways: one has only to watch someone in the process of dying, when the body is no longer viable but the mind remains intact, to imagine the body and mind ultimately must separate.[6]

Given the insights gleaned from these explorations into autoimmunity, I find Freud's use of biological parallels has continued value for expanding our analytic imagination. For example, the biological notion of loss of self-tolerance has proved relevant to the understanding of its psychic counterpart. The most perplexing question remains unanswered, however: why some analysands become ill at the threshold of change and others do not. My work with Ariel suggests a number of possibilities: the presence of penseés operatoire and a diminished capacity for imagination and reverie that predisposes to a regression to the body; the intromission of untranslatable (unrepresentable) unconscious mental content too powerful emotionally to be contained by the psychesoma, leading to a somatic "explosion." The process of Ariel's analysis seems to reinforce Bion's position of an unbridgeable gulf between mind and body in which meaning cannot get through. Her story tells us that an important aim of analysis is to bridge that gulf.

There is much to be learned about the balance between life and death in analysis. This case is also a reminder that what we deal with in analysis has life and death significance in that analytic change may be experienced as a catastrophe both psychically and biologically. An important question concerns how the analyst can support the patient's self-tolerance in the face of the dysregulating impact of change; in this case, the chaos of the sexual death drive as new libidinal energies are mobilized. Which analytic approaches might best help the patient to achieve a new level of organization in the face of psychic and physiological dysregulation? In this chapter I present a perspective influenced by the thinking of Freud, Winnicott, Bion, and Laplanche. New cases will shed further light on how different analytic approaches may help the patient navigate the turbulent waters of analytic change.

One area I've touched upon that merits further exploration is that of mourning. Its role in the dynamics of those with such autoimmune situations remains to be further clarified. As Steiner (1990) reminds us, the guilt involved in relinquishing the tie to a damaged object is an obstacle to mourning and prevents achievement of symbolic functioning.

The issues discussed here, including that of mourning and the ever-present reality of death, take on special significance at this time as the COVID-19 pandemic has restricted activity around the world and brought into focus our relationship with infectious disease and the immune system's varying response to the disease. In this context the immune response of the body–mind, and perhaps of the larger human 'mind,' takes on a new meaning for us all.

Notes

1 In this chapter I use *psyche* and *soma* in three different ways: *psyche-soma*, a term used by Winnicott and Bion; *psyche/soma* for the relationship between psyche and soma; and *psychesoma* for an embodied integration of the two.

2 Note the earlier work of Elizabeth Carter, whose *A Dialogue* (1741) is an intriguingly similar exposition of the mind–body problem, as seen in the excerpt below:

> Says Body to Mind, 'tis amazing to see
> We're so nearly related, yet never agree,
> But lead a most wrangling strange sort of life,
> As great plagues to each other as husband and wife...
>
> Quoted in *The Club: Johnson, Boswell and the Friends
> Who Shaped an Age*, Leo Damrosch, 2019

3 For Laplanche, unconscious maternal sexuality is transmitted to the infant in everyday child care. The child possesses a drive to "translate" this unconscious message into something coherent. When the parental content is particularly disturbing there is a more violent process of "intromission" which resists translation. One may wonder whether this process might bring about the dissociation between psyche and soma written about by Winnicott and others.

4 Schwartz and Cohen (2000), followed by other immunologists, have described a role for "protective autoimmunity." Self-protective autoimmunity is thought to be involved in "self-maintenance," including maintenance of CNS integrity, wound repair, regulation of graft rejection, and tumor surveillance. They note, "A disease in one context may be a boon in another... autoimmunity can be destructive or protective depending on the tissue context: the inflammatory outcome can thus be viewed as a balance" (p. 267).

5 Just as nineteenth-century female hysterics developed symptoms in the context of the sexual repression of their time, it is interesting to think about autoimmune disease in the context of the present moment. Autoimmune disease is on the rise, especially in females. We now have increased life expectancy and fewer external limitations around sexuality. With fewer external restrictions—clear external enemies—for some people destructive forces are aimed at themselves. This raises interesting questions regarding the impact of social factors on the expression of the death instinct.

6 The separation of mind and body at death and the question of whether the mind outlives the body have inspired writers, religious thinkers, and philosophers since the dawn of humankind. The ancient Greeks viewed the soul ("psyche" or *psuchē* in Greek) as the seat of consciousness and other mental faculties. Said Socrates, as quoted in Plato's *Phaedo* (360 B.C.), "Death is the separation of soul and body."

References

Anzieu, D. (1989) *The skin ego: A psychoanalytic approach to the self.* (C. Turner, Trans.). Yale University Press.

Anzieu-Premmereur, C. (2015) The skin-ego: Dyadic sensuality, trauma in infancy, and adult narcissistic issues. *The Psychoanalytic Review, 102*(5):659–681.

Bach, S. (2011) Chimeras: Immunity, interpenetration, and the true self. *The Psychoanalytic Review, 98*(1):39–56.

Bion, W.R. (1962) *Learning from experience.* London: Tavistock Publications.

Bion, W.R. (1970) *Attention and interpretation: A scientific approach to insight in psycho-analysis and groups.* Tavistock Publications.

Bion, W.R. (1991a) *A Memoir of the Future: The Past Presented* (pp. 221–291). Karnac Books.

Bion, W.R. (1991b) *A Memoir of the Future: The Dawn of Oblivion* (pp. 434–435). Karnac Books.

Borradori, G. (2003) *Philosophy in a time of terror: Dialogues with Jürgen Habermas and Jacques Derrida.* University of Chicago Press.

Britton, R. (2004) Subjectivity, objectivity, and triangular space. *The Psychoanalytic Quarterly, 73*(1):47–61.Bronstein, C. (2011) On psychosomatics: The search for meaning. *The International Journal of Psychoanalysis, 92*(1):173–195.

Carter, E. (1741) A dialogue. *Gentleman's Magazine, 11*(Jan.):46.

Damrosch, L. (2019) *The club: Johnson, Boswell and the friends who shaped an age.* Yale University Press.

Freud, S. (1896) Letter 52, from extracts from the Fliess papers. In J. Strachey (Ed. and Trans.) *The standard edition of the complete psychological works of Sigmund Freud* (Vol. 1, pp. 233–239). Hogarth Press.

Freud, S. (1909) Notes upon a case of obsessional neurosis. In J. Strachey (Ed. and Trans.) *The standard edition of the complete psychological works of Sigmund Freud* (Vol. 10, pp. 151–318). Hogarth Press.

Freud, S. (1914). On narcissism: An introduction. In J. Strachey (Ed. and Trans.), *The standard edition of the complete psychological works of Sigmund Freud* (Vol. 14, pp. 67–102). Hogarth Press.

Freud, S. (1917) Introductory lectures on psycho-analysis. In J. Strachey (Ed. and Trans.) *The standard edition of the complete psychological works of Sigmund Freud* (Vol. 16, pp. 241–463). Hogarth Press.

Freud, S. (1920) Beyond the pleasure principle. In J. Strachey (Ed. and Trans.) *The stand-ard edition of the complete psychological works of Sigmund Freud* (Vol. 18, pp. 1–64). Hogarth Press.

Freud, S. (1930) Civilization and its discontents. In J. Strachey (Ed. and Trans.) *The stand-ard edition of the complete psychological works of Sigmund Freud* (Vol. 21, pp. 57–146). Hogarth Press.

Freud, S. (1923) The ego and the id. In J. Strachey (Ed. and Trans.) *The standard edition of the complete psychological works of Sigmund Freud* (Vol. 19, pp. 1–66). Hogarth Press.

Freud, S. (1937) Analysis terminable and interminable. In J. Strachey (Ed. and Trans.) *The standard edition of the complete psychological works of Sigmund Freud* (Vol. 23, pp. 209–254.) Hogarth Press.

Freud, S. (1940). An outline of psycho-analysis. *The International Journal of Psychoanalysis, 21*:27–84.

Green, A. (1975) The analyst, symbolization and absence in the analytic setting (on changes in analytic practice and analytic experience)—In memory of D.W. Winnicott. *The International Journal of Psychoanalysis, 56*:1–22.

Grotstein, J.S. (1997) "Mens sana in corpore sano". The mind and body as an "odd cou-ple" and as an oddly coupled unity, *Psychoanalytic Inquiry., 17*(2):204–222.

Joseph, B. (1989) *Psychic equilibrium and psychic change: Selected Papers of Betty Joseph.* M. Feld-man & E. Bott Spillius (Eds.) New Library of Psychoanalysis, *9*:1–222. Routledge.

Laplanche, J. (1987[1989]) *New Foundations for Psychoanalysis.* D. Macey (Trans.). Basil Blackwell.

Laplanche, J. (2004) The so-called 'death drive': A sexual drive. *British Journal of Psycho-therapy, 29*(4):455–471.

Loewald, H. (1973) On internalization. *The International Journal of Psychoanalysis, 54*:9–17.

Marty, P. (1968) A major process of somatization: The progressive disorganization. *The International Journal of Psychoanalysis, 49*:246–249.

Marty, P. (2010) The narcissistic difficulties presented to the observer by the psycho-somatic problem. *The International Journal of Psychoanalysis, 91*(2):347–360. [Originally published in French, 1952].

Marty, P. & de M'uzan, M. (1978). Das operative denken ("pensée opératoire"). *Psyche – Zeitschrift für Psychoanalyse, 32*(10):974–984.

McDougall, J. (1989) *Theatres of the body: A psychoanalytic approach to psychosomatic illness.* W.W. Norton.

Nataf, S. (2017) Autoimmunity as a driving force of cognitive evolution. *Frontiers in Neu-roscience, 11*:1–16

Ogden, T.H. (1988) On the dialectical structure of experience—Some clinical and theo-retical implications. *Contemporary Psychoanalysis, 24*:17–45.

Plato (360 b.c. [1969]) *Phaedo.* B. Jowett (Trans.) W.J. Black.

Rosenfeld, H. (1971) A clinical approach to the psychoanalytic theory of the life and death instincts: An investigation into the aggressive aspects of narcissism. *The International Journal of Psychoanalysis, 52*:169–178.

Scarfone, D. (2018) Foreign bodies: The body-psyche and its phantoms. In V. Tsolas & C. Anzieu-Premmereur C. (Eds.) *On the body: A psychoanalytic exploration of the body in to-day's world* (pp. 146–158). Routledge.

Schwartz, M., & Cohen, I. (2000) Autoimmunity can benefit self-maintenance. *Viewpoint: Immunology Today, 21*(6):265–268.

Schwartz, M., & Kipnis, J. (2011) A conceptual revolution in the relationships between the brain and immunity. *Brain, Behavior, and Immunity*, 25(5):817–819.

Solan R (1998) Narcissistic fragility in the process of befriending the unfamiliar. *The American Journal of Psychoanalysis*, 58:163–186.

Steiner, J. (1990) Pathological organizations as obstacles to mourning: The role of unbearable guilt. *The International Journal of Psychoanalysis*, 71:87–94.

Toomer H., & Chen Z. (2014) Autoimmunity as a double agent in tumor killing and cancer promotion. *Frontiers in Immunology*, Vol. 5, Article 1161.

Winnicott, D.W. (1949 [1975]) Mind and its relation to the psyche-soma. In *Through Paediatrics to Psycho-Analysis* (pp. 243–254). Hogarth Press.

Winnicott, D.W. (1965) The maturational processes and the facilitating environment. Studies in the theory of emotional development. Hogarth Press.

Winnicott, D.W. (1966) Psycho-somatic illness in its positive and negative Aspects. *The International Journal of Psychoanalysis*, 47:510–516.

Winnicott, D.W. (1971) The mirror role of the mother and family in child development. In *Playing and Reality* (pp. 111–118). Tavistock Publications.

Part VI
Body in virtual space

18 Introduction

Caron Harrang, Drew Tillotson, and Nancy C. Winters

In the early stages of preparing this book we felt a psychoanalytic exploration of the body in cyberspace was an essential aspect of body as psychoanalytic object. With the rapid expansion of the dematerialized virtual world in our daily lives and in the field of psychoanalysis, we need guides such as Marzi to help us think about the complexities of such work.

However, we had no idea the COVID-19 pandemic was just around the corner rendering in-person sessions untenable for an extended period of time. Remote analysis, once a specialized area—one could even say for some it was a 'bête noire' of psychoanalysis—has become a fact of life for analysts and patients worldwide. Thus, Marzi's chapter "The body vanishes? Preliminary thoughts on body and the identity of the analyst in remote analysis" takes on new meaning as psychoanalysts experience their own and their analysands' bodies in the 'meeting space' of virtual reality. This raises the question, whether there can be shared bodily experience or shared emotional experience under these conditions?

Marzi's previous contributions on remote analysis are significant, particularly his 2016 edited collection *Psychoanalysis, Identity, and the Internet*. With case illustrations he explores virtual reality, noting its relation to mental life in having the quality of place/non-place, suggesting cyberspace as a *potential space* comes to life in the analytic field.

In this chapter Marzi builds on his previous contributions, conceptualizing virtual space as a dream space and cyberspace as a dimension of the analytic field. Cyberspace, he says, offers a new perspective for thinking about the mind's 'virtual spaces' and about psychoanalysis itself. He describes the vicissitudes of the 'digital body' in cyberspace, not as material body; rather as imaginal body emanating from "one's own proto-mental inner world."

For Marzi, bodies are mediated and united through the ongoing experimental dimension of analysis conducted via virtual reality. For example, his analysand Cecilia transitions to analysis by Skype after moving away. She dreams of objects (couch, curtains, paintings) coming to life and rescuing somebody who feels bad. Marzi points out the presence of *new* objects such as the internet and Skype, objects there to help. Cecilia moves from dreaming to fantasy. Sometime later she dreams of an experimental procedure using an "epidural catheter" being performed on a suffering woman in "the room next door." Marzi says, "you are still

DOI: 10.4324/9781003195559-18

talking about the internet ... experimental stuff ... you are in a separate room ... the [catheter] tube is like the microphone cable that somehow connects us with the voice without a presence." In making these links the analyst becomes a maternal presence whose container function "repeatedly transforms into the psychic that which is not psychic, identifying almost in a bodily sense with the patient."

The body can remain mute and un-representable, Marzi observes, or it can be

> *thought* of as a digital body if, in this [analytic] relationship, some experience of three-dimensionality is activated, and with it the possibility of thinking, within this space, through the presence of proto-informatic elements which have features similar to the proto-mental elements [are] present in the subject.

His account of how tri-dimensionality is achieved with several analysands offers a way for us to imagine the potential of the virtual world to attain, as he puts it, "a capacious volume" rather than an impoverished one. He cites Ehrlich (2019) who notes with the analyst's emotional engagement *distance* analysis need not be confused with *distant* analysis (p. 270).

References

Ehrlich, L T. (2019). Teleanalysis: slippery slope or rich opportunity? *Journal of the American Psychoanalytic Association, 67*(2):249–279.

Marzi, A. (Ed.) (2016). *Psychoanalysis, identity, and the internet: Explorations into cyberspace.* Karnac Books.

19 The body vanishes?[1] Preliminary thoughts on bodily experience and the identity of the analyst in remote analysis

Andrea Marzi

Introduction

The digital world poses problems and ever more cogent questions for psychoanalysis. Via cyberspace, we are entering the virtual world and using it as a possible perspective for thinking about psychoanalysis itself; the mind's 'virtual spaces' and their possible existence and possible meanings; the internal role of the setting; and the comparison between virtual space and dream-space. This is also a perspective from within which to explore fundamental concepts in psychoanalytic theory and the consequences of all this in the psychoanalytic relationship and the psychoanalytic *field*. For at least two decades, our discipline has been taking an interest in the world of information technology from various vertices, and with opposing and intense emotional and affective responses (see, e.g. Carlino, 2011; Marzi, 2016a; Marzi and Fiorentini, 2017; Mirkin, 2011; Russell, 2015; Savege Scharff, 2015, 2017). For a more detailed discussion of this subject, and the topics addressed in this chapter, see *Psychoanalysis, Identity and the Internet. Explorations into cyberspace* (Marzi, 2016a).

We may ask what the internet has produced and will be capable of producing within psychoanalysis, and at the same time what psychoanalysis will be able to make of the internet. As to the *field*, its concept is intricate and complex.[2] The concept of field not only embraces a theoretical development in science and the social sciences spanning over a long period of time, but veers to psychoanalysis through Lewin and the Gestalt, Rickman and Bion, such that the purely social environment (Lewin's social field) reaches a place where "the social field dynamic between individual and context binds both a social group and a psychoanalytic session into a common pattern" (Hinshelwood, 2018, p. 1414).

One may recall that Lewin himself tried to create mathematical representations of the dynamics and forces at work in the social field—in this respect he tapped into Henri Poincaré's *theorie*—but then he preferred to focus on the vectors and forces in spatial relations. Introducing the spatial dimension in the study of the field is particularly interesting if we think of digital space, and of the subject's interaction with the 'material' in this same space (a space imagined as such by our minds, while in fact it is a mathematical space).

DOI: 10.4324/9781003195559-19

From another perspective, we must bear in mind that the analytic process is a dimension in which sensations and emotions invade the perceptual field and are welcomed in the space where the encounter takes place—the analytic field—so as to permit that transformation which initiates symbolic and representational activity. This involves not only affective states that have not been represented, which are asymbolic, but also the asymbolic affective elements that are inside the body. We must link these affective states awaiting representation to experiential states that can be thought and analytically processed. In my opinion, this is fundamental and one of the frontiers in our field.

In this chapter I provide some preliminary reflections on the fate of the body in the digital world of remote psychoanalysis. I describe the vicissitudes of the body in relation, above all, to the proto-mental system, using some illustrative analytic experiences. To do this, it is first necessary to make some observations on the psychoanalytic nature of both the analyst's identity and virtual reality.

Brief notes on psychoanalysis and the body

In recent years the body has become a focus of interest in the psychoanalytic world, and this is good news.[3] We know that neuroscience has produced fascinating results that have often confirmed what psychoanalysis had previously illustrated. Besides, the mind–body problem, the mysterious leap from mental to physical, provokes an ongoing debate between scientific, epistemological, and generally speaking, philosophical stances, perhaps seeking impossible harmonization.[4]

We may need an adequate reality test in the area of mind–body relations. Hoping that new horizons will open up in the future, it is more realistic to agree with Solms' and Turnbull's (2002) moderate relativism (these authors are prone to accept a "dual-aspect monism") and their claim:

> We (M.S, O.T) are of the opinion that the nature of the relationship between brain and mind (body and soul) is not amenable to scientific proof… It is appropriate to describe certain neuronal processes *causing* consciousness only *within a particular philosophical framework*…
>
> (p. 52)

We might add that "deeper neuroscientific knowledge leads to a greater enrichment of the famed 'mysterious leap', and tends to make this relationship more complex and accomplished" (Marzi, Giovannoni, and Carboni, 1999, p. 3).

Amidst this turmoil, psychoanalysis is renewing its interest in the issues concerning the body, which underwent a sort of eclipse, at least until the 1980s, as Ferrari (2004) suggests. In fact, the body should be considered as "the very origin of the mind…I think that the body dimension also originates the psychic function and immediately establishes with it a more or less harmonic relationship" (Ferrari, 2003, pp. 63–64).

This revived interest in the body–mind relationship has emerged in several respects, although Caldwell (2018) suggests: "a major aspect of the discursive formations of contemporary psychoanalysis did seem to have overlooked that body, especially the impact of its bodilyness, both as material presence and as carrier of other dimensions of the human being" (p. 2).[5] Gaddini (1981) and Lombardi (2008, 2019) have also insisted more than once on the centrality of the body and, mostly, on the internal body–mind relationship.

An opposite attitude—one of psychologizing or even spiritualizing, an idealistic abstraction, broadly speaking—tended to remove the attention paid to the body and our embodied mental life, or at least part of it. This obliteration "risks transforming psychoanalysis more and more into some systemic psychology driven by its own self-referential intellectualism" (Lombardi, 2012, p. 110). No doubt, the development from Freud to Klein, Winnicott and Bion is a semantic and developmental vector of major importance. Among the many authors who have made a significant contribution in this respect, Grotstein (1997), in his intense theoretical effort, has included some of Bion's initial positions about the undifferentiation between physical and mental (especially in *Experiences in Groups*, 1961) as well as Winnicott's ideas of 1949 on the psyche-soma, the latter being a major intuition in this field. Even though both Bion and Winnicott did not directly investigate the body in their psychoanalytic theory (Caldwell, 2018; Oelsner, 2018), theirs are still seminal ideas for a deep reflection on the bodily phenomena and presence and their mutual relationship.[6]

Another path in considering the body is the shifting of the scientific effort to an ambitious interdisciplinary blend, such as Leuzinger-Bohleber (2019) has tried to pursue vigorously through a dialog with the cognitive neurosciences (mostly the so-called "Embodied-Cognitive Science"). In addition it is useful to consider Wilma Bucci's Multiple Code Theory (1997) (See also Solano, 2013, p. 1453; 2016, p. 58). Consider also the role that mirror neurons could play (Rizzolatti and Sinigaglia, 2006), or the very appealing attempts, made consistently by Solms and Panksepp, to find progressive meeting points between neurosciences and psychoanalysis (Solms and Turnbull, 2002; Solms and Panksepp, 2012).

Mind and body can therefore be seen as two vertices from which to observe the same condition, like the two hemispheres of the same brain (Grotstein, 1997; Solano, 2016), where the body seems to progressively take on a full, independent dignity as a feeling, thinking, and relating entity (De Toffoli, 2014; Gaddini, 1981). Constantly monitoring a balancing of such interdisciplinary contributions seems necessary to me. On the one hand, we need to avoid falling into the *Nihil sub sole novum* traps; on the other, it is just as clear that not everything that is in motion is always progress.[7]

Psychoanalysis, the digital world, and the body

While a comprehensive discussion of the proto-mental state (Bion, 1961; Grotstein, 2007), with its numerous developments (see, e.g. Ferro, 2014; Hautmann, 1999, 2002; Neri, 1996), is beyond the scope of this chapter, we know that in the proto-mental system there resides a structure of thought which is a primitive mind, a basic, primordial mental organization, "in which physical and psychological are as yet undifferentiated" (Bion, 1961, p. 103). It can also be considered a primordial condition of a group residing in the mind of an individual, in Bion's sense, a sort of internal group life, a "groupishness", as he underlines (Hautmann, 1999; Meltzer, 1986). In the dynamic evolution of this proto-mental condition, taking on the burden of thinking thoughts, not evacuating them but keeping them inside oneself, is distressing, both because of the contents and because thinking entails detachment from the group state, which represents "the disposition of being and functioning psychologically as a group earlier than as individuals" (Cavagna, 2001, p. 127). It is in fact a matter of becoming "just one", and as a consequence taking responsibility for the conditions of thought, promoting the development of the mind (Neri, 1996).

Using the foregoing discussion of mind and body as background I pose the following question: does coming into contact, in the remote technology session, with the atmosphere created by the information-driven climate affect the possibility of staying within the bounds of one's own previous analytic identity? Or does it violate that possibility?

I have elsewhere emphasized (Marzi, 2016b) how virtuality reflects the "mind" (the object of our analytic work) in that both share the same character of place/ non-place; while having a base that is physical and material (the hardware and the software, the brain and the nervous system), they are both in fact dematerialized by the digitization.

Unlike "two concrete people speaking in a room", here materiality is dematerialized. The body as psychoanalytic object is therefore a dematerialized body. Nevertheless, certain valid and familiar features of analysis in person—the "in the room analysis", as Bolognini underlines (2014, p. 790)—can clearly be achieved here too. I will return to this aspect later on.

The mental space and the virtual space of cyberspace may both be imagined as being endowed with a capacious volume suited to welcoming specific contents of every nature: aspects, states of mind, fantasies, bodies, or numberless dematerialized objects.

Starting from the most primitive or regressive one- and two-dimensionality of a contact/non-contact, of a superficial adhesion which leaves the relationship in a state of potentiality (and is therefore, "virtual"), I propose that a transformation into a structure endowed with depth can come about in the virtual setting where the subject begins to interact projectively and where the communicative and relational impulse originates.

We might postulate that the virtual condition brings an important contribution to the thinking process in analysis in acknowledging that full, satisfying, and genuine immersion in the analysis can be achieved only when the relational quality develops tri-dimensionality—that is, a dimension which entails the presence of space. This makes possible analytic operations such as projection and projective identification within the tri-dimensional space and operations with the (virtual) objects which exist in it.

Reflecting on these features, it has become clear to me that such phenomena as states of mind, fantasies, sensory perceptions, bodies themselves, and dematerialized objects can gradually present themselves, be exchanged, or be connected. In this way virtual space succeeds in being mental space (and vice versa), both of them sharing the character of experiential zones if the subject succeeds in inhabiting this space as a place where "drafts of analytic thought" (Hautmann, 1999, p. 76) are possible, using cyberspace ("dreaming it") as a constant and flourishing source of thoughts. The subject can connect up dispersed or unorganized elements, *proto-informatic elements*, as I proposed calling them (Marzi, 2018), giving to them a form of life, experience, original elaboration (including artistic expressions), and adventures of the mind that are not imbued with omnipotence or destructive narcissism. This conception takes its cue from the Bionian theories of proto-mental states and of beta elements (Bion, 1961, 1962, 1963). I propose the development of these Bionian concepts within the domain of information technology and cyberspace.

The best-known parameters concerning body–mind relations are challenged by the fact that in virtual reality we are confronted with a different fact. We have to deal with a *neverbody*. This highlights analogies and differences. It is very relevant that we can imagine constituents of the body and corporeality as also existing in the digital world, which we need to imagine as a space for our needed representations. We can also imagine this world to be a "digital body" (or that such a body lives and inhabits it) with its specific characteristics and contents, in a dialectical relationship with us, our mind, our mindbody/bodymind system (Grotstein, 1997).

In this way, the possibility of thinking that what happens in the digital world can be thought of as a *digital third* arises. This is a 'third' which is neither a third ear nor an analytic third: it is a datum in the etymological and literal sense of the term, an element which exists separately from the couple at work but which nevertheless keeps coming into the work of that couple. It is at the same time an external and an internal element and, because of all this, "dreamable" (as Ferro would say), processable, and manageable, like an element of analysis itself, and it is, in fact, inevitably intrinsic to it (Marzi and Fiorentini, 2017), and as such can never be neglected in this context.

Of course, the digital body is not a material body, as I just said. It is not a concrete and physical, tangible body; it is rather a body imagined as such by the user. The digital body in cyberspace is not only an external "other" to approach and recognize, but also a (prosthetic?) extension of one's own proto-mental inner world. It is therefore a dimension that we could ascribe to the psyche-soma (Winnicott, 1949) or to the above-mentioned bodymind/mindbody (Grotstein, 1997). It is a virtuality that settles in cyberspace through an interaction of the subject with the digital "space" and its informational contents. It can be *thought* of as a digital body if, in this relationship, some experience of three-dimensionality is activated, and with it the possibility of thinking, within this space, through the presence of proto-informatic elements which have features similar to the proto-mental elements present in the subject (they could even be imagined as being physical). In this situation the proto-informatic elements enlivened by the inter-action with the navigator, and together with the navigator can become primor-dial digital elements liable to be processed, just like the proto-mental elements within the individual.

However, this body can remain mute, uncharted, and unrepresentable, and therefore it can approach the dimension of the "unrepresented primal process" (Aulagnier, in Correale, 2019). In such a case of impossibility or difficulty in evolving to three-dimensionality, one can create hypermaterialization or hy-persensorialization. Then, the virtual space remains "a-spatial" (infinite and/or punctiform); or it can evolve by expanding into three-dimensionality, thus becoming a place of evolution and processing.

It is some kind of unthought, mute "neutrality of sense" beyond the mirror (of the screen) that is revived by the subject interacting with the digital world (of any kind). *Proto-informatic elements*, for that matter, can also be thought of as being part of some sort of "group digital body". The huge digital community supports the latter condition and forms (or perhaps more properly, it can be experienced as) an extended digital body across the planet. This extended body can become an individual through the alphabetization of proto-informatic elements (PIE) themselves. It is some "groupishness" which finds an allusive touchstone in the enormous digital community, a digital body extended right across the planet, the digital community understood as referring back to possible, potential belonging to the human group.

On another note, a qualitative difference between alpha elements in Bion and what we can think of as alpha elements in the digital world should be high-lighted. Bion (1962) stated that alpha elements include both visual images and au-ditory and olfactory patterns along with the material that can be used by dream thoughts and unconscious thinking during the waking state and memory. Yet, the elements one finds in cyberspace ("beyond" the screen), that is, the proto-informatic elements, cannot be categorized as alpha elements. To me they seem to be assimilable to beta elements. They are not elements of thought yet, but rather a precondition to thinking, perhaps. They are raw, asymbolic, and in some respect mute elements. They seem to be closer to the "Thing-in-itself", rather than to other more "metabolized" conditions. Not only do they not have any meaning by themselves, but they do not even have any psychic form. This latter is gained through their transformation into alpha elements in the process of think-ing and through a (creative) interaction with the subject.

This is the characteristic of an authentic psychic birth (or a preparatory pathway leading to it), but within the digital dimension which has much to do with the manifestation and growth of the feeling of being (Hautmann, 2005), in this particular digital context. From there on, more classical analytic di-mensions may arise. I am thinking of dimensions we know well—those classic psychogenetic dimensions, embedded in the Freudian and Kleinian models, for example.

Everything said thus far finds a challenging realization in clinical practice when it has to deal with the digital world, whether this is used simply as material in the session, or as an intrinsic part of the session when the analysis is practiced remotely with digital technology.

In a clinical case I have written about elsewhere (Marzi, 2013, 2016b), which pertains to the internet as material in the analysis, I underlined that a patient, Gianni, detaches himself from the undifferentiated and dangerous dimension of the "proto-mental digital group" in order to become an individual, but one who thus feels himself as a more complete part of the human group, and steadily abandons indistinct and automatic group responses, the urge to impulsive actions and even a short-circuiting action (such as a suicide attempt).

In Gianni's case (discussed in more detail in Marzi, 2016, p. 119), some of a film's characters (which he dreamed *were coming into the room from the computer, doing things which were frightening for him*), can be imagined as the evolving echo of a group dimension within the patient, who has found an unusual but vital call in the cyberspace of his computer. In it, the characters, or their "primitive somatic reality", dematerialized to pure virtuality, could have remained incarcerated forever in the infinite silence of non-form and non-place. Stimulated by analytic work, which succeeded in containing the patient's catastrophic anxiety, they were not broken down into immediate action (of the hallucinatory kind, e.g. expelled as visual efferents). All the film's characters who emerged were instead like the first symbolization of a group identity which steadily found the way to produce a nascent representation of individual identity toward a progressive sketch of psychic birth (see also Hautmann, 1999, 2005).

Gianni exports his most indistinct, primordial dimension—I would call it a sort of digital psyche-soma—into the virtual space, finding a place of welcome but also of developmental gestation. He shows a movement from the "undifferentiated digital proto-mental matrix" to the higher, affective-cognitive level of functioning. I think this may be another feature for research along this psychoanalytic frontier. The steady transition from infinity (but also punctiform: i.e. in any case with no dimension) recognized the computer's "group" places as fundamental steps on the way; then he was able to dream, and finally there was the further evolution in which the possibility of exploiting a psychic birth is recognized. This evolution is also carried out thanks to the nature of potential space, both that of the virtual environment and that of the analytic field and also marks, from a different theoretical orientation, the return from a dangerous and destructive narcissism (Rosenfeld, 1987) toward a healthy narcissism which sustains vital growth.

The specific field of remote analysis

Although the now vast literature on remote analysis is too broad to summarize here (for a review see Marzi and Fiorentini, 2017), the following will address specific areas of interest.

In the field of remote analysis we need to be mindful that running after novelty at all costs is problematic ("what is new is better" is an old basic assumption of modern philosophy), but we also have to defend ourselves against a resistance to novelty which in fact needs to be explored and worked on through our reflective analytic tools (Marzi, 2015).[8]

I propose an open and reflective attitude concerning teleanalysis, that it is not destructive to previous psychoanalytic concepts, but rather can enrich that which is already established. We need to remember that the object relations theory too was once a radical idea which has now contributed much to our discipline.[9]

We know that attention in analysis is not exclusively directed to verbal communication, but also to signals from the senses and importantly, the body as an instrument of great value for getting to know the patient's internal world (through mimicry, posture, tone, voice, sensations of patient, and analyst) and as an indicator of the coloration of the analytic field.

The observations and criticisms of many authors have focused on this and other points. As one example of many, Argentieri and Mehler's (2003) short work (maybe too frequently referenced), Gillian Russell's (2015) interesting book, Turkle et al. (2017), as well as Semi's (2019) writings, and recent papers delivered at the 2019 EPF Congress in Madrid (including Hardt, 2019; Perez Sanchez, 2019). These authors deny more or less any analytic validity of remote analysis (even via telephone), for a variety of reasons, including the fact that telematic devices interfere with the voice. Alongside them, though, other works by several authors (see the three volumes edited by Jill Savege Scharff, 2015, 2017, 2019) have claimed, for a long time, that the voice is a significant strength in a setting where physical presence becomes virtual. They suggest that the voice reaches to the analyst's mind very directly, making connections that are even more intimate than in *in person* analysis. If the visual dimension is missing, other channels take over, and, in addition the voice invariably creates a body image in the analyst's mind, allowing for the transmission of experience in the here and now.

Therefore, in remote analysis the voice, a typical somatic characteristic, is certainly privileged, with a greater requirement for sensitivity to tone, hesitations, pauses, and the quality of silence. We can equally highlight bodily and miming manifestations of the patient with regard to anger, fear, shame and sadness. Besides, the voice is part of the body, and the body enters the analytic field by means of this vocal manifestation, and also by way of the bodily sensations of the analytic couple at work, reciprocally responding to and eliciting the other's tone and vocal rhythm (Savege Scharff, 2015, 2017). Other characteristics have their presence actually diminished: smells, for example, at least until technology finds a way of discovering such total immersiveness as to create olfactory environments. Of course, many other pre- and extra-verbal features can be absolutely similar in both the settings (facial expressions, coughs, and sometimes tactile sensations, projective identifications, and counter-identifications of a visceral nature). The presence of video is certainly very helpful in bringing the two settings closer together, the one "in the room" and the one "not in the room" (See Bolognini, 2014).

One of the most common criticisms against remote analysis is that the whole body, considered as essential, becomes virtual, and if it is not really there concretely, it is said that analysis cannot be carried out, an adequate transference cannot develop, and so on. Regarding this very important observation and other criticisms, a thorough discussion of which are beyond the scope of this chapter I refer to the work of Lena Theodorou Ehrlich (2019), which addresses many topics concerning this issue, with some interesting convergences with what I have argued in my writings on this subject matter.

What actually seems essential is not the physical presence *tout court* (which may be overestimated at times), but rather, as I will show later, to work analytically with the proto-informatic elements in this dimension as well. In other words, it seems to me that, with remote analysis, analytical 'thinkability' and work can develop if the needs for creative exchange are met, whereas its collapse is due to the demise of such relatedness. This potential for creative exchange determines some contiguity with—rather than divergence from—the dimension of the in-person analytic relationship. In other words, we need to consider as one of the essential elements the creation of a genuine three-dimensionality stemming from working through the proto-informatic elements themselves, in the form of an ongoing psychic birth, so that proper psychoanalytic operations and adventures of the mind can come into being.

This point of view is given credence if we bear in mind the words of one of the 'best friends' of psychoanalysis, W.R. Bion (1970, p. 12), who notes that

> ...the physician is dependent on realization of sensuous experience in contrast with the psycho-analyst whose dependence is on experience that is not sensuous. The physician can see and touch and smell. The realizations with which a psycho-analyst deals cannot be seen or touched; anxiety has no shape or colour, smell or sound. For convenience, I propose to use the term 'intuit' as a parallel in the psychoanalyst's domain to the physician's use of 'see', 'touch', 'smell', and 'hear'.

Even if we must underline that this 'intuit' can also be conveyed by the sensory participation of the body, cannot forget that Bion (1970) himself, radically draws our attention to the fact that what counts in analysis is not so much the actual bodily presence, which at times is an obstacle, but rather the primacy of the experience. I argue that such experience can also be there in the case of teleanalysis. Therefore, quoting Bion again

> ... if his [the psychoanalyst's] mind is preoccupied with what is or is not said, or with what he does or does not hope, it must mean that he cannot allow the experience to obtrude, particularly that aspect of it which is more than the sound of the patient's voice or the sight of his postures. What sounds the patient makes, or what spectacle he presents, relates to O only in so far as O has evolved into the K domain […] If the mind is preoccupied with elements perceptible to sense it will be that much less able to perceive elements that cannot be sensed.
>
> (ibid., p. 40)

Erhlich (2019) seems to be following in the wake of Bion's statements of almost 50 years ago, when she underlines: "…underappreciating the importance of the analyst's emotional engagement, and overestimating the importance of the physical presence. I was confusing distance analysis with distant analysis" (p. 270).

Here, strong emphasis is put on the importance not so much of the external sense organs, but rather of the internal sense organ that allows for an opening to the dimension of the unknown, giving up the mostly conscious perception modes.

Finally, Gutierrez (2017) further supports what we are particularly interested in for the purposes of this chapter:

> The reciprocal coordination of the visual and auditory correlates of the interaction makes the dyad seem, to a greater or lesser degree, to share the same place—a phenomenon known in virtuality research as *presence* or the 'subjective experience of being in one place or environment, even when one is physically situated in another' (Witmer and Singer, 1998, p. 225).

And after underscoring some relevant perplexities about online analysis, he ends by highlighting:

> We can thus say that it is not possible to carry out psychoanalytic work complemented by videoconference for all patients, at all times, nor exclusively via videoconference…. The emphasis, however, is not on the structural determinants of the device, but rather on the capacity of each particular analytic dyad to overcome the split in teleanalysis at a given time in treatment…

Also, in my experience, the presence of the body is a "varying-intensity condition". Some patients do not miss it, others suffer, and it is with the latter that we need to think about this mode and the need to explore and examine it further.

Thus, here the analyst needs to pay more attention to what is going on: psychoanalysis itself should be required to concentrate more intensely on a case-by-case basis and on research in the area of remote analysis.

My personal clinical experience underlines the fact that this mode of working is quite adequate on the whole (but not for all patients), and that an analytic relationship can be attained that is to a large extent congruent with the classical model, provided that certain preliminary requirements are respected (i.e. when there are no alternatives, when there have previously been periods of physically present analysis, and if the analytic couple is convinced and confident that the analytic process can continue even at a distance). This specific virtual setting forces us to think not only about the meaning of a specific communication of the patient at a given time in the course of analysis, but also about the potential impact, in that communication and in the listening of the analyst, of the contribution of the actual presence of the IT dimension, its unavoidable presence in terms of technical participation, interference, crashes, and so on. This is a "third" in the sense explained above. We enter a "telecommunicative field", as we might call it, which forms a sort of analytic-digital field. If it collapses, there is the risk of formation of a hypermateriality and a hypersensoriality. It is also a digital body which attracts countless non-metabolized elements, which are incarcerated in this digital body itself, and which need to be signified by the working analytic couple.

Cecilia

In one of the first sessions via Skype, started because she moved far away, Cecilia, who has been in analysis in-person for a few years, relates this dream:

> At my grand-parents' home ... as if all the objects, the couch, the curtains, the paintings were alive, and I interact with them ... I do not know if they are good or bad, they are 'strange'. They don't make me feel at ease. As if they were magic. They leave the house: somebody feels bad, needs some help. And the objects go to rescue ...

I say that there are old objects that convey a sense of disorientation, and she is puzzled ... without, where she is now, but also within. But the objects are also the internet and Skype (I have an insight about it. At first I don't understand anything, then I feel something clicks in my mind, this insight). Everything is scary, now, with these upsetting objects, but if everything is geared to help, then everything becomes more known and less threatening. It is easier to find it again. I also enter this environment. If she feels she is helped—or if she helps the others (through what she is doing and her profession)—then she feels calmer, and the dream becomes more of a fantasy. Besides, what are we saying in this new situation? What object is it? Where does it go? Where is it?

It seems to me that as the patient starts to think about this brand-new experience, she starts to ask herself questions and to create some meaning about it, its functioning and how it relates to us, to her, to her previous analysis. She thinks and fantasizes, like in the dream, where she seems to enter a scene of a Walt Disney cartoon movie, where the inanimate, that is to say the concrete, the unthought yet present, the a-symbolic beta (depending on one's own theoretical options) becomes animated in a (partially) new condition. At first, the material-ized dimension of the objects, the furniture, is experienced as being "strange". It is a dimension (in fact, an a-dimension) that is going to gain suppleness and movement. The patient's β elements, that in this case can be associated with the incipient formation of the new teleanalytic relationship, undergo some transfor-mation, becoming animated, in a supple playful dimension.

Sometime later, the mind of the patient moves forward, processes thoughts and fantasies, some of which manifest restlessness and doubts:

> ... treatment of a woman. Many attempts, experimental things, some kind of epidural catheterization. I discuss it with somebody, I do not know who. An attempt outside the box. Something that has never been done for someone in great suffering. Then, as if we are in a kitchen, with many people, a party,

and the woman is lying in the room next door, she feels unwell and we decide to carry out this experimental treatment...

The analyst suggests to her that she is still talking about the internet... Some "heroic" attempts are carried out, which have never been made together... Who knows what will happen? Experimental stuff... Perhaps the party appears because there is still nourishment in the analytic setting, but there is also an attempt to "commit to" having fun, which often happens to her (a defensive and elusive characteristic of the patient). Then there is the sick woman: she is the needy patient and lies in a "separate" room (just as she actually is now, far from the known place of analysis), and she needs to be "rescued" through these "experimental procedures". After all, the catheter goes to the central nervous system, and the tube is like the microphone cable that somehow connects us with the voice without a presence.

I would say that the dream's atmosphere is also very much characterized by the body, a needy but separate body, once again variously—depending on our theoretical options—a depository of many aspects such as those that are split-off and a-symbolic. In addition to a mind, there is also a "separate" body whose movements are not necessarily mute, but are directed toward a relational component, albeit embryonic, as an initial mental movement which demands a deep acceptance by the couple at work. The analyst is called on to function as a mother who repeatedly transforms into the psychic that which is not psychic, identifying almost in a bodily sense with the patient ($♀ ♂$, Bion's concept of container/contained, 1962). With Cecilia, this must be achieved in a dual but conjoined way, reclaiming the separate and dissociated body but integrating this movement into the new "experimental" dimension of remote analysis. In this dimension, although bodies are mediated through virtuality, the tube or cable of the catheter/internet connection unites us, and is gradually accepted and metabolized as valid and meaningful in the analytic experience.

The objects that come to life in her first dream and then the probes that run into and through the body (like in a re-edition of Asimov's *Fantastic Voyage*) testify to the fact that in the experience of remote analysis the body remains, although in the particular form of a digital body, and the body functions once again as a co-protagonist. The body gives its contribution in a particular de-materialized dimension—where it is neither missing nor undermined—and continues to provide its participation in mental life. With Cecilia, while the body is dematerialized in her telenalysis (but remains well visible, audible, and so on), she recovers analysis itself and herself in analysis with her Disney-style dream, the proto-informatic elements that get animated through alphabetization: distance analysis is not distant analysis (Ehlrich, 2019). The risk may be, in the lack of transformation, a hypermaterialization, a stiff body without the possibility of evolving in metaphor, and of becoming part of a chain of meaning.

So, one of the central points of the analyst's identity resides in the possibility of better understanding how fundamental it is to create, once again, a genuine relational tri-dimensional field which can contain and transform these processes.

It is also what is proposed by, among others, Ogden (2009, 2010) in his discussion of the three forms of thought (magical, dream, and transformative). These forms are very suitable for the field of remote analysis.

Mario

Mario, a young university student, reveals a substantially borderline personality in his analysis, mingling high- and low-functioning features. Against a depressive background, which he often attempts to eliminate by manic choices of an omnipotent kind and with some drug abuse, I note a diffuse identity with some difficulties in sexual identity. Despite this, he is able to study successfully without ever falling behind. The analysis continues for some years, and it seems to me that the central aim is to suggest the presence of emotions to Mario, and to name them, so that he can recognize them in himself, coherently organizing them out of the psycho-emotional chaos which reigns in him. Thus it is very important that the right distance is created in the setting, since if Mario is too distant he fears that the relationship will not survive, while if he gets close, as he intensely desires to, he is still more afraid of disappearing inside me, of being sucked back into a distressing indistinction where he may be lost forever.

This is the frame in which at a certain point the idea of studying abroad for a period of time comes up. Together with the desire for attempting growth through escape, Mario is also anxious about the analysis itself, and the outcome for the two of us. The news also causes me difficulties. I clearly feel how risky and ambiguous this decision is for the patient, as his condition would require a profound intimacy with me/analysis, from which he would naturally like to flee because he fears being sucked in by it. This is the delicate and risky central nucleus of the transferential and countertransferential experience in this case.

It is a technical and ethical dilemma. At the technical level, leaving this patient for almost a year (without a clear physical presence) would have been confirmation of his abandonment, a rupture of the still barely formed analytic link which would have unforeseeable consequences.

At the ethical level, it did not seem acceptable to me to leave this kind of patient on his own or oblige him to begin another therapy with an unknown colleague abroad.

So, I suggest Mario consider the opportunity of continuing analysis remotely (something he had never heard of). In offering this, I am aware of the difficulties I will be encountering with a subject with his personality structure. After initially feeling disconcerted, the patient starts to accept this proposition, though with many doubts about it: will we be able to contact each other? Will "my battery work" over a long distance? Will he still be important to me or will I wash my hands of him? Will doors be shut in his face?

Once we have started these new kinds of sessions, Mario says he finds it better when he puts on the earphones, whereas the other way I seem to be a mechanical, artificial entity: "With the microphone it's as if you were part of the computer, but with the earphones I feel I'm more with you. Without them I'm afraid you can't hear me…". A few weeks later he dreams that I have become half man, half machine, like a monster, and then that he had been welcomed into a village for tourists by a woman/machine to whom he makes sexual advances…

I think—and I tell him this with great caution over several sessions—that with me, he is trying to build a new container/setting for the analytic experience which will strive to preserve the whole of the previous experience, but with difficulty, without our physical presence. He is thinking about our connecting remotely, something he undoubtedly finds disturbing, causing "turbulences". I become half man, half machine, telematic, and human. If I slip away like this, he gets depressed or anxious and wants to possess me concretely. At present, the unstable barrier between fantasy and reality only allows him to express certain contents in this way.

My physical absence is transformed into a persecutory and murderous monster, and this solution sometimes seems largely to lack adequate symbolization. The earphones, on the contrary, are an aspect of proximity, even if it is certainly diminished in teleanalysis, a specific feature of the teleanalytic setting. This "telematic third" takes on the characteristic voice of the analyst which comes directly "into his mind" and is not dispersed: the voice is near, united—perhaps fused—with him as he would like, recreating a sort of common body which at first is blurred, but not sucking him in. It then becomes a total primordial medium and Mario can begin to experience this progressively developing condition, a place where frightening or totally a-symbolic elements (we can also call them β elements *tout court*) can begin to be transformed. Whatever stands in the digital world between us and flows through the digital medium can take the shape of proto-informatic elements, including the problems of the "digital third".

In this case, mainly, the whole new experience of remote analysis—understood as a huge proto-informatic element, comprising numerous proto-informatic components—can begin to move and create a space where some early analytic symbolization is possible. It is ever more evident how much help the digital medium can be in such a case. Alone, without a known voice to keep him together, I believe he would have been much worse off.

Moreover, not being there with his body tends to have prominent meanings in this initial stage of his remote analysis. Although he had much experience with digital media, the impact of the absence of his body in these early sessions caused him real anguish.

Interestingly, this seems to happen even when we meet in person, when there is some disruption of the setting. We could add that the disturbance of the physiological routine, of regular nutrition—expressing the situation in Kleinian terms—induces a great identity-storm, or hinders his identity formation. Teleanalysis shows this alienating difficulty intensely and seems, at least at the start, to absorb a foreign aspect into itself, one that is perhaps persecutory, malignant, certainly arrogant, and scornful toward him.

Mario and I have therefore been called on to address these complex intrapsychic and relational aspects made of meaningless emotional turbulences (the emotional turbulences related somehow to a catastrophic change?), in order to endow them progressively with meaning within our telematic digital field.

In fact, analytic work, the two of us being in the same boat with an enduring faith in analysis and in our way of proceeding, allowed us to address, accept, and contain these troubling conditions, bringing them to a better level of dreamability and thinkability than before, enabling us to take our previous analytic work further, while these conditions dissipated also with more experience and over time.

In conclusion, I emphasize that although virtual reality may, in general, serve as a flight from factual reality, teleanalysis can take on profoundly different and constructive meanings. In this situation with Mario, it also took on the sense of a mysterious place (a digital field) where quasi-psychotic fantasies and anxieties could germinate. It was therefore necessary to work through the fear that there might be an irruption of sensations, emotions, and possibly disorganized proto-thoughts which might so disturb his equilibrium as to unhinge it completely, without a reassuring physical presence. In this case the physical distance, the absence of the material body, has not taken the direction of a total loss of the analytic couple (nor has it upset the analytic field). It has rather entered a renovated dimension of field and greater emotional proximity within the digital analytic field itself. This is what Ehrlich (2019) confirms, while considering the "analytic third", when she says: "Addressing with patients the painful realities of teleanalytic interruptions and malfunctions, or their frustrated yearnings to smell me or lie on my couch, resulted in a stronger sense of emotional connection" (ibid., p. 272). The importance of the physical body has subsequently decreased. The unconscious reality of the patient has managed to gradually understand, within itself, both the absence of an actual body and the presence of a digital analytic body—in all the dynamic multidirectional meanings which I have tried to suggest, with the potential to produce evolution and sense.

I maintain that the re-creation of this field-space, the energizing of emotions and emotional experience which become thought, and the transformation of the (dangerously) inanimate and a-symbolic into animated and symbolic flow represent a fertile field for the evolution of the analyst's ongoing identity. As I have illustrated, they are constituent features of what occurs in the true remote analytic relationship.

Notes

1 The Body Vanishes? refers to *The Lady Vanishes*, a 1938 film directed by Alfred Hitchcock.
2 Many typically divergent meanings converge in the concept of field. Starting from Kurt Lewin's "field theory", deriving from Einstein's and Infeld's theories, we can think of it as a physical or metaphorical place where a system of forces is present, whose characteristic is not given by the single element present but by the whole which is formed with their system of relationships. We can also think of it as a space capable of containing and possibly transforming states of mind and fantasies that germinate in analysis, thanks to the analytic dyad. Ferro et al. (2007) refers to the Barangers for an early basic formulation that would later develop into the notion of an encounter of "multipersonality" of the patient and the analyst. This led to Bion's theorizations about alpha function and waking dream thought, ideas that enrich the picture. Within this framework, each communication in the session belongs to the field, collecting the emotions and "characters" which speak of the present situation of the field itself. In

this way, the proto-emotions come to the fore. Though initially nameless, they can be named, and in this process they also acquire a meaning in figurative terms.

3 We recall here the 2019 FEP Congress on "Body-Corps-Körper", and the Twelfth International Evolving British Object Relations Conference, Seattle, October 12–14, 2018. We also refer to the 2019/1 Rivista di Psicoanalisi, focusing on the body with several papers on this topic.

4 Here I refer to monism and dualism, materialism and idealism, reductionism and integrationism, and nowadays a strong focus on emergentism; although close attention is usually paid to prevent a gradual fall into the (often ideological or ideologized) dominance of psychobiologism that can be connected directly to nineteenth-century organicism (Conrotto, 2003).

5 This is an attitude that also tends to continuously revitalize the psychoanalytic discipline, at the risk of a decline in several other fields. Kandel (1999) endorsed this evolving attitude over 20 years ago: "This decline is regrettable, since psychoanalysis still represents the most coherent and intellectually satisfying view over the mind" (p. 505).

6 Partially contrary to what the above-mentioned authors thought, Lombardi has highlighted that "the reference to the body is central in Bion to the extent that the body provides raw material to be transformed into psychoanalytic elements" (2012, p. 110). In this sense, see Hautmann (1999, 2005), in several contributions on the nature of β elements and γ elements and their fates.

7 The issue of equilibrium, balancing, proper (yet mutual!) fertilization cannot refrain from dealing with what Solms and Turnbull pointed out, simply yet truly, almost 20 years ago:

> We can never literally perceive the stuff we are made of without first representing it through one of our perceptual modalities—which means that we can never escape the artificial mind–body dichotomy. Since we can never transcend the limits of our senses, we can never perceive the underlying mind–body stuff directly. We can only make inferences from the data of perception (from scientific observation) as to the nature of that underlying entity—let's call it the 'human mental apparatus'—and inferences about how it is constructed and how it works. Our picture of the mental apparatus itself will therefore always be a figurative one—a *model*. We possess concrete perceptual images of its two observable manifestations (the brain and the subjective awareness), but the underlying entity that lies behind those perceptual images will never be directly observable. Scientific observation has its limits...
>
> (p. 54)

Interestingly, this clear statement seems to connect to what Bion said more than once about the unknowability of the "Thing-in-itself", except through its derivatives. I will expand on this later on.

8 And we can just hint at the fact that within the psychoanalytic environment we tend to hazardously polarize the debate (an attitude that seems to have spread at a social level globally, like some kind of cheering support in sport) between those who are for it and those who are fiercely against it.

9 Curiously there are, for example, openings for psychopharmacology during an analytic treatment, but extremist and often a priori resistances against remote analysis persist.

References

Argentieri, S. & Mehler, J.A. (2003). Telephone "analysis": "Hello, who's speaking?" *Insight, 12*:17–19.

Bion, W.R. (1961). *Experiences in Groups*. Tavistock Publications.

Bion, W.R. (1962 [1984]). *Learning from Experience.* Karnac Books.

Bion, W.R. (1963 [1984]). *Elements of Psycho-Analysis.* Karnac Books.

Bion, W.R. (1970). *Attention and Interpretation: A Scientific Approach to Insight in Psycho-Analysis and Groups.* London: Tavistock Publications.

Bolognini, S. (2014). L'analisi che verrà.: uno sguardo sul futuro (prossimo) della psicoanalisi in un mondo che cambia. *Rivista di Psicoanalisi, 60*(3):779–794.

Bucci, W (1997). Symptoms and symbols: A multiple code theory of somatization. *Psychoanalytic Inquiry, 17*(2): 151–172.

Caldwell, L. (2018). *Minding the body, embodying the mind.* [Paper presentation] The Twelfth International Evolving British Object Relations Conference, Seattle, WA.

Carlino R. (2011). *Distance Psychoanalysis.* Karnac Books.

Cavagna, D. (2001). Il corpo come *forma mentis.* In D. Cavagna & M. Fornaro (Eds.) *Il corpo negli sviluppi della psicoanalisi* (pp. 123–151). Centro Scientifico Editore.

Conrotto, F. (2003). Corpo e psicoanalisi: Lettura introduttiva a Tononi, Ferrari e M'Uzan. *Psiche, 1:*43–51.

Correale, A. (2019). Unpublished manuscript.

De Toffoli, C. (2014). Transiti corpo-mente. In B. Bonfiglio (Ed.) *Transiti corpo-mente. L'esperienza della psiconalisi* (pp. 285–304). FrancoAngeli.

Ehrlich, L.T. (2019). Teleanalysis: Slippery slope or rich opportunity? *Journal of the American Psychoanalytic Association, 67*(2):249–279.

Ferrari, A.B. (2003). Corporeità e psichicità. Intervista a cura di Nicoletta Bonanome. *Psiche, 1:* 61–73.

Ferrari, A.B. (2004). *From the eclipse of the body to the dawn of thought.* Free Association Books.

Ferro, A., Civitarese, G., Collovà, M., Foresti, G., Molinari E., Mazzacane, F., & Politi, P. (2007). *Sognare l'analisi.* Bollati Boringhieri.

Ferro, A. (2014). *Le viscere della mente.* Borla.

Gaddini, E. (1981). Note sul problema mente-corpo. *Rivista di Psicoanaisi, 27:*3–29.

Grotstein, J.S. (1997). "Mens sana in corpore sano". The mind and body as an "odd couple" and as an oddly coupled unity. *Psychoanalytic Inquiry, 17*(2): 204–222.

Grotstein, J.S. (2007). *A beam of intense darkness.* Karnac Books.

Gutierrez, L. (2017). Silicon in pure gold? Theoretical contributions and observations on teleanalysis by videoconference. *The International Journal of Psychoanalysis, 98*(4):1097–1120.

Hardt, J. (2019). Does psychoanalysis go online without body? Methodical considerations on intercorporeity in analytical encounter [Paper presentation] EPF Annual Conference, Madrid, Spain.

Hautmann G. (1999). Immaginazione e interpretazione. In G. Hautmann (Ed.) *La psicoanalisi tra arte e biologia* (pp. 55–78). Borla.

Hautmann, G. (2002). *Funzione analytica e mente primitive.* Edizione ETS.

Hautmann, G. (2005). Pensiero pellicolare e formazione del sé. In A. Ferruta (Ed.) *Pensare per immagini.* Borla.

Hinshelwood, R.D. (2018). John Rickman behind the scenes: The influence of Lewin's field theory on practice, countertransference, and W.R. Bion. *The International Journal of Psychoanalysis, 99*(6):1409–1423.

Kandel, E. (1999). Biology and the future of psychoanalysis: A new intellectual framework for psychiatry revisited. *American Journal of Psychiatry, 156*(4):505–524.

Leuzinger-Bohleber, M. (2019). The mind–body problem revisited. From: the interdisciplinary dialogue between psychoanalysis and embodied cognitive science [Paper presentation] Madrid Annual Conference, FEP, Madrid, Spain.

Lombardi, R. (2008). The body in the analytic session: Focusing on the body–mind link. *The International Journal of Psychoanalysis, 89*(1):89–109.

Lombardi, R. (2012). *Il corpo nella teoria della mente di Wilfred R. Bion.* Rivista critica della postmodernità. https://www.consecutio.org/2012/o2/il corpo nella teoria della mente di Wilfred Bion.

Lombardi, R. (2019). Il corpo in Freud e Klein: Appunti su continuità e differenze. *Rivista di psicoanalisi, 65*(1):45–66.

Marzi, A. (2015). Analisi remota. O forse no. Stato dell'arte sulla teleanalisi (Remote aanalysis. Or maybe not. State of the art of teleanalysis). [Paper presentation] The Psychoanalytic Center, Florence, Italy.

Marzi, A. (2016a). Introduction. In A. Marzi (Ed.), *Psychoanalysis, identity and the internet. Explorations into cyberspace* 23–50. Karnac Books.

Marzi, A. (2016b). Cyberghosts from the depth. In: A. Marzi (Ed.), *Psychoanalysis, identity and the internet: Explorations into cyberspace* (pp. 111–134). Karnac Books.

Marzi, A. (2018). The analyst's identity and the digital world: A new frontier in psychoanalysis. *The Italian Psychoanalytic Annual, 12*:99–113.

Marzi, A. & Fiorentini, G. (2017). Light and shadow in online analysis. In J. Savege Scharff (Ed.), *Psychoanalysis online* (Vol. 3, pp. 65–83). Karnac Books.

Marzi, A., Giovannoni, A. & Carboni, L. (1999). Parli il corpo: prominenza di elementi somatici in alcuni momenti dell'analisi. [Paper Presentation] The XVII Congresso Nazionale della Società Italiana di Psicosomatica "Significato e senso nella malattia", Siena, Italy.

Meltzer, D. (1986). *Studies in extended metapsychology.* Roland Harris Education Trust.

Mirkin, M. (2011). Telephone analysis: compromised treatment or an interesting opportunity? *The Psychoanalytic Quarterly, 80*(3): 643–670.

Neri, C. (1996). *Gruppo.* Borla.

Oelsner (2018) Does the body have a mind? [Paper presentation] The Twelfth International Evolving British Object Relations Conference, Seattle, WA.

Ogden, T. (2009). Talking as dreaming. In *Rediscovering psychoanalysis.* Routledge.

Ogden, T. (2010). On three forms of thinking: Magical thinking, dream thinking, and transformative thinking. *The Psychoanalytic Quarterly, 79*(2): 317–347.

Perez Sanchez, A. (2019). The body in the "here and now". [Paper presentation] The EPF Annual Conference, Madrid, Spain. Rizzolatti, G., & Sinigaglia (2006). *So quel che fai. Il cervello che agisce e i neuroni specchio.* Cortina.

Rosenfeld, H. (1987). *Impasse and interpretation.* Routledge.

Russell, G.I. (2015). *Screen relations: The limits of computer-mediated psychoanalysis and psychotherapy.* Karnac Books.

Savege Scharff, J. (Ed.) (2015). *Psychoanalysis online* (Vol. 2). Karnac Books.

Savege Scharff, J. (2017). Teleanalysis beyond Skype. In J. Savege Scharff (Ed.), *Psychoanalysis Online* (Vol. 3, pp. 1–19). Karnac Books.

Savege Scharff, J. (2019). (Ed.), *Psychoanalysis online* (Vol. 4). Karnac Books.

Semi, A.A. (2019). Il metodo e il corpo (The method and the body). *Rivista di psicoanalisi, 65*(1): 83–88.

Solano, L. (2013). 14a Joseph Sandler Psychoanalytic Research Conference: *Finding the Body in the Mind* (Ritrovare il Corpo nella Mente). *Rivista di Psicoanalisi, 59*(2): 529–533.

Solano, L. (2016). Al di là di Cartesio: riflessioni sul corpomente. *Rivista di Psicoanalisi, 62*(1): 49–72.

Solms, M. & Panksepp, J. (2012). The "id" knows more than the "ego" admits: Neuropsychoanalytic and primal consciousness perspectives on the interface between affective and cognitive neuroscience. *Brain Science, 2*(2): 147–175.

Solms, M. & Turnbull, O. (2002). *The brain and the inner World. An introduction to the neuroscience of subjective experience.* Other Press.

Turkle, S., Essig, T. & Russell G.I. (2019). Afterword: Reclaiming psychoanalysis: Sherry Turkle in conversation with the editors. *Psychoanalytic Perspectives, 14*(2):237–348.

Winnicott, D.W. (1949[1958]). Mind and its relation to the psyche-soma. In *Through paedriatics to psychoanalysis.* Tavistock Publications.

Witmer, B.G., & Singer, M.J. (1998). Measuring presence in virtual environments: A presence questionnaire. *Presence, 7*(3):225–240.

Index

Note: Page numbers followed by "n" denote endnotes.